AF540225

PARTICIPATIVE MANAGEMENT IN PRIVATE HEALTH CARE INDUSTRY

PARTICIPATIVE MANAGEMENT IN PRIVATE HEALTH CARE INDUSTRY

By

Dr. C. Vijaya Prabha

Associate Professor & Head

Department of Commerce

Sree Devi Kumari Womens College, Kuzhithurai

Kanyakumari Distt.

Tamil Nadu

(INDIA)

DISCOVERY PUBLISHING HOUSE PVT. LTD.

NEW DELHI-110 002

Published by:
Tilak Wasan

DISCOVERY PUBLISHING HOUSE PVT. LTD.
4383/4B, Ansari Road, Darya Ganj
New Delhi-110 002 (India)
Phone : +91-11-23279245, 43596064-65
Fax : +91-11-23253475
E-mail : parul.wasan@gmail.com
discoverypublishinghouse@gmail.com
web : www.discoverypublishinggroup.com

***First Edition:* 2012**

ISBN: 978-93-5056-111-9

Participative Management in Private Health Care Industry

Printed at:
Shree Balaji Art Press
Delhi

Preface

The decline in quality of State-owned health care services, coupled with the growing affluence of Indian society, is leading to more and more people opting for private hospitals for their health care needs. Moreover, India is fast developing as an international health care destination because of the availability of cheap and high quality health care services; in all probability, private health care industry is going to be a vital part of Indian economy.

Health care industry is basically a human organization. So, management with a human touch is a must in any hospital set up. This study was limited to the State of Kerala, as it is one among the leading States in India in terms of number of beds per lakh population. The present study attempts to give significant insights into the management practices of private health care institutions in Kerala, with special reference to participative management, which can help increase efficiency and productivity.

Objectives of the Study

Main objective was to find out the opinion of employees regarding the feasibility of participative management in Private Health Care industry in Kerala. Other specific objectives were:

1. To study the Human Resource Management practices followed in private health care institutions in the State of Kerala.
2. To examine the existing system of participation of employees in the management of private health care institutions in the State of Kerala.
3. To examine the feasibility of participative management in private health care instituitions in Kerala.
4. To suggest a model of participative management for private health care institutions in Kerala.

All the private allopathic health care institutions with inpatient facilities in the State of Kerala constitute the population for the study. The study was exploratory in nature, based on the survey method. The hospitals were divided into three categories—large, medium and small, based on bed strength and were selected randomly from the three zones of Kerala—North, Central and South. The primary data were collected from three groups of employees, namely, Administrators, Doctors and Paramedical/Technical/ Ministerial staff, by conducting interviews using an interview schedule. In all, 45 Administrators, 341 Doctors and 450 PTM staff were included in the sample. The data so obtained were analysed with the help of computer software SPSS.

The study has as its outcome arrived at a participative model. A three-tier participative model is suggested with Work Committees at the grass roots level, followed by Inter-departmental Committees at the intermediary level, and Joint Management Committees at the top level.

It is sincerely hoped that this humble beginning through the suggested model would in future usher in a change in mindset of both the employer and employees, resulting in extra-efficient hospitals which reap rich dividends for the society at large. The authors believe that this book will contribute to the literature and wealth of knowledge about participative management.

C. Vijaya Prabha

Contents

CHAPTER

1

Introduction

India is fast developing as an international health care destination. Availability of cheap and high quality health care services in hospitals in India is attracting patients not only from neighbouring and gulf countries but also from developed countries like those of the European Union. Almost all advanced health care services are provided by the private hospitals in India, especially those in the South. Moreover, with the declining quality of health care services in the State-owned institutions, coupled with the growing affluence of Indian society, more and more people are opting for private institutions rather than government institutions for their health care needs. This trend has resulted in the mushrooming of private hospitals leading to intense competition among them. In all probability, private health care industry is going to be a vital part of Indian economy.

A hospital has many organizational and operational elements in common with other service industrial organizations like hotels and educational institutions. However, there prevail certain conditions which are peculiar to the administrative work in the hospitals. For instance, the consumers of the services provided in the hospital are physically or mentally ill and are rendered services within the four walls of a hospital. As each patient requires highly personalized services, the services in all respects have to be tailored to the needs of each individual customer. Also, many of the services of a hospital are provided continuously round the clock, throughout the year. Hence, it requires a well-knit organizational division of labour and more efficient and responsible management, as its motto is to provide the best possible patient care.

If we examine the organizational structure of a private hospital or any hospital for that matter, it is found to be highly complex and intricately interwoven. A unique management practice in the hospital sector is the dual control by way of professional authority and executive authority, which can lead to management bottlenecks.

In the present scenario with most of the major private hospitals offering more or less the same quality treatment facilities, customer satisfaction as expressed by patients, bystanders and relatives becomes an important factor deciding the success of an organization. Both the service provider and receiver being human beings the attitude and behaviour of the hospital staff is of utmost importance in enhancing the level of satisfaction of patients.

Health care industry is basically a human organization. The staff structure of a hospital includes a wide spectrum of individuals, starting from highly skilled and qualified super specialists to the unskilled labourer. People are involved at every stage. Therefore, humility, devotion to patients, compassion and consideration for the sick and wounded are the hallmark qualities of all those who work there. Management with a human touch is a must in hospital management. Furthermore, each of these employees has his or her own specific role in the total patient care activity, which cannot be substituted or ignored.

The activities in any hospital are highly inter-dependent, and any problem worth tackling is likely to touch a variety of functions and departments. Cross-functional problem solving is a very different and more difficult process because of the turf issues involved, the complexity of coordination, and the nature of the problem itself. Therefore, vertical and horizontal integration, as applicable to multi-institutional systems, is inevitable to health care organizations if they have to pursue excellence.

Our society is becoming increasingly democratic. People are learning to influence the policies and decisions of the management, directly or through their representatives. Viewed against the rapidly changing cultural context, employee participation in management is inevitability with inherent benefits.

Any organization which takes into consideration human feelings and aspirations, and associates staff members in the process of management is likely to be more efficient and healthier compared to an organization which manages the people in an authoritarian way[1].

Participative management is advocated as a management innovation capable of making positive contribution towards the health and effectiveness of the social organization of an enterprise.

The various processes and mechanisms through which workers influence the decisions of a management, discharge managerial responsibility, or enjoy managerial prerogatives are the basic components of the institution of participative management.

SIGNIFICANCE OF THE STUDY

Health care industry is perhaps the world's largest industry, and India is emerging as a major player in the field because of its high population. The WHO in its report points out that India needs to add 80,000 hospital beds[2] every year to meet the demand of its population. The huge shortage of beds reveals the major opportunity of the industry.

The prospects of the health care industry are such that the private sector will have to play a dominant role due to the inadequacy of funds from government sources to invest in this sector. Though we see private hospitals coming up every day at one location or other, many of them do not flourish although there is huge demand. The main reason for this failure is believed to be due to improper, ineffective or inflexible management approaches. As a matter of fact, the age-old bureaucratic practices are not suited to the present era.

The health care sector can sustain itself only through efficient operation which comes through systematic processes. Such processes and operations can be carried out with good management systems. The participative approach with involvement of those in operations is highly desirable. The health care institution, as it is one dealing with human lives, needs employees who are properly nurtured, motivated, rewarded and counselled to bring about the best results. Hence, a dynamic and flexible management with active involvement of the employees is most desirable. In this context, a study on participative management is of high topical relevance.

The present study is an enquiry into the existing management practices and the attitudes of various groups of employees regarding participative management in the private health care industry.

SCOPE OF THE STUDY

Health care industry is the most important service industry in India. The Indian health care industry is estimated to be around Rs. 1000 billion at present and expected to reach Rs. 2000 billion by 2012 with 17 per cent annual growth rate[3].

Health care industry is run by teams consisting of highly skilled and specialist doctors down to illiterate sweepers. In such an organization with several independent and inter-dependent functions, it is a daunting task to solve various types of problems that crop up day by day. To tackle these problems is a real challenge faced by institutions in the sector. It is essential to study the working of health care institutions keeping in view the national objective of providing health care to all.

Even though, there is the central health ministry, health care services are directly under the purview of each individual State, health being a

State subject under the constitution. Each State delivers health care through private and public sectors. Government sector is delivering health care through a hierarchical network of government hospitals which provide free health care services and hence it cannot be called an industry. All over India, the bulk of health care activities are, however, provided by the private health care industry through private hospitals—especially those with inpatient facility.

One major yardstick that indicates the adequacy of health care service is the number of beds available per lakh population. From the available data it is apparent that Kerala with 584 beds per lakhs population[4] (335 rural and 249 urban) stands far ahead of all other States of India. Number of primary health centers in the State in terms of population is also the highest. Taking into account the fact that 70 per cent[5] of the health care needs of the people of Kerala are provided by the private sector it goes without saying that Kerala is the State having maximum number of beds per lakh population in the private sector compared to other States in India.

Over and above this, since the study is regarding employees' participation in management the availability of literate and enlightened work force in the private health care institutions also is an important parameter to be considered and in this regard also the State of Kerala with 100 per cent literacy is ideal. Hence *the State of Kerala was selected for the study.*

The health care services in the State of Kerala are provided by the Government, ESI, Co-operative, Autonomous and Private sectors. Among these, the private sector occupies a very dominant position, as its bed strength is more[6] than that of all the other sectors put together. Hence this study is confined to the private health care sector of the State of Kerala.

In Kerala, both government and private health care institutions provide health care services through different systems of medicine viz, allopathy, ayurveda, homoeopathy, unani, naturopathy, etc. Out of 48,834 beds in the government sector, 89 per cent (43,619)[7] are allopathic. In the private sector also, out of the total 63,386 beds available, 90 per cent (57,071) beds[8] are in the allopathic sector. As allopathic hospitals in general and private allopathic hospitals in particular, constitute the major health care providers to the people of Kerala, this study concentrates on the private hospitals following the allopathic system of medicine in the State.

The various activities of a hospital may be classified as *operational activities* related to health care, and *managerial activities* related to administration. Operational activities include anything from diagnosing and treating a patient to conducting lab tests, dispensing medicines, providing nursing services, offering dietary services, etc. These activities are excluded from the scope of the study.

The second major activity in a hospital is that of making sure that these operational activities are carried out qualitatively and quantitatively, in order that they help the hospital achieve its objectives. This aspect of the activities of a hospital in getting things done by and through its personnel is what is called managerial aspects. The present study attempts to give significant insights into the *management practices* of private hospitals in Kerala, with special reference to *participative management* which can help increase efficiency and productivity in this sector. This, in turn, would not only benefit the patients, but the organization and above all the society at large.

The legally responsible group in the hospital, entrusted with formulating policy is the Board of Trustees. The day-to-day activities of the hospital are carried out by the available administrative, medical, paramedical, technical and ministerial staff. The study covers only the *day-to-day managerial activities* and the *parties performing such activities*, i.e., Administrative personnel, Doctors, Paramedical, Technical and Ministerial staff.

DEFINITIONS

For the purpose of this study, definitions of the following terms have been adopted from the Report on Private Medical Institutions in Kerala[9].

1. Private Medical Institutions

Medical institutions run by individuals or an organization (e.g. Trust, Co-operative Society, Company, etc) other than government institutions receiving government grants are also considered as private medical institutions.

2. Doctor

Any person in the institution authorized to diagnose illness, prescribe medicine, conduct surgery and other therapies are considered as doctor for the purpose of the study. He may be paid or not, and may work full-time or part-time.

3. Para-medical and Technical Staff

Paramedical staff includes Nurses, Assistant Nurses, Pharmacists, Medico/ Psychiatric social workers and Attenders. Technical staff includes Laboratory technicians, X-ray technicians, Scan technicians, etc.

4. Ministerial Staff

These include the Office Staff, Drivers, Attenders, Lift Operators and other Non-Para-Medical Staff (Clerical staff, Accounts and Medical records librarians, Dieticians, Catering officers, Engineering and maintenance personnel and Electricians).

OPERATIONAL DEFINITIONS

1. Administrators

Administrators means persons who are involved in the general and overall administration of the institutions like Medical Administrator, Non-medical administrator, General Manager and Managing Director. Functional heads like Purchase Manager, Finance Manager, and Accounts Officer are not considered as General Administrators. The Board members, who are the policy makers and have overall institutional responsibility are also excluded from the definition of administrators.

2. Large hospital

A hospital which has *200 or more* beds is treated as a *large* hospital.

3. Medium hospital

A hospital which has bed strength *between 100 and 199* is termed as a *medium* hospital.

4. Small hospital

A hospital which has bed strength *up-to 99* is considered as a *small* hospital for the purpose of this study.

OBJECTIVES OF THE STUDY

The prime aim of the present study was to find out the opinion of employees regarding the feasibility of participative management in Private Health Care industry in Kerala. The study focussed on the following specific objectives:

1. To study the Human Resource Management practices followed in private health care institutions in the State of Kerala.
2. To examine the existing system of participation of employees in the management of private hospitals in the State of Kerala.
3. To ascertain the possibility of implementation of participative management in the private health care industry in Kerala.
4. To suggest a model of participative management system for private health care institutions in Kerala.

HYPOTHESES

1. There is no significant difference in the opinions of employees in different types of hospitals on the extent of satisfaction regarding communication systems.

The parameters relating to communication systems to be tested separately were:

(*i*) The effectiveness of information sharing system;

(*ii*) Upward communication;

(*iii*) Horizontal communication;

(*iv*) Downward communication;

(*v*) Communication skill of subordinates;

(*vi*) Communication skill of superiors; and

(*vii*) Communication skills of peers.

2. The different categories of employees in the private hospitals of Kerala are motivated by 'the opportunity to participate in managerial decision making' rather than by 'remuneration'.
3. There is no significant association between forms of participation in different types of hospitals.
4. There is no significant association between parties controlling the hospital in different types of hospitals.
5. There is no significant association between 'tenure of office of Members of Committees' in different types of hospitals.
6. There is no significant association between 'the concepts of participation for different categories of staff' in different types of hospitals.
7. There is no significant association between the opinions about 'implementing participative management for different categories of staff' in different types of hospitals.
8. There is no significant association between the opinion about 'the success or not of the scheme of participative management in Kerala' for different categories of staff in different types of hospitals.

METHODOLOGY

Source of Data

This study conducted in a selected number of the private allopathic hospitals with inpatient facilities in Kerala is exploratory in nature and the required data was collected through a survey. The variables for the study relate to participative systems of management and opinions on its effectiveness or otherwise. Secondary data was used to assess participative systems in place and HR initiatives in the records of sample units surveyed.

Pilot Study

The interview schedule, first drafted, was tested by conducting a pilot study covering a selected number of hospitals, giving due representation to *small*, *medium*, and *large* hospitals, and interviewing a total of 5 Administrators, 25 Doctors, 50 Para medical, Technical and Ministerial staff.

The pilot study gave valuable insights into the day-to-day functioning of the hospitals, about the various staff members and their duties, and helped in acquiring practical knowledge to elicit proper response from the interviewees. In the light of the observations made and suggestions received through the pilot survey, the draft interview schedule was finalized.

An important fact revealed during the pilot study was that hospitals with a very limited number of beds (mostly with less than 50 beds) follow no standard management practices and that the majority of the staffs in such institutions were unable to answer most of the questions in the interview schedule. So, hospitals with number of beds below 50 were excluded from the study.

Universe

All the private allopathic hospitals in the State of Kerala having inpatient facilities with 50 or more beds represent the universe for the study. District-wise information of all the institutions with names, addresses, total number of beds, and ownership was obtained.

Sample Units

For the purpose of the study hospitals were classified into three categories on the basis of bed strength. Those with bed strength 'up to 99' are grouped as *small* hospitals, those with '100-199' beds as *medium* size hospitals and those having '200 and above' beds as *large* size hospitals.

The sample size was determined considering the heterogeneity of the population. Due representation was given to each segment of the population; the segments considered being size of the population, location and type of employees. A statistical minimum of 30 hospitals were chosen giving due representation to all the above variables. The 30 hospitals were chosen from the *small* (excluding those with bed strength below 50), *medium* and *large* sector in the *proportion they held in the entire population.*

The sample units were selected from the total list of hospitals covering the whole State of Kerala. For this, the State was divided into three zones, viz., North zone, Central zone and South zone. The *North zone* included 5 districts—Kasargod, Kannur, Wynad, Kozhikode and Malappuram; the *Central zone* included 5 districts—Palakkad, Thrissur, Eranakulam, Idduki and Kottayam; the *South zone* included four districts—Alapuzha, Pathanamthita, Kollam and Thiruvananthapuram.

Proportionate numbers of sample units were selected from each zone on the basis of the total number of hospitals in each zone under each type. Table.1.1. shows the number of hospitals selected from each zone.

Table 1.1 : Number of sample Units Selected

Type of hospital	Zone	Population size	Sample size
Small	South	26	3
	Central	56	7
	North	28	3
Medium	South	20	2
	Central	43	5
	North	20	3
Large	South	19	2
	Central	34	4
	North	11	1
Total		**257**	**30**

Source: Computed

A list of *small*, *medium* and *large* hospitals (totaling 257 in number) in the three zones was prepared and the sample units (totalling 30) were selected on the basis of simple random sampling technique. Approximately 10 per cent of the units in each sector were included in the sample. In a few cases, where the authorities refused permission to the researcher to meet the employees, substitute sample units were selected from among hospitals of the same type in the same zone.

Sample Respondents

For selecting the respondents, the employees in the hospitals were grouped into three major categories, such as:

(*i*) Administrators;

(*ii*) Doctors; and

(*iii*) Para-medical, Technical and Ministerial staff.

Hereafter, the third category of staff will be referred to as *PTM staff*.

As a first step the category-wise list of all the staff working in the sample hospitals was obtained. Of the total Administrative personnel, seventy-five per cent (45 in number), fifty per cent of the total Doctors (341 in number) and twenty per cent of the total Para-medical, Technical and Ministerial staff (450 in number) were selected randomly. They were considered as respondents for conducting interview and for collecting the necessary information for the study. Those employees who were extremely reluctant to give information were excluded from the sample and substituted by other employees of the same category in the same hospital. The composition of the sample is depicted in Table.1.2.

Table 1.2 : Composition of the Sample

Type of employee	Total Population	Sample Size
Administrators	60	45
Doctors	681	341
PTM staff	2220	450
Total respondents		**836**

Source: Computed

Data Collection

Structured interview schedules were used to collect data from the Administrative personnel, Doctors and PTM staff. A Malayalam translation of the interview schedule was prepared and used for interviewing employees who were not well-versed in English. The interview schedule sought information on various variables ranging from human resource management practices and participative management practices actually existing in the hospitals to opinions of employees about participative management.

Secondary data were used in the study to develop the theoretical frame-work of hospital management. Such data were gathered from the published and unpublished records of private hospitals. Some informal methods had to be used to secure rare data relating to human resource management. Secondary data were also collected from several libraries and research centres across the country.

Analysis of Data

All the data collected for the study were carefully scrutinised and tabulated. They were edited and analyzed with the help of computer software SPSS. Tools used for analysis of primary data were mathematical and statistical techniques, such as:

(*i*) Percentages;

(*ii*) Mean;

(iii) Two-way ANOVA technique;

(iv) Chi-square analysis; and

(v) Factor analysis.

Limitations of the Study

Even though the study is pioneering, innovative and extensive, on aspects of human resource management and participation of employees in management, in the private health care institutions in the State of Kerala, the conclusions arrived at in this study are not without limitations. The major limitations are the following.

The present study envisaged understanding employees' perspectives on participative management in the health care segment. A final conclusion on effectiveness requires ascertaining the views of patients as well.

The study was mainly based on the data collected through an interview schedule, and the analysis is purely statistical in nature. Evaluation of the responses of the subjects is within the limits of the interview schedule.

Since the study is based on opinions and attitudes of Administrators, Doctors, Para medical, Technical and Ministerial staff, it may not be totally free from bias. The verification of the accuracy of the data was difficult. Such being the case, whatever data could be obtained had to be accepted and made use of for analysis. However, sufficient care was taken to keenly observe all the aspects so as to make the analysis and interpretation meaningful and logical.

The sample size for the large scale units in terms of number of respondents is small as their proportion in the population is also small. This has often resulted in inconsistent statistical results with regard to the large-scale units in terms of association within the sample.

In spite of all these limitations, an earnest attempt has been made to cross-check the responses and to make the conclusions meaningful and rational.

Presentation of the Report

The study begins with an introduction which discusses the significance of the study, the scope of the study, definitions and operational definitions, objectives of the study, hypotheses and methodology.

Chapter two briefly reviews the previous studies and observations made regarding the subject and related areas.

In the third chapter, the health care industry, with special reference to the scenario in Kerala, has been dealt with. In addition to the profile of the sample units and respondents, the concept of participative management, forms of participation, participative management in hospitals, parties involved in private health care delivery, and the role of doctors in administration are discussed.

Chapter four gives the profile of the sample units, the sample respondents and an analysis of HR management practices in the private hospitals of Kerala.

An analytical evaluation of the existing participative management practices in the private hospitals of Kerala is made and presented in chapter five.

In the sixth chapter, the opinion of employees of private hospitals in Kerala towards participative management is analyzed.

Summary of findings and suggestions including the model of participative management systems for private hospitals are presented in chapter seven.

REFERENCES

1. Alexander, K.C., *Participative Management: The Indian Experience*. Delhi : Sri Ram Centre for Industrial Relations and Human Resources, 1972, p. 4.
2. Pestonjee, D.M. *et al.*, 'Image and Effectiveness of Hospitals: An HR Analysis', *Journal of Health Management*, Vol. 7, No.1, Jan-June 2005, p. 42.
3. Sankaranarayanan, K.C., 'Education, Health and Housing' in Rajasenan, D. *et al.* (Ed), *Kerala Economy, Trajectories Challenges and Implications,* Cochin: Directorate of Publications and Public Relations, 2005, p. 263.
4. Government of Kerala, *Report on Private Medical Institutions in Kerala-2004,* Department of Economics and Statistics, Thiruvananthapuram: 2006, p. 2.
5. Bhaskaran, M., 'IMA and Medical Profession', *Kerala Medical Journal*, Vol. 41, No. 2, April 2000, p. 17.
6. Government of Kerala, 'Health Care Infrastructure', *Economic Review*, State Planning Board, Thiruvananthapuram: February 2006, p. 358.
7. *Ibid*, p. 357.
8. *Report on Private Medical Institutions in Kerala – 2004,* Op. cit. p. 5.
9. Government of Kerala, *Report on Private Medical Institutions in Kerala-1995,* Department of Economics and Statistics, Thiruvananthapuram: 1995, p. 3.

CHAPTER 2

Review of Literature

Hospitals, unlike other industrial units, with their inherent complex organizational structure and functions, are well known to have serious managerial problems which can significantly affect their performance. Despite the gravity of these problems, there have only been very few detailed comprehensive studies regarding hospital management, that also with regard to human resource management. With a view to identify the gaps in the research studies already undertaken in this area, published studies by eminent scholars in and outside India have been reviewed.

The review here gives a detailed presentation on findings pertaining to participative management approaches in the health care industry, followed by a brief description of the management perspectives in the health care sector.

PARTICIPATIVE MANAGEMENT APPROACHES IN THE HEALTH CARE SECTOR

The concept of participation in management is fast catching up in all industries. Even international and multinational companies have started recognizing participative management as an essential ingredient for the sustainable growth of any organization. This awareness regarding participative management has generated many studies in large industrial enterprises, but only very few studies in the health care industry. A sincere attempt has been made here to review all available literature and published data relating to studies focussing on Administrators, Doctors, Para-medical, Technical and Ministerial staff—a heterogeneous group responsible for patient care activities in a hospital, and their role and participation in managerial activities.

Carol Huss[1] (1973) analyses the impact of participative management on the personnel and their interpersonal relationships, and revealed that participation produced personal satisfaction, improved service to the sick and settlement of differences by collaborative means—all done by joining hands to bridge the gap between professionals and non-professionals.

Mowday, Richard and Lyman[2] (1974) report that in the health sector, employees were expected to strengthen the organization's image among customers through co-operative behaviour. Organizational commitment portrays employees with high organizational commitment not only as greatly productive and satisfied, but also as extremely responsible with a high civic sense. All these are important pre-requisites to ensure adequate quality of health care services. Hence, the importance of commitment of employees cannot be over-emphasized in the health sector.

Pylee[3] (1975) cites the analysis made by the administrator regarding the difficulties found in a hospital. The administrator's solution was to institute participative management through the Information Decision System which sets up a mechanism whereby subordinates at all levels feel obligated to initiate information that will assist in solving problems, formulating policies or improving procedures.

Austin[4] (1975) concludes that the underlying cause of difficulty in managing hospitals is the lack of interpersonal participation and problem-solving skills on the part of administrators and staff.

In (1981)[5], the Secretary of State for social services established a small enquiry team with business experience to examine the NHS management arrangements in England, chaired by Roy Griffths. The Griffiths Inquiry focussed on the absence of a clear line of management responsibility in the NHS and reported about the existing method of decision making. As per this report, management teams were drawn from a variety of backgrounds including administration, finance, nursing and medicine. In principle, no member of the management team had superior status and each had the power to veto decisions. Although this form of decision making had advantages, the management team was forced to consider a wide range of perspectives before arriving at a decision; it was held responsible for delay in decision making, avoidance of tough decisions and blurring of responsibility.

Coveleski and Dirsmith[6] (1981) point out that what appears to be necessary for hospitals is a 'free float' approach to MBO. Here, rigid procedures are not necessary, since hospital leaders believe in the inter-personal participative philosophy behind MBO.

James J Polezynski and Larry E Shirland[7] (1983) reveal that there is significant positive relationship in the degrees of satisfaction derived from inter-personal relations and positive opinion about the participative component processes of MBO.

Sinha[8] (1987) in his dissertation has assessed the staffing requirement of doctors in surgical units of a large hospital.

Barger, Hofmann, Shumake and Davies[9] (1987) observe that hospitals must learn to involve their lowest-paid para professionals in decision making since often these people have more contact with patients than have physicians and nurses. The study concludes that effective employee involvement techniques through problem solving group result in higher morale, greater satisfaction with management and a more favourable attitude towards their job.

Boissoneau and Mc Pherson[10] (1991) observe that employee participation and involvement are at the leading edge of management thinking. They also state that although employee participation has been a major issue in management for many years, the emphasis still is on traditional quantitative subjects of accounting, finance, statistics and systems engineering rather than on qualitative or behavioural aspects of management which will improve the functioning of an organisation.

Schwartz[11] (1991) points out that the associations between Participative Management and absenteeism, and between work autonomy and turnover, are found to be more negative in nursing.

Schrubb[12] (1992) in his study conducted in Good Samaritan Hospital, Ohio, USA, has found that the workers' participation through self-managed team has produced new levels of productivity, commitment among workers and optimism about meeting the challenges of competition.

Herman J Gilligan[13] (1995) in his research paper, studied the importance of Leadership Development Programme at all levels of employees in the Lutheran Hospital. The conclusion of the study is that Leadership Development Programme has a major organizational impact by virtue of its contribution to the breaking down of professional, inter-departmental, and facility-based barriers and the enhancement of organization-wide connectivity.

Savita Sharma and Cherry[14] (1996) observed from the study conducted at Arthur Andersen & Company and the American College of Hospital Administrators that considerable managerial ability to harness the talent and skill of human resources was essential in health care. The study asserts that organizations can stretch themselves only if they allow employee participation in setting individual and/or work group goals.

Brigid L Bechtold[15] (1997) who explores how organizational culture is created, estimates its impact in industry including health care industry, and studies how inclusion and participation become cultural norms in an organisation. He concludes that we need to change our fundamental assumptions about human nature, organisational philosophy, and business strategy to self-organization. Only then will participation work effectively.

Goyal[16] (1999) examines the various methods of organizing human resource department in a hospital. He also explains how the use of scientific techniques would invariably improve the overall services of the hospital. The study also covers areas like the functioning of hospitals, hospital ethics, need for and benefits of manpower planning, employees' performance appraisal and methods of maintaining cordial human relations in the hospital.

Nico W Van Yperen, Agnes E Van den Berg[17] (1999) conclude that commitment leads to intrinsic desire among employees to contribute more to improved services in service sectors; it also reduces the need for external monitoring mechanisms. Committed employees need less supervision to control their behaviour. In the health sector, employees are expected to strengthen the organization's image among customers through co-operative behaviour.

Bhagyalakshmi Sankar[18] (2000) in her study 'Human Resource Management in the Apollo Hospital', examines the working of the principles and practice of human resource management in the Apollo Hospital and concludes that the doctors, using their professional skills with the support of the paramedics and modern state-of-the-art technology, have helped a lot to build Apollo as a world-class institution. The concept of the right person for the right job is Apollo's credo. The effective quality systems supported by the highly qualified personnel have created an ideal work environment.

Chandra Sekar[19] (2000) states that the health team includes not only doctors and nurses, but also para-professionals, para- medicals, pharmacists, etc.

Lee Hyun[20] (2001) reveales that effective implementation of health services requires adequate co-operation from health professionals. Such behaviour instigates concern for patients, their relatives, peers and other health service providers. It facilitates team work and strengthens team functioning in organizations. Co-operative behaviour is an outcome of professional and organizational commitment. Hence, the quality of care in the health sector is dependent on both professional and organizational commitment.

Lynn M Morgan's [21] (2001) paper addresses how participation has been analyzed by anthropologists and other social scientists and by epidemiologists, health service managers and policy makers, and how to operationalize, implement and measure levels of participation. He concludes that the complexities of participation are better understood today and the possibilities for pragmatic compromise are more widely accepted by a generation of planners, practitioners and analysists.

Sharon Fonn and Makhosazana Xaba[22] (2001) who explored the provider-client relationship, tested several participatory methods with health workers. Health workers identified many constraints on the provision of adequate health services and these constraints affected their work in general and their relationship with women clients in particular. Constraints included inadequacies and inefficiencies in management and lack of gender sensitivity training. The participatory approach was found to be acceptable to the participants and effective in exploring interpersonal relationships.

Elisa J Sobo and Blair L Sadler[23] (2002) in their article, describe a Project conducted in a children's hospital at San Diago to improve the morale of employees by fostering constructive expression of dissatisfaction and innovative ideas to senior executives, in the context of Employee- Leadership Council meetings.

A pre-project survey showed that three-fifth of the employees had low motivation and two-third felt that there was no inter-departmental communication. There was significant depression, anxiety, emotional exhaustion, job insecurity deterioration in team work, and lack of clarity of roles, among Para-medical staff leading to dissatisfaction in other occupational groups.

Through monthly Employee Leadership Council meetings, the employees' views and suggestions were incorporated in the management process, and within one year employees' satisfaction was doubled, and open, honest and direct communication improved by 50 per cent. The senior leadership team was able to make sound decisions with the whole-hearted support of the employees and 90 per cent of the employees' recommended that the children's hospital was a good place to work, and thereby the hospital productivity improved.

Terry, H. Wagan[24] (2002) conducted a study among union leaders of private health care institutions in Canada, regarding co-operative labour management relations and found that labour management cooperation in the form of joint labour management committees has been adopted in many health care work places, which augmented work place performance.

Parameswaran[25] (2003) points out that organized HRD programmes will

- help, achieve and maintain good human relations within the hospital;

- enable each employee to make his/her maximum contribution to the recovery of patients;
- ensure respect and well-being of other employees;
- ensure maximum development of an individual who provides quality care to the patient;
- ensure participation in decision making; and
- ensure satisfaction of various needs of the patient in order to help realize the hospital's goals.

Lunblad and Jennifer Paige[26] (2004) have conducted a research among physicians and staff to describe and analyze team work climate and safety climate in small rural hospitals. The correlation and multiple regression analysis showed that the combination of job/position, length of experience, age, gender and hospital explained only a very small percentage of the variance in team work and safety climates. It was found that the relationship between team work and safety climates and staff turn-over rates, was weak and not of any practical significance.

Buwa Drugudi[27] (2004) suggests that regular planning and review meetings, to streamline programmes, and to identify strengths weaknesses and potential areas for improvement, would be informative and useful. He also suggests that for the improvement of quality of service an experienced team with a suitable mix of staff is essential.

Magnus Lindelow, Pieter Serneels, and Teigist Lemma[28] (2005) report about the need for effective human resource policies and management. They reveal that both policies and the way they are implemented need to be revised and strengthened on the basis of the understanding of how health workers make constrained choices, both in their career and in their day-to-day professional activities.

Ramesh Bhat and Sunil Kumar Maheshwari[29] (2005) examine the human resource challenges in the health sector. One of the findings of the study is that most respondents expressed the desire to assume higher levels of responsibilities and expect more transparency and involvement in manpower planning and development of people. Most health officials felt that management systems were highly centralized constraining them from experimenting with ideas to improve services. This proves that the department can secure commitment of their staff by involving them in human resources planning.

Pestonjee, Kajal, H Sharma and Sonal Patel[30] (2005) conclude that there is need for applying managerial functions in order to make the HRD system a more effective operative function of human resources management in the hospital. The study also offers some suggestions to reduce the stress level of doctors and nurses. A specific model of HRD for hospitals that could be 'patient focused' on the one hand and 'employee central' on the other was suggested.

Margitta B and Beil-Hildebrand[31] (2005) have critically analysed the day-to-day life in the nursing division of hospitals. They reached the conclusion that the results lend little support to the official claim that, if managerial objectives are realized, they are achieved through some combination of shared values and employee participation.

Abhay Shukla[32] (2005) points out the need to promote decentralization of health care, and build up integrated, comprehensive and participatory approaches through the Jan Swasthya Abhiyan. JSA, a unique and growing nationwide coalition of civil society organizations working on health issues, people's organizations, social activists, health professionals academics and researchers working together consistently towards the goal of 'Health for All' on a common platform since the year 2000.

Norbert Dreesch and Carmen Dolea[33] (2005) who present an overview of various methods for planning human resources for health, with their advantages and limitations, and propose a methodological approach to estimate the requirements of human resources to achieve the goals set forth by the Millennium Declaration.

David Heel, John Sparrow and Robert Ashford[34] (2006) in their study, attempt to identify the features of the work environment that facilitates or impedes reflective practice endeavours. The study focused on workplace events and meetings where uni- and multi-disciplinary groups interacted by discussing contemporary issues. An emergent assessment tool arguably provided the workplace practitioner with the ability to measure critical reflection and as such determined personal strategies that might overcome obstacles. Moreover, the study enabled improved awareness of workplace issues that either impeded or facilitated the practice of critical reflection.

Christopher G.Worley[35] (2006) suggests that teams are fairly productive but have not generally influenced the more substantive aspects of hospital operations.

The review attempted above gives a brief description about the published data obtained from various studies conducted in hospitals regarding the co-operation of employees', Information Decision System, problem solving skills of Administrators, management teams, inter-personal relationship, employee involvement through problem-solving groups, workers' participation through self-managed teams, essentials of human resources in health care, methods of maintaining cordial human relations, working of the principles and practices of HRM, components of health team, incorporation of employees' ideas through councils, team work, desire to assume higher levels of responsibilities and decentralization. Now, an attempt is made to trace the major studies on the management practices in the health care industry.

MANAGEMENT PERSPECTIVES IN HEALTH CARE SECTOR

John Leslie Livingstone[36] (1974) has analysed the need for the introduction of Management Accounting System in hospitals. He recommends the need to develop an efficient Accounting System for improving the effectiveness of management in a hospital.

The Voluntary Health Association of India[37] (1975) conducted a study with a view to finding out the accurate cost involved in the running of hospitals. The study report suggests the method of charging the amount from patients on the basis of cost incurred in those Departments from where the patient gets service.

Gupta and Juyal[38] (1978) in their work, have made an attempt to find out the accurate cost of various activities performed by the staff in voluntary clinics. They have also tried to determine the cost of various services provided by the clinic to the patient community. In this report, they suggest that the whole activities of the staff of the clinic should be divided into two categories, namely, (*i*) productive and (*ii*) non-productive, and the cost may be computed for each activity and for each category of staff.

Gouri S.Gupta[39] (1982) in his article, 'Complaint Management in Hospital' concludes that the missionary purpose of a hospital is best served, if medical care is accompanied by an integrated system comprising (*i*) quick and effective services; (*ii*) patients' comfort; and (*iii*) proper and adequate guidance to the visitors. This is, to a great extent, made easy by having efficient management of complaints. Adequate arrangements for voicing and redressal of public grievances help create an atmosphere of optimum service to the patients and keep the authorities informed of the quality of services rendered in the hospital.

Bhadkamkar[40] (1983) in an article, observes that in order to run the hospitals efficiently and effectively, a good management information system with continuous evaluation of the hospital activities is essential.

Mahendra Dutta, Chawla and Sharma[41] (1983) undertook a study of the utilization of hospital beds in major teaching hospitals in the country. The study concludes that (*i*) Though the recommended bed-population ratio has almost been achieved on all-India basis, additional beds need to be provided at appropriate levels (*ii*) Average length of stay in hospital indicates that in the large teaching hospitals the authorities may be under pressure to discharge the patients early.

Mitra and Anand[42] (1983) in their article, conclude that 'if a ward sister has to manage her ward competently, she must understand thoroughly and follow some important factors which are involved in good ward management'. They list out the most important factors in the article.

Ray[43] (1983) conducted a study about the functioning of filter clinic of a large-size hospital during the peak activity period. For the improvement of organizational climate, he suggested that:

(*i*) The principle of unity of command must be adhered to;
(*ii*) Opportunity of free dialogue must be provided by the superiors with increasing awareness of the problems at lower levels;
(*iii*) Optimum use of the capabilities of the functionaries need be made with adequate recognition of instances of good performances;
(*iv*) Inter-departmental work, relevant information and problem-solving adaptation must be available.

Iyer[44] (1983) prepared a paper on modern management systems for hospitals based on the experience of the author and his colleagues in hospitals. He concludes that modern management systems have an important role to play in efficient utilization of resources invested (be they government or private) in hospitals and contribute to better patient care.

Khurana[45] (1984) conducted a study to identify the operational problems of the present information system existing in the hospitals. He identified the problems as those of accuracy, timeliness and over-burdening.

Chandran[46] (1984) examines the scope for the application of Queuing theory to the various problems that any hospital has to face, and suggests how a queuing theory approach can solve them. He has made this case with reference to the X-ray department. He reports that applying queuing theory to the X-ray departments of a general hospital is expected to result in estimating the optimal number of facilities in terms of reducing the total waiting time of the patients. The system will be more efficient when marginal cost of the additional facilities and staff is equal to the marginal benefits of the patients.

Anand[47] (1985) in a paper presented has stated that Medical Specialists are over-burdened by administrative tasks for which they are not professionally trained. He stresses the need for appointing professionally trained medical administrators in the hospitals.

Khanna[48] (1986) points out that government doctors experience a higher level of stress than private doctors. Both government and private doctors experience this stress (role expectation conflict), because they are not able to satisfy the conflicting demands of people, peers, juniors or bosses. They feel that they are over-burdened and their work load affects their quality of work. Both exhibit average stress because of their desire to have more skills to handle responsibilities. Because of the feeling that their role has not been defined clearly and is vague, doctors experience average 'role ambiguity stresses'. Although government doctors have more intense feelings than private doctors, both on an average feel lack of resources and facilities needed in their role.

Anantha Padmanabhan[49] (1986) has conducted a study on the cost of hospitals and suggested some important methods and techniques to control the cost in general and to reduce the cost of materials provided in hospitals in particular.

Guleria[50] (1986) has examined the feasibility of introducing computers in a Hospital Information System with special reference to the areas of patient information system and in patient medical records.

Harold Trader[51] (1986) in his article entitled, 'Management Accounting in a Hospital,' has made an attempt to develop a new accounting system for the successful management of hospitals. Three types of reports, such as: (*i*) Managers' Report, (*ii*) Productivity Report, and (*iii*) The Capital Budget analysis have been proposed to achieve this.

Hella and Toshniwal[52] (1986) in their report, have made an attempt to review the practices and procedures followed for the proper management of materials in hospitals.

Rao[53] (1986) in his dissertation, has examined the need for developing computerized Management Information System for the successful running of small hospitals.

Lohe[54] (1987) emphasizes the need and importance of the system of Drug Inventory Control in nursing homes. He suggests a new method of inventory control of drugs for nursing homes.

Sheela Datta[55] (1988) in her paper, has identified the various areas in the functioning of hospitals where computers can be applied successfully to achieve the objective of providing right information to the right person at the right time.

Yesudian[56] (1988) has found that the communities living in slums in Deonar and Naiguam in Mumbai preferred private sector facilities to public facilities for the short-term and minor ailments.

Duggal and Amin[57] (1989) conducted a study in Maharashtra and this study shows that out of 100 people who fell sick, only 13 went to government hospitals, 77 sought the services provided by the private sector, and the rest resorted to home remedies. This study also shows that the private sector is also a significant provider of primary health care, which includes services like immunization, which are available in both rural and urban areas for all income groups.

Viswanathan and Rohde[58] (1990) estimate that in cases of diarrhoea, nearly 80 per cent of the rural people in India approach private practitioners, while only 10 per cent utilise government facilities.

Lloyds G.Reynolds[59] (1990) conducted a study on the importance of the health care industry. He states that the peculiarity of the industry is, it is the supplier rather than the customer who determines the demand for health care. The important problems identified by him in the health care industry are the problems of access to medical services, inefficient utilization of doctors' time and the use of specialized paramedical personnel.

Tiwari[60] (1990) in his article, has narrated the significance of budgeting in hospitals. He states that the budget committee in a hospital should collect and consolidate necessary data for various budgets, and draft the master budget.

Klinger[61] (1991) calls for the decentralization of many hospital pharmacy departments in order to provide pharmacists and other health care professionals with access to patient records. He finds that this change in department structure decreases the manager's ability to supervise the clinical activities of staff pharmacists. A policy for pharmacist intervention should be developed by the pharmacy department. The policy identifies actions to be taken in specific situations, thus serving to standardize care.

Sankara Rao[62] (1992) examines the organization and administration and suggests that incentives like better promotional prospects, better emoluments and better service conditions would add to their satisfaction. The study suggests some steps necessary to improve the 'administrative potential' of the hospital.

Sundaresan[63] (1993) in his doctoral dissertation, has attempted to design a suitable cost control technique to reduce the ever-increasing hospital costs. He suggests the need for introducing cost accounting system and techniques in the specific areas of materials and supplies, hospital labour and other expenses.

Bhat[64] (1993) concludes that there has been an increase in health care service provided by the private sector.

The study conducted by George[65] (1993) has revealed that the utilization of the private sector services for acute episodes was 69.5 per cent in Madhya Pradesh.

Santosh Jain[66] (1995) has conducted a study on the management information system (MIS) in the LNJPN Hospital, New Delhi. In his report, he has stated the need and importance of MIS for the successful running of hospitals. Further, he offers certain suggestions for improving the present system of MIS in hospitals.

The Medical Services Development Committee[67] (1995) analyzed the strategy of nurses and stated that 'Nurses now have greater management responsibilities at both the ward and hospital levels'. The major reason is that the management's role is so alien to medical professionals that they are more burdened with the additional workload. The developments in medical science and technology, rapid patient turnover, the rising dependency level of patients, and the emergence of professionalism have increased the complexity and volume of nursing care.

A survey was made by the Department of Economics and Statistics[68] 1995 to find out the number of private medical institutions in the State under various systems of medicines, the number of medical and paramedical staff employed in them and the type of facilities available.

Anand[69] (1996) has discussed managerial issues, management concepts and techniques of management in hospitals. He has illustrated the application of some of the management concepts and techniques on medical aspects such as Pathology and Radiology Services, Nursing Services, Blood Banks, etc. Further, he offers some suggestions for managing and improving hospitals and nursing homes.

Cox and Griffiths in their study in the International Labour Organisation (ILO) manual[70] (1996), revealed that the role of nursing is associated with multiple and conflicting demands imposed by nurse supervisors and managers and by medical and administrative staff. This situation appears to lead to work overload as well as to role conflict.

Mox and Chan[71] (1996) have viewed that one difficulty faced by nurses in the ward is increased demand for administrative accountability. The nurses have to produce more statistics and written reports of their activities in the ward. They often feel torn between spending time in direct patient care and administrative duties in the ward.

Premavathi[72] (1998) studied the role of private health care institutions in Tamil Nadu and concluded that the private sector in the State had played a significant role in the delivery of health service. Private health care is mostly of curative nature. In recent times, nearly 60-80 per cent of the people use private sector hospitals and the share of the public health sector has come down. People believe that private health care stands for quality.

Baghotia and Sethi[73] (1998) in their study, identify various gaps/ shortfalls in the practices adopted for collection, segregation, storage, transportation, treatment and disposal of hospital waste. The study reveals that though guidelines on hospital waste management exist, the same are not properly printed and circulated among hospital employees. The study has further observed that the size of plastic bags was not consistent with the size of the dustbins, sharps were not being segregated properly, and the average quantum of waste generated in the hospital was found to be 1.45kg per bed per day.

The Voluntary Health Association of India (VHAI)[74] (1998) of Rajasthan revealed that while the number of beds in the private sector in rural and semi-urban areas in Jaipur had increased 13 times in the past two decades, the number of inpatients in the private sector had increased 18 times during the same period.

Narayan, Menon and Spector[75] (1999) observed that while workload and poor remuneration are the most important factors of stress for nurses in a burn unit, whereas work overload, interpersonal conflict and lack of support are the major constraints.

Saini[76] (1999) has conducted a study on the existing MIS in hospitals. He has identified the magnitude of the information problem and assessed the actual information needs of various sections of the hospital.

Rajaram and Swathi Pandey[77] (2000) conducted a survey to assess the current status of medical audit in India. Most of the respondent doctors agreed that medical audit was required in a hospital as it ensures better patient care, but its success would depend on who conducted the audit, and what method was applied.

Lakshman Rao[78] (2000) quoted that with the application of Queuing theory, the doctors' arrival time was rescheduled and the afternoon was allocated to the members of the employees' families (so that they could get priority in servicing). This enabled servicing of 30 per cent more cases per day.

Onyango-Ouma, Rose Laisser, *et al.*[79] (2001) have indicated that overall health system development is essential for improved service including quality of care. A number of research tools were developed to study different aspects of health workers for change from the perspectives of clients, the facility itself and the larger health system.

Onyango-Oum, Frederick W. Thiong, O., *et al.*[80] (2001) have suggested that with external support and help, especially from the health system level, health workers can work towards improving health services and their job satisfaction can lead to better 'health worker–client' relations.

Green, Ali, Naeem and Vassall[81] (2001) conducted a study to provide information on the levels of resources being used in the government sector and on the resource requirements for facilities in order to improve the resource allocation from provincial to district level. The collection of data on the actual costs of running primary facilities was done through a combination of survey and examination of existing district records. Activity information was obtained from the new HMIS. The main findings of the study are of use in developing more bottom-up budgeting systems.

Birna Trap and Charles[82] (2001) pointed out that following supervision, overall stock management improved significantly. The study also showed that allocating resources to supervision was likely to result in improved performance of health workers with regard to the rational use of essential drugs, resulting in improved efficiency and effectiveness.

McKingsey[83] (2002) in his paper tries to explain the growth of private health care centres in the country. He finds that there has been a significant growth in the number of general and specialist hospitals, nursing homes, individual practices and proliferation of sophisticated diagnostics, and pathological service centres. Further, he has found that the undue growth of private sector hospital services shrink the development of hospital services in the public sector, which ultimately leads to the narrowing of the access of health care to a large section.

Venkat Reddy[84] (2002) in his paper titled, 'Hospital Materials Management', presents a comparative picture of material management practices related to hospitals with the practice prevalent in an engineering industry.

Nguyen Thi Hong Ha, Peter Berman and Ulla Larsen[85] (2002) found that there was no difference by education, sex or place of residence in the use of private ambulatory health care. The private sector served young children in particular. Expenditure on drugs accounted for a substantial percentage of household expenditure in general and health care expenditure in particular. These findings call for a prompt recognition of the private sector as a key player in Vietnam's health systems.

Sagaya Doss[86] (2003) has studied the choice of health care services and estimated the relative influence of variables determining the choice. He concludes that the lower income group preferred government service and the high income group availed themselves of private service. Those who utilized private service attributed the reasons for their choice like: better service and immediate treatment. This study concluded that 81 per cent of the respondents were satisfied with the private doctors.

Sena Eken David A. Rabilino. and George Sehieber[87] (2003) have conducted a study on the existing health system in the Middle East and North African countries. They suggested that the low income countries should continue to focus on providing public health services, promoting good nutrition, ensuring safe water supply, preventing and treating communicable diseases and improving material and child health outcomes.

Mathai K.Mathiyazhagen[88] (2003) has observed that the private health care provider has emerged as the people's choice. However, the choice is significantly linked with socio-economic conditions of the rural people. The discussion suggests that policy makers in India should take serious note of the growing popularity of the private sector in providing health care services, and that it would be advisable to opt for a private– public mix for regulatory and supportive policy interventions.

Mala Ashok[89] (2003) has presented the need for specialization in hospital management, updating of skills among the personnel involved in the medical sector, keeping abreast of up-to-date methods of medication and techniques.

Thomas Bossert, Mukosha Bona and Diana Bowser[90] (2003) made an assessment of the degree of decentralization, with an analysis of available indicators of performance suggests that decentralization may not have either a positive or negative impact on services.

Sweta D'Cunha and Sanjeev Rai[91] (2004) undertook a study to find out the effectiveness or otherwise of management information system in the out-patient department. The study findings revealed that there were deficiencies in the information supplied to the different categories of personnel associated with the outpatient department and frequency of information made available to the personnel.

The objective of the study by Varatharajan, Thankappan and Sheeba Jayapalan[92] (2004) is to provide an approach to assess the performance of PHC's under decentralized governance in Kerala. The analysis here pertains only to PHCs and does not include the private sector. The study concludes that decentralization brought no significant change to the health sector. Active panchayat support to PHCs existed in only a few places, but wherever it was present, the result was positive.

Parikh, Taukari and Bhattacharya[93] (2004) studied occupational stressors and coping mechanisms among nurses. They concluded that among nurses occupational stress did vary according to individual and job characteristics, and work-family conflict. Common occupational stressors found among nurses were work overload, role ambiguity, and interpersonal relationships. Emotional stress, burnout and psychological morbidity could also be a product of occupational stress. Nurses' common coping mechanisms included problem solving, social support and avoidance. Coping and job satisfaction were found to be reciprocally related.

Janat Shah and Murty[94] (2004) observe that a sense of compassion and commitment and a strong leadership are the key elements of the 'Aravind model'. Productivity is fundamentally related to demand. Volume brings down the cost and ensures the viability of the enterprise. Volume, in turn, is ensured by the combination of low cost, high quality and efficient procedures, as well as the appropriate use of information technology in spreading awareness among the people. The model can be replicated, and some of its principles are universally applicable, like the appropriate use of man-power, reduction of time and costs, strong innovative practices to improve quality, and so on.

JDH Porter, Ogden and Ranganadha Rao[95] (2004) have reported on the feasibility and appropriateness of incorporating operating research into the management and decision making of a leprosy NGO. They determined the advantages and disadvantages of introducing operations research to assist in decision making and programme implementation within the organization. This study helps to ensure the creation of appropriate infectious disease control policies that support the needs of patients.

Vivek Handa, Sood and Rajini Bagga[96] (2004) have analysed the status of HRD mechanisms and issues in a government health organisation, and Employees State Insurance Corporation (ESIC). As per the responses, the process of recruitment was slow. Though the performance appraisal was as per the prescribed norms, many were of the opinion that it was subjective, generalized and not reflective of the actual performance. The study also identified that rewards were invariably delayed. No separate Training Cell existed for doctors.

Tran Tuan, Van Thi Mai Dung and Ingo Neu[97] (2005) have concluded that private providers are successfully competing with public health centre system in rural areas. The quality of private health care services is not controlled and is significantly poorer than public services. The current practice in both systems has fallen below the national standard, especially for the management of chronic health problems.

Pol De Vas[98] (2005) in his article, states that in spite of the economic hardships during the 1990s, Cuba has achieved health indicators that are among the best in the world. Today, health care continues to be of high quality and free for all Cubans. It remains exclusively in the hands of the public sector and privatization is not an option.

Ekta Sharma[99] (2005) in her study, shows that both private and government hospitals should consider conducting stress audits regularly, so that, affected doctors can be identified and their stress levels reduced, which will, in turn, improve the quality of work.

The main purpose of the study by Vander Plaetse, Hlatiwayo and Van Eygen[100] (2005) was to generate data on the cost of health care of a relatively high standard, in a context of decentralization of health services and increasing importance of local cost-recovery arrangements. The study results make a clear case for the management of the different elements of the budget at the decentralized district level. The study also shows that it is possible to deliver district health care of a reasonable quality at a cost that is by no means exorbitant.

The findings of the study by Nilambar Jha, Premarajan and Nakesh[101] (2005) is that teaching and learning during MBBS have to focus more on areas like communication, leadership and managerial skills.

Chet N.Chaulagni and Christon M Mayo[102] (2005) observe that lack of reliable data and grossly inadequate appreciation and use of available information in planning and management of health services are two main weaknesses of the health information systems.

Mohanan Nair[103] (2005) conducted an in-depth analysis on the working of hospitals in the private sector in comparison with that of hospitals in government and co-operative sectors functioning in the State of Kerala. He concludes that the private hospitals in the State are performing well in their operation. The operational problems of private, government and co-operative hospitals are different. Only the private hospitals in the State are conscious, while framing and implementing various marketing strategies, to conquer a lion's share of the market. He also concludes that in deciding patient satisfaction in respect of services of doctors, private hospitals are better placed than the government and co-operative hospitals. In the case of services of nursing staff and miscellaneous services, the patients in the co-operative hospitals are more satisfied. He recommends that the government should take the initiative to declare health sector as priority sector and give proper directions to the banks and other financial institutions for providing adequate financial assistance at concessional rates.

Geetika Tankha[104] (2006) conducted a study to investigate the effect of role stress in nursing professionals of government and private hospitals. The results reveal that male nurses experience a significantly higher stress level, compared to females. Secondly, male nurses from private hospitals show significantly higher stress levels than the government nurses. The major reason is that private nurses need to be more vigilant and alert as they may lose their job more easily than government nurses. This means that there is job insecurity for nurses in private hospitals.

The Department of Economics and Statistics[105] (2006) conducted a survey to find out the number of private medical institutions in the State under various systems of medicines, the number of medical and paramedical staff employed in them and the type of facilities available. The recent survey throws light on the achievement made by the private sector in health care facilities of the State.

Ali Mohammad Mosadegh Rad[106] (2006) in his thesis 'Developing a Total Quality Management Model in Health Care Systems of Iran', has identified the strengths and weaknesses of TQM in Health Care Organizations. He developed a model which health care organizations aiming at using TQM to achieve excellence can follow easily.

The review made here clearly indicate that various studies were conducted relating to Materials management, Financial Management, application of Modern Techniques of Management, Ward Management, Complaint Management, Stress Management, Time Management, Waste Management, Application of Queuing Theory, etc.

Even though the health care industry has been earning much profit and rendering service and is vital to the economy of Kerala, no study regarding Participative Management in hospitals, which can significantly improve patient care service and profitability, has been conducted in Kerala. The present study is an attempt to bridge this gap.

REFERENCES

1. Carol Huss, 'Experiment in Participation' in Thakur, C. P. and Sethi, K. C. (Eds), *Industrial Democracy: Some Issues and Experiences,* Delhi: Sri Ram Centre for Industrial Relations and Human Resources, 1973, pp. 186-204.
2. Mowday, 'Unit Performance, Situational Factors and Employee Attitudes in Spatially Separated Work Units', *Organisational Behaviour and Human Performance,* Vol. 12(2), 1974, pp. 231-248.
3. Pylee, M.V., *Worker Participation in Management: Myth and Reality,* Delhi: N.V Publications, 1975, pp. 169–183.
4. Austin, M., 'Evaluating the Training of Mental Health Administrators', *Administration in Mental Health*, Vol. 3, 1975, pp. 62-72.
5. Rob Baggott, *Health and Health Care in Britain*, London: Macmillan Press Ltd, 1998, p. 133.
6. Coveleski, M. and Dirsmith, M., 'MBO and Global Directedness in a Hospital Context', *Academy of Management Review*, Vol. 6, No. 3, pp. 409-418.
7. James, J. Polezynski, *et al.,* 'Determining Readiness of Hospital Administrators to Accept Management by Objectives', *Hospital Administration,* Vol. 20, No. 2, September, December 1983, pp. 138–146.
8. Sinha, R. K., 'A Study to Assess Staffing Requirements of Doctors in Surgical Units of a Large Hospital', *MHA Dissertation*, New Delhi: AIIMS, 1987.
9. Barger, G. Hofmann, P., *et al.,* 'Improving Patient Care through Problem Solving Groups', *Health Progress*, Vol. 68, No. 7, September 1987, pp. 42-45.
10. Boissoneau, R. and Mc Pherson, J., 'Practicing Participative Management in the Clinical Laboratory: Foster a Productive and Satisfying Staff', *Clinical Laboratory Management Review,* May-June 1991, Vol. 5, No. 3, pp. 176–182.

11. Schwartz, R. H., 'Nurse Decision Making Influence: A Discrepancy Between the Nursing and Hospital Literatures', *Health Policy Economics and Management,* Vol. 27, Issue 1, 1991, p. 27.

12. Schrubb, D. A., 'The Implementation of Self-managed Teams in Health Care', *Health Information Management*, Vol. 13, No. 1, August 1992, pp. 45-50.

13. Herman J Gilligan, 'Evaluating Self-managed Learning Part-3: Developing Leaders in a US Health System', *Health Man power Management,* Vol. 21, No. 6, 1995, pp. 25–34.

14. Savita Sharma, K. Cherry, *Hospital Management*, Delhi: Commonwealth Publications, 1996, pp. 53, 54.

15. Brigid, L. Bechtold, 'Towards a Participative Organizational Culture: Evolution or Revolution', Empowerment *in Organisations,* Vol. 35, No. 1, 1997, pp. 4-15.

16. Goyal, R. C., *Human Resource Management in Hospitals,* New Delhi: Prentice-Hall of India, 1999.

17. Nico, W. Van Yperen, et al. 'Towards a Better Understanding of the Link Between Participation in Decision-making and Organizational Citizenship Behaviour: A Multilevel Analysis', *Journal of Occupational and Organizational Psychology,* Vol. 72 (3), 1999, pp. 377-393.

18. Bhagyalakshmi Sankar, 'Human Resources Management in the Apollo Hospital Administration', *Ph.D.Thesis,* Department of Public Administration, University of Madras, September 2000.

19. Chandra Sekhar, S. F., 'Hospital Organization Structure' in Srinivasan, A.V. (eds), *Managing a Modern Hospital,* Delhi: Response Books, Sage Publications, 2000, p. 79.

20. Lee, Hyun–Jung, 'Willingness and Capacity: The Determinants of Pro-social Organizational Behaviour Among Nurses in the UK', *International Journal of Human Resource Management*, Vol. 12 (6), 2001, pp. 1029–1048.

21. Lynn M Morgan, 'Community Participation in Health: Perpetual Allure, Persistent Challenge', *Health Policy and Planning,* Vol. 16, No.3, September 2001, pp. 221–230.

22. Sharon Fonn and Makhosazana Xaba, 'Health Workers for Change: Developing the Initiative', *Health Policy and Planning*, Vol. 16, Supplement 1, September 2001, pp. 13–18.

23. Elisa, J. Sobo and Blair, L. Sadler, 'Improving Organizational Communications and Cohesion in a Health Care Setting Through Employee-Leadership Exchange', *Human Organisation*, Vol. 61, No. 3, 2002, pp. 277–286.

24. Terry H Wagan, and Kent V. Rondeau, 'Labour-Management Forums and Work Place Performance: Evidence from Union Officials in Health Care Organisations', *Journal of Management in Medicine*, Vol. 16, No. 6, 2002, pp. 408-421.

25. Parameswaran, E. G., *Perspective in HRD*, Hyderabad: Neelkamal Publication, 2003.

26. Lunblad and Jennifer Paige, 'Team Work and Safety Climate in Small Rural Hospitals', *International Dissertation Abstracts,* Vol. 65, No.10, April 2005, p. 3728–A.

27. Buwa Drugudi, 'A Day in the Life of a District Medical Officer', *Health Policy and Planning,* Vol. 19, No. 1 January 2004, p. 68.
28. Magnus Lindelow, *et al.*, ' The Performance of Health Workers in Ethiopia—Results from Qualitative Research', *Policy Research Working Paper,* The World Bank Development Research Group, Public Services Team, April 2005.
29. Ramesh Bhat and Sunil Kumar Maheswari, 'Human Resource Issues. Implications for Health Sector Reforms', *Journal of Health Management,* Vol. 7, No. 1, January-June 2005, pp. 1-36.
30. Pestonjee, D. M., *et al.*, 'Image and Effectiveness of Hospitals: An HR Analysis', *Journal of Health Management*, Vol. 7, No. 1, Jan–June 2005, pp. 41–90.
31. Margitta, B. Beil- Hildebrand, 'Instilling and Distilling a Reputation for Institutional Excellence—A Critical Reflection on Organizing Practice', *Journal of Health Organisation and Management,* Vol.19, No.6, 2005, pp. 440–465.
32. Abhay Shukla, 'Jan Swasthya Abhiyan', *Yojana,* Vol. 49, July 2005, pp. 14–17.
33. Norbert Dreesch., *et al.* 'An approach to Estimating Human Resource Requirements to Achieve the Millennium Development Goals', *Health Policy and Planning,* Vol. 20, No. 5, September 2005, pp. 267–275.
34. David Heel, *et al.,* 'Work Place Interactions that Facilitate or Impede Reflective Practice', *Journal of Health Management,* Vol. 8, No. 1, Jan – June 2006, pp. 1–9.
35. Christopher, G Worley, *Implementing Participation Strategies in Hospitals: Correlates of Effective Problem Solving Teams*, California: School of Business and Management, 2006.
36. John Leslie Livingston, *Accounting for Social Goals*, New York: Hooper and Raw, 1974, pp. 289–293.
37. The Voluntary Health Association of India, *An Accounting Guide for Voluntary Hospitals in India,* New Delhi: 1975.
38. Gupta, J. P. and Juyal, R. K., 'An Exploratory Study on Cost Analysis of an Urban Maternal and Child Health and Family Welfare Centre', *Hospital Administration,* Vol.15, No.3, 1978, pp.28-35.
39. Gouri S. Gupta, 'Complaint Management in Hospital', *Hospital Administration,* Vol. 19, No. 1 & 2 March & June 1982, pp. 5–11.
40. Bhadkamar, S. M., 'Management Information System and Ranking of the Hospitals', *Hospital Administration*, Vol. 21, No. 2, September & December 1983, pp. 194–198.
41. Mahendra Dutta, *et al.*, 'Pattern of the Bed Utilization in Large Hospitals of India', *Hospital Administration*, Vol. 20, No. 1 & 2, March & June 1983, pp. 60–63.
42. Mitra, P. and Anand, T. R., 'Ward Planning and Management', *Hospital Administration,* Vol. 20, No. 1 & 2, March & June 1983, p. 28.
43. Ray, D. B., 'A Study of the Filter Clinic of a Large Size Hospital', Hospital Administration, Vol. 20, No. 1 & 2 September & December 1983, pp. 148–156.
44. Iyer, R. S., 'Modern Management Systems in Hospitals', *Hospital Administration,* Vol. 20, No. 2, September & December 1983, pp. 121–126.
45. Khurana, Renu. B., 'Computers in Indian Hospitals—A Market Study', Bangalore: *IIM Project Report*, 1984.

46. Chandran J. S., 'A Queuing Model for Hospital with Reference to Routine X-rays', *Journal of Hospital Administration*, Vol. 21, No. 2 June 1984, pp. 73–76.

47. Anand, K. K., 'Professionalising Management in Hospitals', *Paper Presented at National Hospital Convention*, New Delhi: IHA, December 1985.

48. Khanna, B. B., 'Relationship Between Organizational Climate and Organizational Effectiveness: A Case Study', Unpublished *Ph.D. Thesis*, Varanasi: Banaras Hindu University, 1986.

49. Anantha Padmanabhan, U. K., 'Relevance of Cost Control and Cost Reduction Techniques in Hospital Material Management', *Hospital Administration,* Vol. 23, No. 6, 1986, pp. 408–420.

50. Guleria, M. S., 'A Study of Hospital Information System with Particular Reference to Patient Information System and Inpatient Medical Records', *MHA. Dissertation,* New Delhi: AIIMS, 1986.

51. Harold Trader, 'Management Accounting in a Hospital', *Hospital Administration*, Vol. 23, No. 3, 1986, pp. 1–8.

52. Hella, A. K. and Thoshniwal, A. K., 'Material Management Practices and Procedures in a Hospital', *Project Report*, Mumbai: Bombay Management Assn., 1986.

53. Rao, M. N., 'Development of Computerized MIS for Small Hospitals', Bangalore: Unpublished *Ph.D.Thesis*, IIM, 1986.

54. Lohe, L. P., 'Drug Inventory Control in Nursing Homes', *Project Report*, Mumbai: Bombay Management Association, 1987.

55. Sheela Datta, 'Application of Computers in Hospitals', *Hospital Administration*, Vol. 25, No.11, 1988, pp. 54 – 59.

56. Yesudian, C. A. K., *Health Services Utilization in Urban India: A Study,* New Delhi: Mittal Publications, 1988.

57. Duggal, R. and Amin, S., *Costs of Health Care Household Survey in an Indian District,* Mumbai: Foundation for Research in Community Health, 1989.

58. Viswanathan, V. and Rohde, J. E., *Diarrheea in Rural India: A Nation-wide Study of Mothers and Practitioners,* New Delhi: Vision Books, 1990.

59. Lloyds G. Reynods, *Micro Economic Analysis and Policy*, New Delhi: Universal Book Stall, 1990.

60. Tiwani, C. K., 'Hospital Budgeting', *Hospital Administration*, Vol. 27, No.3, 1990, pp. 101–105.

61. Klinger, P., 'Protocols for Pharmacists Intervention in a 160 Bed Hospital', *Health Policy Economics and Management,* Vol. 27, Issue. 1, 1991.

62. Sankara Rao, M., 'Hospital Organization and Administration', *Deep & Deep Publications,* Delhi: 1992, pp. 7–179.

63. Sundaresan, P. K., 'Cost Accounting and Cost Control-Hospitals', Unpublished Ph.D.Thesis, Kochi: Cochin University of Science and Technology, 1993.

64. Bhat, R., 'The Private/Public Mix in Health Care in India', *Health Policy and Planning,* Vol.8, No.1–4, 1993, pp. 43–56.

65. George, A., 'Household Health Expenditure in Madhya Pradesh', Mumbai: *Foundation for Research in Community Health*, 1993.

66. Santhosh Jain, 'Management Information in Hospitals—A Case Study of LNJPN Hospital', New Delhi: *MBA Project Report*, 1990.

67. Medical Services Development Committee, *Nursing Strategy: Towards the Year 2000,* Hong Kong: Hospital Authority of Hong Kong, 1995.

68. Government of Kerala, *Report on the Census of Private Medical Institutions in Kerala—1995*, Thiruvananthapuram: Department of Economics and Statistics, 1995.

69. Anand, K. K., *Hospital Management—New Perspectives*, New Delhi: Vikas Publishing House, 1996.

70. Cox, T. Griffiths, A. and Cox, S., 'Work-related Stress in Nursing: Controlling the Risk to Health', *International Labour Organisation (ILO) Manual*, 1996, web site:www.ilo.org.

71. Mox and Chan, 'Work and Family Roles of Female Nurses: Sources of Stresses and Coping Strategies', *The Hong Kong Nursing Journal*, Vol.73, 1996, pp. 12–19.

72. Premavathi, K., 'Health Care Administration in Tamil Nadu; A Study in Public Policy', *Unpublished Ph.D. Thesis,* Madras: Anna Centre for Public Affairs—University of Madras, November 1998.

73. Baghotia, K. S. and Sethi N. K., 'A Study of Hospital Waste Management in a Territory Care Hospital', *Health and Population Perspectives and Issues,* Vo. 21, No.1, Jan – March 1998, pp. 12–25.

74. Voluntary Health Association of India (VHAI), New Delhi: India's Health Status, 1998.

75. Narayan, L. S. *et al.*, 'Stress in the Work Place: A comparison of Gender and Occupations', *Journal of Organisational Behaviour,* Vol.20, No.1, 1999, pp. 63–73.

76. Saini A. K., *Management Information System in Hospitals. A Computer-based Approach for Quality in Hospital Services and Administration,* New Delhi: Deep & Deep, 1999.

77. Rajaram, N and Swati Pandey, 'Medical Audit and Its Administration' in Srinivasan, A. V. (ed), *Managing a Modern Hospital,* Response Books, Delhi: Sage Publications, 2000, pp. 364–365.

78. Lakshman Rao, H. K., 'Application of OR to Management Practice: An Introduction', *Management Review*, Vol. 12, No.4, 2000, pp. 53–54.

79. Onyango-Ouma, Rose Laisser, *et al.*, 'An Evaluation of Health Workers for Change in Seven Settings: A Useful Management and Health System Development Tool', *Health policy and Planning,* Vol.16, Supplement 1, September 2001, pp. 24–42.

80. Onyango-Ouma, Frederick W Thiang'o, *et al.*, 'The Health Workers for Change Impact Study in Kenya', *Health Policy and Planning,* Vol. 16, Supplement 1, September 2001, pp. 33–39.

81. Green, A., Ali, B., *et al.*, 'Using Costing as a District Planning and Management Tool in Balochistan, Pakistan', *Health Policy and Planning*, Vol. 16, No. 2, June 2001, pp. 180–186.

82. Birna Trap, Charles, H. Todel, *et al.*, 'The Impact of Supervision on State Management and Adherence to Treatment Guidelines: a Randomized Controlled Trial', *Health Policy and Planning,* Vol. 16, No.3, September 2001, pp. 273–280.

83. Kinsey Mc, 'Health Care—Expansion for Profit', *Economic and Political Weekly*, Vol.37 (34), 2002, pp. 34–76.

84. Venkat Reddy, *Hospital Materials Management*, New Delhi: Response Books, 2002.

85. Nguyen Thi Hong Ha, *et al.,* 'Household Utilization and Expenditure on Private and Public Health Services in Vietnam', *Health Policy and planning*, Vol. 17, No.1, March 2002, pp. 61–70.

86. Sagaya Doss, S., 'An Economic Analysis of Health Care Services', *Unpublished Ph.D. Thesis*, Department of Economics and Research, University of Madras, June 2003.

87. Sena Eken David A., *et al.,* 'Living Better', *Finance and Development*, Vol. 40, No.1, 2003, pp. 15–17.

88. Maathai K Mathiyazhagan, 'People's Choice of Health Care Provider: Policy Options for Rural Karnataka in India', *Journal of Health Management,* Vol. 5, No.1, January–June 2003, pp. 111–137.

89. Mala Ashok, 'Doctor's Day', *The Hindu*, 28 June, 2003.

90. Thomas Bossert, *et al.,* 'Decentralization in Zambia: Resource Allocation and District Performance', *Health Policy and Planning*, Vol.18, No.4, December 2003, pp. 357–369.

91. Sweta D'Cunha. and Sanjeev Rai, B., 'A Study on the Management Information System Used in the Outpatient Department', *Journal of the Academy of Hospital Administration (JAHA),* Vol. 16, No.2, July–December 2004.

92. Varatharajan, *et al.,* 'Assessing the Performance of Primary Health Centres under Decentralized Government in Kerala, India', *Health Policy and Planning*, Vol. 19, No.1, January 2004, pp. 41–51.

93. Parikh, P., *et al.,* 'Occupational Stress and Coping among Nurses', *Journal of Health Management,* Vol. 6, 2004, pp. 115–127.

94. Janat Shah. and Murty, L. S., 'Compassionate, High Quality Health Care at Low Cost: The Aravind Model', *IMB Management Review,* Vol. 16, No.3, September 2004, pp. 31–43.

95. JDH Porter, *et al.,* 'Introducing Operations Research into Management and Policy Practices of a Non-governmental Organisation (NGO): A Partnership Between an Indian Leprosy NGO and an International Academic Institution', *Health Policy and Planning,* Vol. 19, No. 2, March 2004, pp. 80–87.

96. Vivek Handa, A. K., Sood, *et al.,* 'Human Resource Development in a Government Health Organization: Views of Doctors', Health and Population Perspectives and Issues, Vol. 27, No. 2, April–June 2004.

97. Tran Tuan, *et al.,* 'Comparative Quality of Private and Public Health Services in Rural Vietnam', *Health Policy and Planning*, Vol. 20, No. 5, September 2005, pp. 319 – 327.

98. Pol De Vas', 'No One Left Abandoned Cuba's National Health System Since the 1959 Revolution', *International Journal of Health Service,* Vol. 35, No. 1, 2005, p. 189.

99. Ekta Sharma, 'Role Stress among Doctors', *Journal of Health Management*, Vol. 7, No. 1, Jan–June 2005, pp. 151–156.

100. Vander Plaetse, B. *et al.*, 'Costs and Revenue of Health Care in a Rural Zimbabwean District', *Health Policy and Planning*, Vol.20, No. 4, July 2005, p. 243.

101. Nilambar Jha, K. C. *et al.*, 'Five Star Doctors for the 21st Century: A BPKIMS Endeavour for Nepal', *Journal of Health Management*, Vol. 7, No. 2, July–December 2005, pp. 237–247.

102. Chet N. Chaulagai, *et al.*, 'Design and Implementation of a Health Management Information System in Malawi: Issues, Innovations and Results', *Health Policy and Planning,* Vol. 20, No. 6, November 2005, pp. 375–384.

103. Mohanan Nair, V. R., 'A Study on the Working of the Hospital Industry in Kerala', *Unpublished Ph.D.Thesis,* Department of Commerce, University of Kerala, 2005.

104. Geetika Tankha, 'A Comparative Study of Role Stress in Government and Private Hospital Nurses', *Journal of Health Management,* Vol. 8, No.1, January–June 2006, pp. 11–21.

105. Government of Kerala, *Report on the Private Medical Institutions in Kerala—2004,* Department of Economics and Statistics, Thiruvananthapuram: 2006, pp. 1–167.

106. Ali Mohammad Mosadegh Rad, *Developing a Total Quality Management Model in Health Care Systems of Iran,* m.mosadeghrad@rhul.ac.uk2006.

CHAPTER

3

Health Care Industry

The maxim that 'health is wealth' highlights the importance of health for a happy life. Good health is of utmost importance in social development, and hence it can very well be equated with wealth. Considering its importance, all over the world, 6th April is celebrated as World Health Day.

Health is an ephemeral mirage which is difficult to measure and assess. Non-health, a wide spectrum ranging from dysphoria to death[1] is also difficult to assess but easier to record. The WHO has defined health as a state of complete physical, mental and social well-being and not merely the absence of disease or infirmity.[2] Further, the WHO constitution states that '. . . . the enjoyment of the highest attainable standard of health is one of the fundamental rights of every human being without distinction of race, religion, political belief and economic or social condition'[3].

More specifically, health can also be seen as process of adaptation to the environment, a capacity to function, and strength to cope both with specific illness and with life in general. A wide range of social factors and environmental features, as well as individual and personal behaviour, affect the health of individuals and of the nation. The distribution of income, level of employment, the state of housing, the presence or absence of environmental pollution of various sorts and a variety of both socially and individually determined life styles affect health status.[4]

Health was first recognized as a fundamental human right at the International Conference on Primary Health Care at Alma Ata in Kazakhstan, Soviet Socialist Republic, in 1978. India is one of the signatories to the Alma Ata Declaration of 1978. The Declaration aimed at 'Health for

All by 2000'. But India will be quite far from realizing this dream even in 2010. One of the reasons for non-realization of the objective has been consistent reduction in public fund allocation for the health sector. The allocation is only less than one per cent of the GDP, which again is a mere one-fifth of the total health-spending in the country[5]. A number of health projects are being implemented in India with assistance from the WHO in the form of experts, and supplies and equipment.

In spite of all these, the objective of 'Health for All' remains a dream. It is in this context that the role of private health care organizations, which are increasing in number day by day, becomes significant in helping the nation reach its objective.

This chapter mainly deals with private health care industry in the State of Kerala and covers the evolution, unique aspects, peculiarities, advantages and criticisms of the health care industry in general and also explains the concepts and forms of participation, parties involved in health care, participative management in hospitals and role of medical practitioners.

EVOLUTION OF HEALTH CARE INTO AN INDUSTRY

For a long time, health care was not thought of as business because health care involves basic human needs, the expertise of physicians, and a large amount of local practice variations.[6] Until the 1960s:

— The health care industry was dominated by voluntary, not-for-profit, hospitals and a strong, independent medical profession;

— Physicians were well respected, very busy and left to their own judgements in almost all medical affairs;

— There was a strong legal doctrine against the corporate practice of medicine;

— There were strong professional norms against advertising or other competitive behaviour among physicians;

— Many patients were uninsured and the sums of money to be made in the health sector were small.

For these reasons, health care looked very little as an industry and people viewed its provision more as a public service than as a business.

However, starting around the 1960's, a series of changes took place that transformed the health sector into an industry. The most important of these changes were:

(1) The entry of government as a large-scale health purchaser through Medicare and Medicaid;

(2) There was an increase in the number of people covered by employer-provided insurance.

These two changes injected huge amounts of money into the health care industry and people began seeing the provision of health care not solely as a way to serve humanity, but as a way to make money.

UNIQUE ASPECTS OF HEALTH CARE INDUSTRY

An industry is a group of organizations that produce the same or similar products. Though health care is being more and more considered as an industry, many of its features are unique.

The business of health care is labour and capital-intensive, and the utilization of some of the equipments or machinery rarely reaches the break-even level. The obsolescence rate is high. Cost of equipment, land and building, personnel and other inputs have kept spiralling up constantly. The demand for service is unpredictable, while new hospitals are coming up at an incredible pace. They are growing in number by leaps and bounds, and the existing hospitals are adding bed strength every year. Price war is crawling slowly into the health care industry. Health insurance opens up new opportunities for many hospitals. Hospitals established in joint ventures with foreign participation seem imminent.[7]

Nowadays, with the corporatization of hospitals, it has not only remained the place for medical treatment, but has emerged as a sophisticated service industry in which the major players compete with each other in terms of types and number of services, extra facilities, speed of service, expert doctors and staff, and the price.

The unique aspects of hospitals[8] are:

(*i*) Health care organizations operate 24 hours a day. Service or, in the language of the industrial complex, production cannot be shut down at night and on the weekends; the facility must remain open to admit the sick and injured round the clock to carry on normal business.

(*ii*) Hospital patients and visitors present unique problems not found in most other social settings. Patients are involuntary customers because they generally have no desire to be in the hospital or to undergo major treatment. The visitors' actions and reactions to management practices may not always be completely rational. Thus tolerance for abnormal behaviour within limits resulting from stress must be a major consideration in any hospital protection programme.

PECULIARITIES OF THE HOSPITAL AS AN ORGANIZATION

The peculiarities of a hospital as an organization[9] may be many, such as:

(1) The product of the hospital is service which cannot be quantified in economic terms.

(2) The service in the hospital is always personalized, professional and directly rendered by the medical, nursing and other specialized personnel according to the needs and requirements of each individual.

(3) Hospital service is normally emergent in nature and no two situations are similar, needing the same treatment.

(4) The wide spectrum of people involved in the hospital activity ranges from the highly skilled professional to a person who may not have visited a school.

(5) The dual control by way of the professional authority and the executive authority in the hospital invariably leads to management conflicts which is a peculiar situation every hospital administrator has to face in the day-to-day operation.

(6) A hospital has to be highly responsive to the health needs and service expectations of the community.

(7) The work in a hospital tends to be both variable and uneven.

(8) There is great concern arising from clarity and responsibility. The cost of making mistake in patient care is likely to be very high, with serious life and legal consequences.

(9) Health facility has abstract goals, diffuse authority, low inter-dependence, few measures, and require extensive coordination of efforts, resources and demands.

Business engages in price competition to gain customers. However, price has not been the major competitive issue for hospitals when attracting patients. Hospitals act to gain revenue by maximizing the quality of their service and consequently gain more patients. Quality, rather than price is the main form of competition between hospitals[10].

HEALTH CARE IN KERALA—A COMPARISON WITH ALL-INDIA AVERAGE

Health care industry is the most important service industry in India. The Indian health care industry is estimated to cost around Rs.1000 billion at present and is expected to reach Rs.2000 billion by 2012, with 17 per cent annual growth rate. In spite of 55 years of planning, India's achievement in the field of public health is not very impressive[11].

Health care is only one of the several factors which influence the health status of the population. The data regarding the health care services in India as a whole and a few major States of India[12] are given in Table 3.1

and from this Table, it is clear that Kerala has attained high health standards when compared with the all India level health indicators.

Kerala has unique achievements in immunization status. The vaccination coverage of infants against polio, BCG and measles was reported to be 100 or near 100 per cent in 1998-99 itself. The State has succeeded in preventing the incidence of communicable diseases like leprosy, tuberculosis, filariasis and malaria to a large extent. Paradoxically, the morbidity levels in Kerala are also exceptionally high compared to other States. Scholars consider that this is due to the 'positional objectivity'; a Keralite who has ready access to health care facilities perceives illness and seeks medical care more readily than one in a less favourable environment.

Table 3.1 : Health Care Services in India and a Few Major States of India

State	Number of Hospitals per 100000 population (1998)		Number of Beds per 100000 Population (1998)		Number of Primary Health Centers per 100000 population (1998)		Number of Doctors and Nurses per 100000 population (1998)	
	Rural	Urban	Rural	Urban	Rural		Rural	
					PHCs	SCs	Doctors	Nurses
India	0.7	3.7	23.25	188.5	3.3	19.7	47.19	36.88
Bihar	0.1	2.0	3.94	226.69	2.7	17.9	30.55	10.29
Andhra Pradesh	2.0	9.5	27.28	255.44	3.2	20.3	49.67	23.34
Orissa	0.3	3.1	5.56	189.77	4.6	20.0	35.19	50.23
Rajasthan	-	1.6	2.95	159.55	4.3	25.3	32.01	22.38
West Bengal	0.2	1.3	9.12	224.57	2.8	14.7	61.38	25.26
Gujarat	0.6	13.7	24.16	381.01	3.3	24.5	52.98	59.0
Karnataka	0.1	1.6	11.26	213.19	4.7	24.0	98.58	52.21
Maharastra	0.0	8.3	20.72	219.70	3.3	18.6	62.72	48.64
Tamil Nadu	0.2	1.6	11.14	218.99	3.7	22.4	81.94	60.49
Delhi	-	-	-	-	0.6	3.3	-	-
Kerala	9.1	0.9	334.81	249.11	4.3	22.9	56.72	78.41
Madhya Pradesh	0.9	0.7	11.79	75.55	3.0	20.9	16.92	88.00

Source: Report on Private Medical Institutions in Kerala–2004, Government of Kerala

Kerala has attained enviable health status indicators like low infant mortality rate, low birth rate, low death rate and high rate of expectancy of life at birth[13]. Low infant mortality rate, low birth rate, low death rate, and high rate of expectancy of life at birth indicate that the health status of Kerala is far advanced and higher than the all India average[14] and is even comparable to that of developed countries. The figures for birth rate, death rate and infant mortality rate in Kerala and India are given in Table 3.2.

Table 3.2 : Health Development Indicators: Kerala and India – 2004

Health Indicators	Kerala	India
Birth rate (per '000 population)	16.70	24.80
Death Rate (per '000 population)	6.30	8.00
Infant mortality rate (per '000 population)	11.0	60.0
Maternal mortality rate (per '000 population)	0.30	4.37
Life at birth		
Male	71.67	64.10
Female	75.00	65.80
Total	**71.00**	**64.80**

Source: Economic Review—2005, Kerala State Planning Board

Kerala has attained this health status despite being an economically weaker state with a per capita expenditure on health of $28 compared to $3925[15] by the United States of America. Socio-economic factors like female literacy, social reforms, nutritional programmes, accessibility and availability of health services, public distribution system and other forms of State intervention have contributed to the achievements in the health sector of Kerala.

HEALTH CARE IN KERALA UNDER VARIOUS SECTORS

This outstanding progress in the health status of a Keralite, as outlined above, is achieved through widespread growth of the three systems of medicine (allopathy, ayurveda and homoeopathy) in public, private and co-operative sectors, combined with people's health awareness. In Kerala, in the public sector, health care is provided through a network of sub-centres, Primary Health Centres in the rural areas and Hospitals and Dispensaries in the urban areas. The private sector delivers health care through a vast number of institutions, ranging from clinics with no inpatient facility, to more than 1000-bedded multi-specialty corporate hospitals, distributed throughout the State.

For providing health care, Kerala has 48834 beds under the Government sector, 1123 beds in ESI hospitals, 5272 beds under the Co-operative sector, 510 beds under the Autonomous sector, and 70506 beds under the private sector[16]. The relevant details about the availability of number of beds and beds per lakh population under various sectors in Kerala are given in Table 3.3.

Table 3.3 : Total Beds under Different Sectors

Category	No. of beds	Beds per lakh population
Government sector (including 3 systems)	48,834	153
ESI Hospitals	1,123	4
Co-operative Sector	5,272	17
Autonomous Sector	510	2
Private Sector	70,506	221
Total	**1,26,245**	**396**

Source: Economic Review, 2005, Kerala State Planning Board

The striking feature from Table 3.3 is that the bed strength in the private sector is greater than the bed strength in all other sectors put together.

HEALTH CARE IN KERALA UNDER VARIOUS SYSTEMS OF MEDICINE

Furthermore, health care is delivered through various systems of medicine like Allopathy, Ayurveda, Homoeopathy, Unani and Naturopathy. The latest data relating to medical institutions revealed that the three systems of medicine together have 2,696 institutions and 48,834 beds in the Government sector. Out of the total institutions, 47 per cent (1,278) are under allopathy, 32 per cent (857) under ayurveda and 21 per cent (561) under the homoeopathy system of medicine[17]. Out of the total beds, 89 per cent (43619) are under allopathy, 8 per cent (3920) under ayurveda, and 3 per cent (1295) under homoeopathy system. The three systems together treated 22.98 lakh inpatients and 941.90 lakh outpatients during 2004. In the case of inpatients treated under different systems of medicine also, allopathy had a lion's share. The data relating to various systems of medicine under government sector are given in Table 3.4. *(See on next page)*

In the case of number of institutions, number of beds, number of inpatients and outpatients treated under different systems of medicine also, allopathic system has a lion's share.

PRIVATE MEDICAL INSTITUTIONS IN KERALA

The condition of private hospitals in the State of Kerala[18] may be assessed as follows. Even though more than 70 per cent of the health care needs of the people of Kerala are met efficiently by the private sector, the government

Table 3.4: Medical Institutions, Beds and Patients Treated Under the Three Systems of Medicine in Government Sector during 2004.

Sl. No.	Systems of medicine	Institutions		Beds		Patients Treated (Lakhs)			
						IP		OP	
		No.	%	No.	%	No.	%	No.	%
1.	Allopathy (Excluding sub centres)	1278	47	43619	89	17.42	75.81	431.16	45.78
2.	Ayurveda	857	32	3920	8	5.18	22.54	253.29	26.89
3.	Homoeopathy	561	21	1295	3	0.38	1.65	257.45	27.33
	Total	**2696**	**(100)**	**48834**	**(100)**	**22.98**	**(100)**	**941.90**	**(100)**

Source: Economic Review, 2005, Kerala State Planning Board

does not properly recognize their services. The private hospitals are viewed purely as commercial institutions by the government so that even the benefits enjoyed by the industries in the State are denied to them. High rate of interest for hospital loans, high electricity tariff and water charges equal to those of star hotels, non- availability of subsidy to hospital buildings and equipment etc. throw light on this fact. Over and above this, laws and regulations from various Departments of government and from local bodies often adversely affect the smooth running of the hospitals. However the liberalization policies of the government have led to the mushrooming of private hospitals in the State.

The Department of Economics and Statistics, Thiruvananthapuram, Kerala, has conducted State-wide Census of Private Medical Institutions in Kerala in 1986, 1995 and 2004 and published the data so collected. The total number of private medical institutions in the State[19] as per that report is given in Table 3.5.

Table 3.5 : Number of Private Medical Institutions in Kerala

Year of survey	Number of Institutions	Increase of Institutions	Rate of increase
1986	9663	-	-
1995	12618	2955	30.58
2004	12918	300	2.38*

Source: Report on Private Medical Institutions in Kerala–2004, Government of Kerala

* Although the increase in Private Medical Institutions was 30.58 per cent (2955) during the decade 1985-1995 it was negligible during the next decade 1995-2004. This is due to the difference in concepts followed during the second and third surveys. Doctors' consultation centres were also taken as hospitals during 1995, but not during 2004.

District-wise Details about the Private Medical Institutions

The Ernakulam district ranks at the top and Wynad district at the bottom in respect of the total number of institutions and of beds. District-wise details about the number of medical institutions, number of beds and average number of inpatients and outpatients per year[20] under all different systems of medicine are given in Table 3.6.

Table 3.6: District-wise Number of Private Medical Institutions and Average Number of In-patients and Out-patients per Year

Sl. No.	District	Number of Institutions	Number of Beds	Number of Inpatients	Number of Outpatients
1.	Kasaragod	439	1549	110220	2062716
2.	Kannur	962	5081	225480	4170600
3.	Wynad	341	1521	93708	1431828
4.	Kozhikkode	1235	3081	233880	4614060
5.	Malappuram	944	4108	325392	5176932
6.	Palakkad	796	2653	130692	3243756
7.	Thrissur	981	7272	444432	4209396
8.	Eranakulam	1857	9850	1200612	7720092
9.	Idukki	496	5149	234624	3627876
10.	Kottayam	1341	5285	304692	5659656
11.	Alappuzha	1005	2922	294636	3959820
12.	Pathanamthitta	598	4323	274956	3000312
13.	Kollam	860	4886	314136	4824564
14.	Thiruvananthapuram	1063	6811	327288	4925544
	State	**12918**	**64491**	**4514748**	**58627152**

Source: Report on Private Medical Institutions in Kerala – 2004, Government of Kerala

System-wise Details of Private Medical Institutions

In Kerala, we have various systems of treatment, viz., allopathy, ayurveda, homoeopathy, naturopathy, unani, etc. There were 64,491 beds in 2004 in all the systems together, as against only 50,766 beds in 1986. The number of institutions under the ayurveda system of medicine has been almost equal to the number of institutions under the allopathy system. But the number of beds under the ayurveda system is negligible when compared to the number of beds under the allopathy system[21], in all the surveys. Hence, we can conclude that the major health care delivery system in the State for all major illnesses, especially those requiring hospitalization, is under the allopathy system.

System-wise details of private medical institutions in the State under the main systems during the years 1986, 1995 and 2004 are presented in Table 3.7.

Table 3.7: System-wise Details of Private Medical Institutions—Number of Institutions and Number of Beds during the Years 1986, 1995 and 2004

Sl. No.	System of Medicine	Number of Institutions			Number of Beds		
		1986	1995	2004	1986	1995	2004
1	Allopathy	3565	4288	4825	49,030	67515	57,071
2	Ayurveda	3925	4922	4332	1301	2595	5,502
3	Homoeopahy	2078	3118	3226	296	394	813
4	Others	95	290	535	139	418	1105
	Total	**9663**	**12618**	**12918**	**50766**	**70924**	**64491**

Source: Report on Private Medical Institutions in Kerala, 1986, 1995 and 2004, Government of Kerala

Comparison of all Private Health Care Institutions

The role played by private allopathic institutions in health care delivery can be understood by studying the bed strength in allopathic hospitals compared with the same of other systems of medicine. Of the total number of beds 88.49 per cent are in the allopathic system[22]. Idukki district stands at the top with 96.58 per cent beds in allopathic institutions, while Malappuram District stands at the bottom with only 73 per cent. For details refer Table 3.8.

Table 3.8: Number of Beds in All Private Health Care Institutions and Allopathic Private Health Care Institutions, District-wise Comparison

Sl.No.	District	Number of beds		
		In all private health care institutions.	In Allopathic private health care institutions	Percentage of Allopathy to the total number of institutions
1	2	3	4	5
1.	Kasargod	1549	1441	93.03
2.	Kannur	5081	4766	93.80
3.	Wynad	1521	1429	93.95
4.	Kozhikode	3081	2908	94.38

...(Contd.)

1	2	3	4	5
5.	Malappuram	4108	3000	73.03
6.	Palakkad	2653	2192	82.62
7.	Trissur	7272	6612	90.92
8.	Ernakulam	9850	8770	89.04
9.	Idukki	5149	4973	96.58
10.	Kottayam	5285	4873	92.20
11.	Alappuzha	2922	2342	80.15
12.	Pathanamthitta	4323	3801	87.93
13.	Kollam	4886	4236	86.7
14.	Trivandrum	6811	5728	84.1
	State	**64491**	**57071**	**88.49**

Source: Compiled from the Report on Private Medical Institutions in Kerala–2004, Government of Kerala

Private Allopathy Medical Institutions in the State

Table 3.9: Number of Private Allopathy Medical Institutions in Kerala

Year	Number of Institutions	Growth	Growth rate (%)
1986	3565	-	-
1995	4288	723	+20.28
2004	4825	537	+12.5

Source: Report on Private Medical Institutions in Kerala – 2004, Government of Kerala

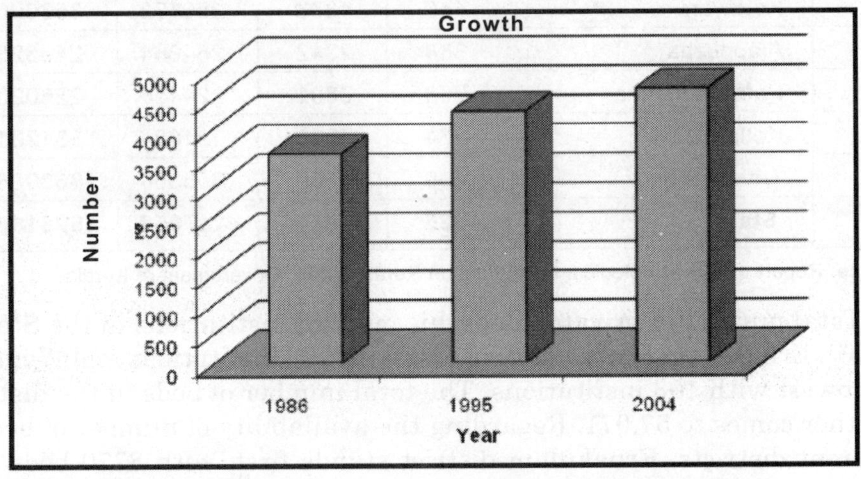

Fig. 3.1 : Number of Allopathy Private Medical Institutions

In the present context, a detailed analysis of the allopathy medical institutions providing health care services in the State is relevant. Table 3.9 and figure 3.1 shows the number of private allopathy medical institutions[23] in the State as obtained from the three surveys conducted by the Department of Economics and Statistics, Thiruvananthapuram, during the years 1986, 1995 and 2004.

District-wise Details about Allopathy Medical Institutions

Table 3.10 gives a clear idea regarding the district-wise distribution of the various allopathic institutions including the number of beds, in-patients and out-patients.

Table 3.10: District-wise Distribution of Medical Institutions and Average Number of In-patients and Out-patients per Year–Allopathic System of Medicine

Sl.No.	District	Number of Institution	Number of Beds	Number of Inpatients	Number of Outpatients
1.	Kasaragod	184	1441	104016	1303872
2.	Kannur	300	4766	216624	2692860
3.	Wynad	106	1429	86484	909936
4.	Kozhikkode	352	2908	225936	3079716
5.	Malappuram	333	3000	297912	3089904
6.	Palakkad	262	2192	120264	1929396
7.	Thrissur	316	6612	407928	2895336
8.	Eranakulam	793	8770	1161996	5325132
9.	Idukki	238	4973	223488	2826960
10.	Kottayam	440	4873	286632	3530064
11.	Alappuzha	384	2342	264864	2495256
12.	Pathanamthitta	263	3801	224460	2260200
13.	Kollam	374	4236	291084	3312312
14.	Trivandrum	480	5728	305364	3630864
	State	**4825**	**57071**	**4217052**	**39281808**

Source: Report on Private Medical Institutions in Kerala–2004, Government of Kerala

Total number of private allopathic medical institutions in the State is 4825[24]. Ernakulam district stands first with 793 institutions and Wynad at the lowest with 106 institutions. The total number of beds in the districts together comes to 57,071. Regarding the availability of number of beds in different districts, Ernakulam district stands first, with 8770 beds. The number of in-patients being related to number of beds, the districts of

Ernakulam, Thrissur and Thiruvananthapuram rank first, second and third, with 1161996, 407928 and 305364 inpatients respectively. For providing outpatient services also Ernakulam district holds the first place. The total number of outpatients served in the State during the year 2004 was 39281808.

Type of Ownership

The ownership-wise private hospitals can be categorised as proprietorship, partnership, co-operatives, trusteeship, limited companies and others. In Kerala out of the 12467 units 87.14 per cent (10864) were owned by individuals[25], and the rest 12.86 per cent (1603) only belonged to all the other sectors together. Further, it could be noted that, 5.4 per cent (674) of the units were owned on partnership basis, 2.92 per cent (365) under trusteeship, 0.74 per cent (93) under co-operatives, 1.41 per cent (176) under limited companies and 2.39 per cent (295) under other categories.

An overall picture of the total number of private medical institutions, coming under all the systems, according to the type of ownership in the State of Kerala, is given in Table 3.11.

Table 3.11 : Private Medical Institutions in Kerala According to the Type of Ownership during 2004

Sl. No.	Type of ownership	Number of institutions	Percentage of total
1.	Proprietorship	10864	87.14
2.	Partnership	674	5.40
3.	Cooperatives	93	0.74
4.	Trusteeship	365	2.92
5.	Limited Companies	176	1.41
6.	Others	295	2.39
	Total	**12467***	**100**

Source: Report on Private Medical Institutions in Kerala–2004, Government of Kerala

Note: The total number of private medical institutions under all systems of treatment together comes to 12467. But when we take the system-wise number of institutions, the total number comes to 12,918. This is because in a few institutions more than one system of medicine is used for treatment.

Private Allopathic Medical Institutions According to Type of Ownership

Ownership-wise majority of the private allopathic medical institutions in the State come under proprietorship. As per the survey 79.36 per cent (3403) of the institutions in 1996, and 79.11per cent (3817) of the institutions in 2004, belonged to proprietorship. 7.84 per cent (336) and 8.56 per cent

(413) of the institutions were on partnership basis during the year 1996 and 2004 respectively[26]. In line with the changing and sophisticated demands of the public, more and more multi-specialty and super-specialty hospitals are mushrooming on limited company basis. As per the 2004 Report, 2.47 per cent (119) of private allopathic medical intuitions in Kerala were owned and managed on Limited Company basis. Table 3.12 shows the details of ownership of private allopathy institutions in Kerala.

Table 3.12: Number of Private Allopathy Medical Institutions According to Type of Ownership During the years 1996 and 2004

Type of ownership	1996		2004	
	Number of Institutions	Percentage of the total	Number of Institutions	Percentage of the total
Proprietorship	3403	79.36	3817	79.11
Partnership	336	7.84	413	8.56
Cooperatives	75	1.75	60	1.24
Trusteeship	336	7.60	266	5.51
Ltd Companies	—	—	119	2.47
Others	148	3.45	150	3.11
Total	**4288**	**100**	**4825**	**100**

Source: Report on Private Medical Institutions in Kerala, 1996 and 2004, Government of Kerala

Parties Involved in the Health Care Institutions

The composition of manpower employed within a health care unit is wide compared with other organizations. As there are doctors, nurses, engineers, technicians, computer staff, finance officers, ministerial staff etc., managing such a wide range of occupations and professions is difficult. The complexity is enhanced by the wide range in professional qualification, diversity and interdependence of services provided, political and economic factors, the influence of the professional organizations and unions.

The survey conducted by the Department of Economics and Statistics on private health care institutions in Kerala revealed the district-wise details about the number of employees working in various health care institutions as on 31-3-2004[27]. Table 3.13 gives the details and this Table shows that the majority of the doctors, para-medical and non-medical staff were working in allopathic institutions.

Table 3.13: District-wise list of Doctors, Para-medical and Non-medical Staff in Private Health Care Institutions—in *All the Systems* together and in the *Allopathic System* as on 31-3-2004

Sl.No.	District	Number of Doctors/ Physicians		Number of Nurses, Para-medical Technical staff		Ministerial Staff/ Non-medical staff	
		All systems	Allopathic system	All systems	Allopathic system	All systems	Allopathic system
1.	Kasargod	648	400	925	821	223	200
2.	Kannur	1511	844	2470	2145	595	489
3.	Wynad	520	259	847	768	277	199
4.	Kozhikode	2250	1326	3087	2690	1233	917
5.	Malappuram	1838	1127	3562	2989	1290	972
6.	Palakkad	1497	742	1861	1396	826	536
7.	Trissur	2586	1733	4958	4430	1524	1194
8.	Ernakulam	3600	2272	5649	5014	1713	1414
9.	Idukki	745	478	1241	1192	234	224
10.	Kottayam	2207	1265	3169	2736	974	814
11.	Alappuzha	1545	883	2028	1775	658	576
12.	Pathanamthitta	1362	998	2665	2518	780	722
13.	Kollam	1616	1097	3015	2684	786	622
14.	Thiruvananthapuram	2478	1857	3589	3275	994	845
	State	**24401**	**15281**	**39066**	**34433**	**12107**	**9724**

Source: Report on Private Medical Institutions in Kerala–2004, Government of Kerala

MANAGEMENT IN HOSPITAL

A hospital is a highly complex social, economic and scientific organization, whose main function is to provide comprehensive health care to the society and to act as a referral centre. Complexity of functions in hospitals is increasing due to the growth of various specialities and super specialities. Every hospital desires to acquire the latest technology so that treatment of the sick can be accurate and quick. More complex the organization, more difficult is its management.

The *principles of management* or the truths of management shall increase the efficiency of management and it helps to crystallize the nature of the management, to improve research, and to attain social goals. The hospitals in the private sector—corporate, trust or the religious kind, will have to be administered as self- supporting institutions. Hence, there is need to apply management principles for planning, resource allocation, investment analysis, pricing and cost control in hospitals[28].

Hentry Fayol, father of modern management, propounded 14 principles of the management in 1911. Hospital management is a special branch of general administration and out of the principles of management; the principles like unity of direction, unity of command and scalar chain are not applicable to hospitals[29].

The *organizational structure* of the typical general hospital differs substantially from the bureaucratic model of other large-scale organizations. The hospital has a unique relationship between the formal authority of position as represented by the administrative hierarchy and the authority of knowledge as represented by medical practitioners and other professionals. This creates a somewhat diffused and unique formal structure.[30]

There is *diverse source of authority* and no one line of authority, in hospitals. The authority in the hospital is shared (not equally) by the Board of Trustees, the Doctors and the Administrator—the three centres of power in the organization. In the hospital, authority does not emanate from a single source and does not flow along a single line of command as it does in most formal organizations.

Each of these groups has a basis for the exercising of authority; however, they are not clearly delineated and separate:

(*i*) The legally responsible group in the hospital, charged with legislating policy, is the board of trustees; therefore these men must be the *policy makers;*

(*ii*) The essential activity in the hospital is medical care for the sick, rendered by specialist physicians; therefore they should *determine the policies* of the organization;

(*iii*) The person most knowledgeable about all phases of life in the hospital, the only full-time professional with wide perspective, is the Administrator; therefore, he should *decide matters of policy.*

It is difficult to select any one of the three as having the central authority. Authority is disbursed and shared rather than adhering to the scalar hierarchy. There are three separate sources of authority exercising within the same social organization; there are diverse sources of authority.

HUMAN RESOURCE IN HOSPITALS

When patients enter a hospital their primary contacts are with their doctor and the nurses. However, the tasks of the hospital are carried out by a large number of co-operating participants whose educational background, training, skills and functions are diverse and heterogeneous.

The personnel of Health Care Organizations[31] consist of doctors who provide the medical treatment, nurses who take care of peripheral treatment, paramedical staff, who give support services to the medical staff and non-medical staff who render ancillary, supportive, administrative and other services.

A hospital is basically a human organization. People are involved at every stage-the staff and the patients. Humanity, devotion to patients, compassion and consideration for the sick and wounded are the hallmark qualities of all those who work there. Management with human touch is a must in hospital management. It is a human organization run on business lines.[32]

The *Medical Staff (Doctors)* are specialized because of the growing complexities of medical technology. The group dynamics within the medical staff is very complex. Although each physician engages in independent practice, he must coordinate his hospital activities with other doctors, nurses, various service departments and paramedical personnel. This requires the development of effective group relationship[33].

Within the hospital, the physician's rank is that of specialized decision-maker about patient care needs and the hospital resources necessary for that needs.[34] The medical staff of the wards and departments of the hospital should be arranged, wherever practicable, on a team basis, particularly in the main specialties of medicine, surgery and obstetries and gynaecology.

If the medical staff is strong, the nursing, technical and other staffs needed are likely to be attracted by the quality of the work. In a significant judgment, the Kerala High Court has held that 'a doctor would be a workman' as defined under Section 2(s) of the Industrial Disputes Act[35]. The five areas of expertise of doctors were identified as care giver, decision maker, communicator, community leader and manager[36].

The *Administrator* of the hospital may be a medical expert or a non-medical executive. Whether the administrative head should be a doctor or a layman, he should be well-versed in hospital administration and should possess those qualities of mind and spirit that make for the smooth working of the hospital and encourage all staff members to give willingly their best.

The function of the Administrator was primarily clerical and housekeeping in nature. With the growing complexities the greater need for coordination of the hospital activities and the increased demands for sophisticated equipments and its effective use, physicians became administrators. However, as hospital affairs grew more complicated, skilled administration has come to be recognized as vital to the effective functioning of a hospital[37].

A hospital is essentially a medical institution; and logically, one would expect the head of it to be a doctor, just as one would expect the captain of ship to be a sailor or the head of a school to be a teacher. If the head of the hospital is a medical director, he should have as his deputy a layman thoroughly trained and experienced in hospital administration. He should relieve the medical director of non-medical administrative duties and leave him free to advice on hospital policy; co-ordinate the medical services of the hospital; deal with medical staff within and medical agencies outside the hospital, and supervise the medical records department, the pharmacy, the medico-social workers, and through the heads of the respective departments, the technicians employed therein. The lay administrator and the finance officer are responsible for all matters of a financial nature.

Para Medical, Technical and Ministerial Staff: Scientific and technical staff in professions allied to medicine (e.g. Physics, computer science) is increasing because of the increasing needs for specialist skills resulting from developments in medical science and technology[38]. Compared with industries, technological advances in the hospitals tend to increase the need for specialist staff. Medical technicians work in the laboratories, X-ray departments and other units. Para-medical, Technical and Ministerial Staff include the following:

- *(i)* ***Nurses:*** The Nursing staff includes graduate professional nurses in various supervisory and non-supervisory positions, practical nurses, and nurse's aides. The nursing staff has the difficult but important function of co-ordination between the 'care' functions of the hospital, i.e. the administrator and his staff, and the 'cure' functions of the physician. In this role, the nurse often serves as a negotiator, compromiser and influencer. The nursing role is moving away from the doctors' assistant towards increased specialized and technical functions. When doctors find it difficult to make or communicate decisions about the management of patients, nurses bear the brunt of relatives' questions and answers;
- *(ii)* ***Pharmacists:*** Pharmacists prepare and dispense medicines as well as advise physicians on their dosage, use and side-effects. The Chief Pharmacist, who is in charge of the hospital pharmacy, supervises the accurate dispensing of drugs prescribed by the doctors;
- *(iii)* ***Medico-social Workers:*** Medico-social workers can collaborate with the clinicians; without it, much of the skill and energy of the doctors

and nurses may be wasted. A medico-social worker needs to have knowledge of local conditions, customs, traditions, and general mode of life of the people among whom she works;

(iv) ***Physiotherapists:*** Physiotherapists concentrate on specific exercises for patients to regain physical function after injury or illness;

(v) ***Occupational Therapists:*** Occupational therapists help individuals develop, maintain, or regain skills needed for work on daily living. Occupational therapy is intended mainly to arouse a patient's interest and to take his mind off his illness;

(vi) ***Radiographers:*** The radiographer is responsible, under the supervision of the radiologists, for the smooth working of the X-ray department, for the keeping of registers, and for the ordering, checking and safe custody of films and reagents;

(vii) ***Laboratory Technicians:*** The pathological laboratory attached to a large hospital is likely to be divided into sections dealing with microbiology, blood chemistry, hematology, anatomy, and histology. Each of these sections needs its own staff of technicians and laboratory aids. All technicians should be trained in all branches of pathological work so that they can, when necessary, be interchanged;

(viii) ***Dieticians and Nutritionists:*** The dietician is in charge of the diet kitchen and supervises the special diets required by patients with diabetes or with renal, gastric, or other disorders. He also has to instruct patients referred to him by physicians;

(ix) The ***Non-medical Staff*** includes records librarian, maintenance staff and mechanics, managers of finance, personnel departments and supplies, electricians, clerical and secretarial staff working within clinical areas to support professional and technical staff, laundry managers, etc.;

(x) ***Medical Secretaries*** support clinical staff by relieving them of administrative, clerical and secretarial tasks and so allow them to concentrate on matters for which they have been professionally trained;

(xi) ***A Records Officer*** must have intelligence and training of a fairly high order if the medical records are to be subjected to statistical analysis or data processing. The Records Officer should keep strict confidence about the records entrusted to his care, in as much as some of them may contain intimate details about the lives of patients;

(xii) The tendency today is towards mechanization and so, ***mechanics and maintenance staff*** are required in a modern hospital. The greater the number of the complicated equipment more will be the need of highly skilled mechanics, electricians, and others to maintain and to deal promptly with breakdowns.

Apart from these direct participants, in the hospital system, there is usually *Board of Trustees* having overall institutional responsibility for the organization.

Hospital personnel, be they those in administration, medical staff, paramedical staff or general employees, must all be concerned with one goal, (i.e.) to provide the best possible patient care. It is unfortunate that administration frequently loses sight of the fact that patient care is dependent upon the skills and attitudes not only of the medical and paramedical staff but also of the hospital personnel whom the patients may never see.[39]

Human beings need to be dealt with, with empathy and compassion because they do have feelings. We may force people to work but we cannot force people to work well. We can only motivate them to do so and 'achieve excellence,' as we know people who feel good about themselves produce good results and people who produce good results feel good about themselves[40]. The personnel policies of a hospital should help employees to realize their individual goals and needs and ultimately to improve the quality of patient care.

People need to be motivated in order to work well. The current theories of motivation demand that managers delegate subordinates and give them full responsibility for what they are doing. Supervisors should be given as much freedom to manage as is possible within the framework of the organization's objectives. On the lower levels, the staff must be allowed similar freedom, even to the extent of organizing the work themselves in any way they think fit. They may be encouraged to work in groups, building up a team spirit and a sense of belonging. This is the basis of participative management.

THE CONCEPT OF PARTICIPATIVE MANAGEMENT

The tasks of the hospital are carried out by a large number of cooperating participants whose educational background, training skills and functions are diverse and heterogeneous. Much of the treatment task is performed by the doctors who require the collaboration and assistance of many paramedical professional personnel.

To make the employees produce their best, they need to be motivated with more serious factors like job satisfaction, achievement orientation, recognition, acceptability, etc. These can be ensured only if the individual is recognized and appreciated for the quality of work that he or she is putting in. Through delegation and job enrichment, and by introducing participative management, people may be made to feel that they are important for the organization and that they are recognized and appreciated wherever necessary.

Frederick Taylor, the father of Scientific Management, believed that men were usually driven by the fear of hunger and search for profit and, therefore, they could be motivated for peak performance through economic inducements and material rewards.

The human relationists held that non-economic rewards also played an important role in determining the motivation and happiness of the worker; workers react to management and its norms and rewards not as individuals, but as members of groups. The human relationists further emphasized the role of communication, participation, and leadership in the management of organizations.

Some other studies revealed that the group under 'democratic' leadership was superior to the one under 'authoritarian' as well as 'laissez faire' leadership. Some of the studies emphasized the importance of participation by lower ranks in making decisions, especially those decisions that directly affect them.

Even though the terminologies used by these scholars varied to some extent, the central theme stressed by all of them is that an organization which takes into consideration human feelings and aspirations and associates members in the process of management is likely to be more efficient and healthier compared to an organization which manages the people in an authoritarian way. Therefore, participative management is advocated by these scholars as a management innovation capable of making positive contribution towards the health and effectiveness of the social organization of an enterprise.

The idea of participation has become very popular and has been embraced by international and multilateral agencies as an essential ingredient for sustainable development programmes.[41]

Participative management is a vague concept which has different meanings for different people. Participation refers to a process in which two or more parties influence each other in making certain plans, policies and decisions.[42] Participative management aims at involving every individual in the organization to participate to his full capacity in the management of the organisation[43]. Participation is a means to accomplish the aims of a project more efficiently, effectively, or cheaply[44]. For the management, it is joint consultation prior to decision making. It is a tool for improving the overall performance of an enterprise. For labourers, it is just like co-decision or co-determination. The trade unions view that the objective of participative management is to gain control over decision making process within an enterprise.

Participation means mental and emotional involvement, rather than mere muscular activity[45]. A person's self is involved, rather than just one's skill. This involvement is psychological rather than physical. A person who participates is ego-involved instead of merely task involved. Some managers insist on task involvement for true participation.

Participation[46] is the mental and emotional involvement of a person in a group situation which encourages him to contribute to group goals and to share responsibility.

DETERMINANTS OF PARTICIPATION

The determinants of participation can be classified under two broad headings, viz., external or situational factors and internal or human factors.

The political, social and economic environments of the participants concerned form the *external factor*. For example only a democratic set up is congenial to meaningful participation. Similarly, a society with clearly drawn lines that segregate classes is unsuitable for participation. Effective participation is possible only if the society that forms the background of the industry is economically sound and growing. Another important external determinant of participation is the nature of an enterprise. The ability of employees to influence managerial decision varies from enterprise to enterprise. The size of the enterprise too may be different. If the employees are to participate in the management directly, the management should be free and autonomous to take final decisions without reference to a higher authority.

Internal factors include employees' propensity to participate and management's acceptance of the participation. Employees' attitude towards participation, their capacity to participate, and their perception of own powers jointly form the propensity to participate. Management's acceptance of employees' participation depends upon the management's attitude towards participation, capacity to participate and perception of its own powers.

Suggestions for Meaningful Participative Management

The main considerations for meaningful participative management[47] are the following:

(*i*) Participative management must be decentralized. Putting a worker on the Board of Directors is not enough. Emphasis should be on face-to-face groups in the various sections of the industry. But, starting from bottom, there should be participative forums at various levels right up to the Board of Directors;

(*ii*) Real power and responsibility must be given at every level;

(*iii*) Incentives should be built-in in the form of recognition and monetary rewards for outstanding performance. These incentives should be both individual and collective;

(*iv*) An attitude of respect for the individual should be developed. Workers should be considered partners in the enterprise and not mere wage-earners;

(*v*) Status distinction between various categories should be de-emphasized. This can be done by providing similar uniforms, lunch rooms, medical facilities, recreation and leisure, washrooms, etc., to all levels of workers;

(*vi*) Communication should be in the language of the workers, and efforts should be made to disseminate information about the enterprise widely and in a form easily understandable to workers;

(*vii*) Too much division of labour should be avoided. Instead, each worker should be encouraged to learn several types of relatively similar jobs. If this is done, workers can change jobs, help each other, and take collective responsibility for production in their respective sections.

The successes of participative management would depend on the degree of autonomy and participation that the managers and supervisors themselves enjoy. Participation is based on leadership exchange; one who does not receive participation may find it difficult to initiate it for his subordinates.[48]

Forms of Participation

The form, or the way in which workers can and do participate in management varies a great deal. To some extent, this variation is related to the differences in the level of management, the subjects or areas in which participation is sought, and the pattern of labour-management relations. The relevance of the level of management may also vary from organization to organization, depending upon the level of power or authority enjoyed by managers at different levels in different types of organization.

This means that even in an organization there may be a high level of participation in certain spheres, whereas the level of participation in certain other spheres may be low. Empirically, it has been found that the level of participation varies from situation to situation even in the same organization.[49]

The important forms in which workers could participate in management are: information sharing, consultation, joint decision-making and administration, and collective bargaining. [50]

Information-sharing is the form of participation wherein workers are informed of certain aspects of the enterprise, such as the financial results of its operations, plans for expansion, etc.

In the ***Consultative form,*** the management only consults workers-their desires, opinions, ideas, suggestions, etc., but retains to itself the authority and responsibility of making decisions and executing them.

Some management may go beyond consultation and involve workers to play a more active role in making decisions and executing the same. It is generally the issues on which the interests of workers and management are identical that provide scope for such ***Joint decision-making*** and administration. In joint decision-making, the relationships of parties are based on mutual faith and reciprocity of interests. They sit *around* the table and make decisions.

Workers often influence managerial decisions through ***Collective bargaining***. The issues over which the interests of workers and management are competitive are usually decided through collective bargaining. Collective bargaining is based on power relationship and it is the relative power of each party which is the main factor in deciding issues. It is the manner in which workers influence managerial decisions that distinguishes joint decision making from collective bargaining. The relationship between the parties is based on the respective power; the gains of one are the losses of the other. The parties sit *across* the table, negotiate, and try to arrive at an agreement.

Since workers and their representatives are able to exert greater influence on management decisions through joint decision-making and collective bargaining, these two forms of participation may be considered as the ***higher forms of participation***, and consultation and information sharing as the ***lower forms of participation*** of workers in management.

If the workers are given an opportunity to influence managerial decisions at higher levels through their elected representatives, it is *ascending* participation. Where the workers may be given more power to plan and make decisions about their own work, it is *descending* participation. [51]

Since the attitudes of the parties concerned are so important in the functioning of participation systems, any introduction or reform of such a system must be preceded by explanations and consultations on the systems, nature, aims and operation. A minimum of consensus between employers' intermediate staff and workers must be secured on the kind of system to be applied and on aims and expectations.[52]

Participative Management in India

With the growth of democracy and socialistic ideas, participative management has become a popular concept all over the world. Workers participate in management through Joint Consultative Committees in the U.K, Joint Enterprise Councils in Sweden, Works Committees in France, Works Councils and Co-determination Committees in the Federal Republic of Germany, and through collective bargaining in the USA. Participative management was achieved in these countries through both evolutionary and legislative processes. A recent survey of the extent of workers' participation in these countries showed the institutionalization of higher forms of participation in all of them.[53]

Our private sector organizations are still run in an outdated, authoritarian manner. Decision-making powers are in the hands of a few enterprises, and investors continue to be favored over employees in matters of policy. Hence, a colonial type of bureaucratic system prevails, which allows little or no share of power to the employees. In fact, many of the managers of these enterprises are drawn from the civil service or the military, and have a strong status quo orientation. Exceptions, of course, are there.[54]

Outside the organizations, our society is becoming increasingly democratic. People are learning to choose their representatives and through them to influence the policies and decisions. Their conception of their rights and powers as citizens is rapidly changing. Viewed in the rapidly changing cultural context, participative management in Indian institutions has become an imperative.

Participative Management in Hospitals

The hospitals are managed with the objective of providing prompt, adequate, continuous and satisfactory services to the patient community, because their prime consideration is providing quality health care, as well as earning profits.

The experience from other organizations and indeed from within the Health Service shows that maximum efficiency can only be achieved if all the staff in the organization works together and contribute to the management.[55]

Full staff participation is important both as a means of tapping the practical and intellectual resources of all the health personnel for the benefit of the health organization and as a way of making work in the organization more meaningful for everyone.[56]

Top level managers set the basic stones for planning, determine overall goals for the organization and give direction on the content of policies and similar planning documents. This is not done in isolation, but based on information provided through the direct participation of personnel in each department or division.[57]

The running of a hospital is not simply the responsibility of a limited number of administrative staff but is a complex interplay between medical, paramedical and administrative staff. [58]

The employees in general expect to be treated with dignity. Therefore all the hospital executives concerned must work together with all categories of employees and gain their genuine and whole-hearted contribution to achieve the hospital goals by providing them opportunities for participation even at the planning stage. Every individual engaged in the singular service of promoting the cause and mission of a hospital is a vital link in its overall chain, be he a skilled surgeon or an unskilled sweeper. The lower level hospital staff should, in fact, be considered essential to hospital functioning as a physician or a nursing orderly.[59]

Joint effort is important, as there are different types of health personnel who make the health systems more effective in providing health services. Without their joint effort a health service worth its name is not possible.[60]

Clinical management teams should give all professional staff, including Doctors, Nurses and Administrators working together, the responsibility for the quality of care provided and control over the use of resources necessary for service provision. Effective team work not only improves staff morale, but provides more efficient and effective service to the patient.[61]

The organisation should give considerable management responsibility to clinical or locality groups, and value and encourage staff participation in making decisions.[62]

Studies of doctors' views[63] on management show that differences in attitude range from those doctors who consider management to be a waste of time and feel that it would be better to left to a professional, possibly non-medical managers, to those who see grave dangers, if doctors do not participate actively in health service management.

While summarizing the Griffiths report, Rob Baggott[64] stated that management team was drawn from a variety of backgrounds including administration, finance, nursing and medicine. In principle, no member of the management team had superior status and each had the power to veto decisions. He also urged that doctors should become more closely involved in processes of management and budgeting.

Thus, many experts were of the idea that participative management is good and essential in hospitals. The *advantages* of involving all levels of staff in participation[65] are many like:

— individual's knowledge and experience is expanded and initiative is encouraged;
— involvement in the planning process boosts morale;
— inter-professional and inter-departmental cooperation is enhanced;
— low level managers become familiar with policies;
— targets set by the budget are more likely to be accepted; and the
— staff knows where they fit in the department or specialty.

But the author concludes that motivating staff in these ways sounds easy but takes time and energy.

The range of occupations and professions within the Health Care unit is huge compared with other organizations. There are doctors, nurses, engineers, technicians, computer staff, managers, finance officers, etc. The complexity is enhanced by political and economic factors and the influence of the professional organizations and unions. Managing such a wide range of occupations and professions is difficult.

DOCTOR MANAGER

It was not until the late 19th century that the doctor began to play an important role in the hospitals. Doctors maintained complete and total authority over his own area and he was not involved and indeed had no need to be involved in the management of hospitals. In the second half of the twentieth century, the hospital management and medical treatment have both become more complex. There are large numbers of people involved in treatment and the organization has grown in size with a move away from professional independence to inter-dependence.[66]

Ten years ago or less, a doctor who expressed an interest in management was, at best, suspected of eccentricity, but more generally accused of a lack of clinical commitment. Now, however, a move into management especially on a part-time basis is widely regarded as a healthy and interesting development in a clinical career. This has been reinforced by a well-established trend in other countries, primarily the USA, Canada and Australia, where doctors with specific talent in management move into senior positions in the management of their organization. The reason why doctors should get involved in management is clearly explained by Tony White as follows: If doctors do not take collective actions to rationalize their own behaviour, then others will seize on this evidence and use it for their own probably unacceptable ends.

Doctors' views on management show that if they do not get involved in managing their own affairs they will be subject to external control by others who lack personal insight into the problems of caring for patients.[67]

Doctors are Managers

Doctors are inescapably managers first and foremost, because they are responsible for the clinical management of patients who come to or are referred to them. For doctors of hospitals with admitting facilities this personal responsibility for clinical management exists at three levels[68]

— they are responsible for clinical management of the individual patient, from diagnosis to treatment. They are also responsible for managing inpatient and/or outpatient waiting lists.

— another very important part of their task is to decide who gets treatment now and who waits - whose access to resources takes priority over someone else.

— the third level of clinical management, which is now the most controversial, is the management and leadership of the multi-disciplinary clinical team or network that focuses on the care of the individual patient. Traditionally, doctors are responsible for seeking to ensure that treatment is both timely and appropriate to the patients' needs.

Why Doctors Should be Involved in Management?

Doctors should be involved in management for the following reasons[69]:

(*i*) Optimizing resources is the most effective way to ensure that resources are used to the best advantage. Doctors must be at the centre in such decision-making;

(*ii*) There are some very capable clinicians, who can offer leadership, the ability to motivate a passion for the work being undertaken, and an understanding of law to build a team to work together;

(*iii*) The doctor has an involvement of a different sort, and his long-term view should be reflected in discussions of management problems;

(*iv*) A doctor is free to express contrary points of view, which may be the important aspects of democratic debate;

(*v*) Once a doctor is convinced of the soundness – or perhaps the inevitability – of a particular course of action, he or she is likely to be the most persuasive voice in altering the views of his or her clinical colleagues;

(*vi*) If the area or issue is one in which hospital managers do not have any interest, there may be no effective management input even when it is needed like for e.g. the handling and storage of medical notes, which will be managed by somebody else;

(*vii*) An open-minded interaction with colleagues in management, finance and other disciplines gives an illuminating perspective of the problems and complexities arising in the running of a modern hospital and can also make a doctor aware of the ability and dedication of colleagues in many other disciplines;

(*viii*) It is often extremely difficult for a lay manager to judge the validity of the seriousness of some patients. But efficient doctors will give credibility and support to those cases which are genuine.

Resistance of the Doctors in Management

Doctors resist taking management responsibility. The reasons may be many as:

— they are already extremely busy;

— they probably have had no formal training in management;

— many regard financial management skills as being irrelevant to their careers;

— the undergraduate training they have had is to provide the best possible care for their patients, regardless of cost

Some experts are of the view that as medicine and management start from such different points they cannot be mixed.[70]

Appointing doctors as general managers has the effect inevitably of removing them from their clinical practice, thereby emphasizing the split between the management and the professional culture of the organisation.[71]

Role of Medical Practitioners

The theoretical analysis revealed the status of the health care professionals as follows: Within health care, doctors enjoy superior status. Other health care professions also act for the most part under medical direction and instruction. They have less autonomy and are weaker in terms of their political organization and leverage.

A forecast made about the future of doctors in management revealed that most of posts like Medical Director of the Trust Board, Clinical Director, Chief Executive Officer, etc., would probably be occupied by doctors in the future as the medical profession is become more aware of the opportunities in management. For doctors to occupy any of these roles, training and support is necessary, although often lacking.[72]

Doctors want to be involved in management, to protect their interests and prevent an erosion of their discretionary decision making; yet, they do not want to sacrifice their valuable clinical time for the successful performance of a management role. In the longer term, doctors may not wish to compromise their clinical independence by assuming management functions. At the same time, securing a share of resources and determining priorities can only be done through involvement in management activities.

With these ideas in mind, the extent of involvement of different categories of employees in the management of private hospitals of Kerala in the present system is assessed in the next chapter.

REFERENCES

1. Peter Orton and John Fry, *U K Health Care: The Facts*, London: Kluwer Academic Publishers, 1995, p. 1.
2. Rob Baggott, *Health and Health care in Britain*, London: Macmillan Press Ltd, 1998, pp. 1, 2.
3. Andrew Green, *An Introduction to Health Planning in Developing Countries,* Tokyo: Oxford University Press, 1994, p. 8.
4. Calum Paton, *Health Policy and Management*, London: Chapmen and Hall, 1996, p. 3.
5. Sankaranarayanan, K. C., 'Education, Health and Housing' in Rajasenan, D. and General de Groot (Eds), *Kerala Economy, Trajectories Challenges and Implication,* Cochin: Directorate of Publications and public Relations, 2005, p. 262.
6. David Calkins, *et al., Health Care Policy*, USA: Blackwell Science, 1995, pp. 8-10, 61.
7. Jangaiah, P., 'Financial Management for Hospitals' in Srinivasan, A. V. (Ed), *Managing a Modern Hospital*, Delhi: Sage Publications, 2000, p. 110.
8. Russell L Colling, *Hospital and Health Care Security,* USA: Butter worth Heinemann, 2001, pp. 47-48.
9. Syed Amin Tabish, *Hospital and Hospital Services Administration Principles and Practice*, Oxford: Oxford University Press, 2001, p. 156.
10. Rushika J Fernandopulle, and David Chin, 'The Health Care Industry' in David Calkins, *et al.* (Eds), *Health Care Policy*, USA: Blackwell Science, 1995, pp. 63, 64.
11. Sankaranarayanan, K. C., *Op. cit.*, p. 263.
12. Government of Kerala, 'Report on Private Medical Institutions in Kerala—2004', *Department of Economics and Statistics,* Thiruvananthapuram: 2006, p. 1.
13. Nayar, K. R., and Anant Kumar, 'Kerala and Bihar: A Comparison', *Yojana*, Vol. 49, July 2005, p. 9.
14. Government of Kerala, *Economic Review 2005,* State Planning Board, Trivandrum: Feb. 2006, p. 356.
15. Nayar, K. A., and Anant Kumar, *Op. cit.,* p. 9.
16. *Economic Review 2005, Op. cit.*, p. 358.

17. *Ibid*, p. 357.
18. Bhaskaran, M., 'IMA and Medical Profession', *Kerala Medical Journal*, Vol.41, No.2, April 2000, p. 17.
19. Report on Private Medical Institutions in Kerala–2004, *Op. cit.*, p. 3
20. *Ibid*, p. 18.
21. Report on Survey of Private Medical Institutions in Kerala, *Op. cit.*, 1986, 1995, p. iv and 2004, pp. 19-26.
22. *Ibid*, 1986, 1995, p. iv and 2004, pp. 18, and 19.
23. Report on Private Medical Institutions in Kerala 2004, *Op. cit.*, p. 7.
24. *Ibid*, p. 19.
25. *Ibid*, p. 45.
26. Report on Survey of Private Medical Institutions in Kerala, *Op. cit.*, 1996, p. 1 and 2004, p. 46.
27. Report on Survey of Private Medical Institutions in Kerala 2004, *Op. cit.*, pp. 97, 98, 106,107, 115, 116.
28. Subha Rao, K. B., 'Planning a Modern Hospital' in Srinivasan, A.V. (Ed), *Managing a Modern Hospital*, Delhi: Response Books, 2000, p. 44.
29. Ghei, P. N., 'Principles of Hospital Management', *Hospital Administration*, Vol. 14, No. 2, June 1977, p. 139.
30. Fermont E Kast and James E Rosenzweig, *Organization and Management: A Systems Approach*, New York: McGraw Hill Book Company, 1970, p. 539.
31. Pestonjee, D. M., *et al.*, 'Image and Effectiveness of Hospitals: An HR Analysis', *Journal of Health Management*, Vol. 7, No.1, Jan-June 2005, pp. 44-45.
32. Desai, V. B., 'Principles of Management as Applicable to Hospitals', Hospital *Administration*, Vol. 21, No. 1&2, March & June 1984, pp. 10-14.
33. Fermant E Kast, *et al.*, *Op.cit.*, pp. 539-549.
34. David Calkins, *Op. cit.*, pp. 47-48.
35. Staff reporter, 'A Doctor is a Workman, Says High Court', *The Hindu,* Wednesday, Feb.28, 2007, p. 4.
36. Nilambar Jha, K. C., *et. al.*, 'Five Star Doctors for the 21st Century; A BPKIHS Endeavour for Nepal', *Journal of Health Management*, Vo. 7. No. 2, July-Dec. 2005, pp. 237-247.
37. Sudhir Dawra, *Hospital Administration and Management,* Delhi: Mohit Publications, 2002, Vol. II, p. 448.
38. John Sutherst, *et al.*, *The Doctor Manager*, Tokyo: Churchill Livingstone, 1994, pp. 133.
39. Sudhir Dawra, *Op.cit.*, p. 447.
40. Davar, S. R., *Personnel Management and Industrial Relations,* New Delhi: Vikas Publishing House, 1976.
41. Ricardo Gomez, 'Facilitating Participatory Action Research' in Shirley A White (Ed), *The Art of Facilitating Participation*, Delhi: Sage Publications, 1999, p. 152.

42. George F Thomason, 'Workers Participation in Private Enterprise Organisation' in Campbell Balfour (Ed), *Participation in Industry,* London: Croom Helm, 1973, p. 139.
43. Pylee, M. V., *Worker Participation in Management Myth and Reality*, Delhi: N.V Publications, 1975, pp. 172-173.
44. Lynn M Morgan, 'Community Participation in Health Perpetual Allure, Persistent Challenge', *Health Policy and planning*, 16 (3), Sept. 2001, pp. 221-230.
45. David, K., *Human Behaviour at Work*, New York: Mc Graw- Hill, 1977, p. 140.
46. Keith Davis, *Human Relations at Work*, New York: McGraw-Hill Publishing Company, 1957, p. 288.
47. Pratap C Aggarwal, 'Cultural Milieu in India and Participative Management' in Thakur, C. P. and Sethi, K. C. (Eds), *Industrial Democracy Some Issues and Experiences,* Delhi: Sri Ram Centre for Industrial Relations and Human Resources, 1973, pp. 9-10.
48. Roy, S.K., 'Participative Management in Public Industry: Organizational Ground Work Necessary' in Thakur, C. P. and Sethi, K. C. (Eds), *Industrial Democracy: Some Issues and Experiences,* Delhi: Sri Ram Centre for Industrial Relations and Human Resources, 1973, pp. 61-62.
49. Alexander, K. C., *Participative Management: The Indian Experience*, Delhi: Sri Ram Centre for Industrial Relations and Human Resources, 1972, p. 7.
50. Alexander, K. C., 'Workers Participation in Management' in Thakur, C. P. and Sethi, K. C. (Eds), *Industrial Democracy: Some Issues and Experiences,* Delhi: Sri Ram Centre for Industrial Relations and Human Resources, 1973, pp. 162-163.
51. Manoj Kumar Sankar, *Personnel Management*, Delhi: Crest Publishing House, 2000, p. 358.
52. International Labour Office, *Workers Participation in Decisions Within Undertakings,* Geneva: 1981, p. 89.
53. Alexander, K. C., 'For a Survey of Workers' Participation in Management in France', *Federal Republic of Germany and the United States of America, Bulletin,* International Institute of Labour Studies, No. 6, June 1969, pp. 54-186.
54. Partap C Aggarwal, *Op. cit.*, pp. 1, 2.
55. Cyril Chantler, 'Introduction—Should Doctors be Involved in Management: Personal Perspective—3' in Maurice Burrows, *et al.* (Ed*), Management for Hospital Doctors,* Oxford: Butterworth Heinemann Ltd. 1994, p. 11.
56. Goel, S. L., *Health Care Management and Administration*, Delhi: Deep and Deep Publications Private Ltd, 2004, p. 54.
57. John Gratto Liebler, *et al., Management Principles for Health Professionals*, Mary land: An Aspen Publication, 1999, p. 88.
58. Syed Amin Tabish, *Op. cit.*, p. 44.
59. Goyal, R. C., *Handbook of Hospital Personnel Management*, Delhi: Prentice Hall of India Private Ltd, 1993, p. 231.
60. Redwariur Rahman, M. 'Health Services System in Bangladesh; An Overview', *IASSI Quarterly*, Vol. 18, No. 3, January/ March 2000, p. 73.

61. Cyril Chantler, *Op. cit.*, p. 12.
62. Jenny Cowpe, 'Managing within the Organisation' in David M Hansell, Brian Salter, *et al.* (Ed), in *The Management of Health Care*, London: W B Saunders Company Ltd, 1995, p. 76.
63. David J Hunter, 'Doctors as Managers: Poachers Turned Gamekeepers?' Rosemary Stewart (Ed), *Management of Health Care,* England: Dastmouth Publishing Company Ltd, 1998, p. 357.
64. Rob Baggott, *Health and Health Care in Britain*, London: Macmillan Press Ltd, 1998, pp. 133-134.
65. John Sutherst, *et al., The Doctor Manager*, Tokyo: Churchill Livingstone, 1994, pp. 70-71.
66. Tony White, *Text Book of Management for Doctors,* Tokyo: Churchill Livingstone, 1996, pp. 21, 39, 400.
67. David J Hunter, *Op. cit.,* pp. 357-361.
68. Roger Dyson, 'Personal Perspective-2', in Maurice Burrows, *et al., Management for Hospital Doctors,* Oxford: Butterworth Heinemann Ltd., 1994, p. 10.
69. Hugh Saxton, 'Personal Perspective—I' in Maurice Burrows, *et al.* (Ed), *Management for Hospital Doctors*, Oxford: Butterworth Heinemann Ltd., 1994, pp. 4-5.
70. *Ibid*, p. 6.
71. David J Hunter, *Op. cit.,* pp. 359, 362-363.
72. Ron Parker, 'The Management Challenge' in David M Hansell and Brian Salter, *The Management of Health Care,* The Clinicians Management Hand Book, London: W.B Saunders Company Ltd, 1995, p. 9.

CHAPTER 4

Profile and HRM

This chapter presents a profile of the sample units and that of the respondents, followed by an analysis of the survey results. Before presenting the survey results, it is apt to get a picture of the sample units and the respondents, as the survey aims to analyse the opinions of the said respondents. *Profile of the Sample Units* (Part-A) includes size-wise number of units, the nature of ownership, year of establishment, staff strength and bed strength. *Profile of the Respondents* (Part-B) includes details such as sex, age, academic qualifications, specialized qualifications, and experience of the respondents. The analysis of the *Existing Human Resource Management Practices* (Part-C) covers some aspects of HRM, like communication, motivation, interpersonal relations, cooperation and resistance, which are relevant in the context of participative management in the Health Care Institutions.

PART A
PROFILE OF THE SAMPLE UNITS

The universe of the study comprises the private hospitals in Kerala. A sample of 30 units has been selected in proportion to the existing number of hospitals in each size and in each zone

- 13 *small*-sized hospitals—3 from the South zone, 7 from the Central zone and 3 from the North zone;
- 10 *medium* sized hospitals—2 from the South zone, 5 from the Central zone and 3 from the North zone; and
- 7 *large* sized hospitals—2 from the South zone, 4 from the Central zone and 1 from the North zone—were selected as sample units.

Thus the sample covers, *small* hospitals: 43.3 per cent, *medium* hospitals: 33.3 per cent and *large* hospitals: 23.3 per cent. The number of units selected is given in Table 4.1 and Figure 4.1.

Table 4.1: Distribution of Sample Units, Size-wise

Region	Type of the hospital			Total
	Small	Medium	Large	
South	3	2	2	7
Central	7	5	4	16
North	3	3	1	7
Total / Percentage	**13** **43.3%**	**10** **33.3%**	**7** **23.3%**	**30** **100.0%**

Source: Field Survey

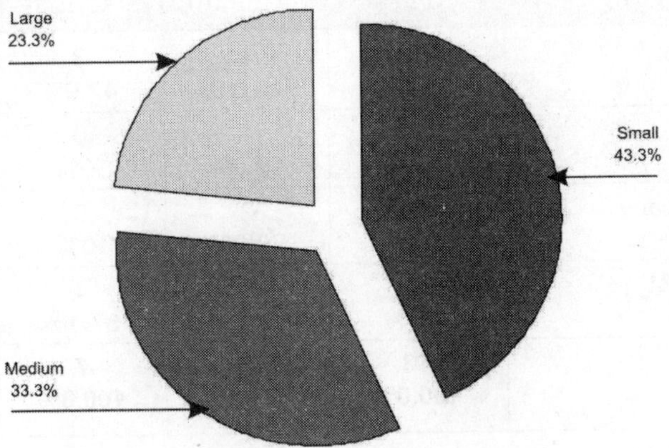

Fig. 4.1 : Pie diagram showing sample units

Nature of Ownership of the Sample Units

Ownership of business is represented by the right of an individual or groups of individuals to acquire legal title to assets for the purpose of controlling them and enjoying the gains or profits from such possession and use. There are different possibilities for a hospital ownership. It may be organized by an individual as sole proprietorship, or by an association of persons by mutual agreement as a partnership firm, or by an association of persons who form a co-operative society for the purpose, or else, it may be organized by a number of persons as a joint stock company.

In Kerala we have proprietorship, partnership, cooperatives, missionary and trusteeship, Private Limited and Public Limited hospitals. Of the 13 small-sized hospitals selected as sample, 69 per cent (9) fall under proprietorship, 15 per cent (2) under partnership, 8 per cent (1) under private limited company and another 8 per cent (1) under missionary/trust. Of the 10 *medium* sized hospitals, 40 per cent (4) were proprietorship, 10 per cent (1) partnership, 20 per cent (2) private limited company and 30 per cent (3) missionary / trust hospitals. Lastly, of the 7 large-sized hospitals, 43 per cent (3) were proprietorship and 57 per cent (4) missionary / trust hospitals.

Of the total 30 sample units, 53 per cent (16) were proprietorship, 10 per cent (3) partnership, another 10 per cent (3) private limited companies and 27 per cent (8) missionary / trust hospitals. The details of the hospitals selected for the study on the basis of ownership are given in Table 4.2 and Fig 4.2.

Table 4.2 : Type of Ownership of Sample Units, Category-wise

Ownership	Type of the hospital			Total
	Small	Medium	Large	
Proprietorship	9 69.2%	4 40.0%	3 42.9%	16 53.3%
Partnership	2 15.4%	1 10.0%	0 .0%	3 10.0%
Pvt. Ltd. Company	1 7.7%	2 20.0%	0 .0%	3 10.0%
Missionary/trust	1 7.7%	3 30.0%	4 57.1%	8 26.7%
Total	**13 100.0%**	**10 100.0%**	**7 100.0%**	**30 100.0%**

Source: Field Survey

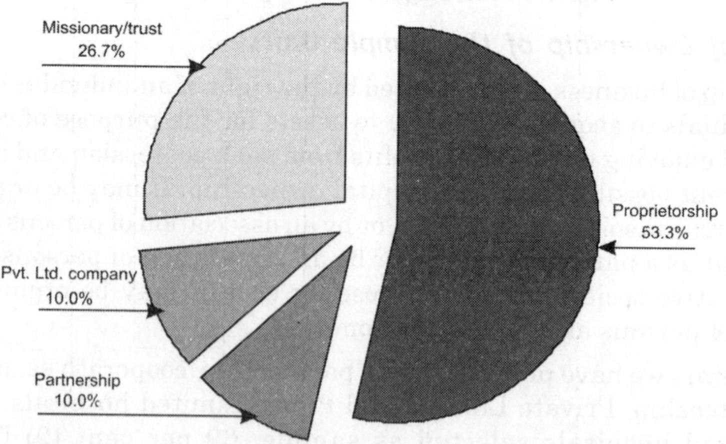

Fig. 4.2 : Pie diagram showing ownership of sample units

Year of Establishment of the Sample Units

The year of establishment denotes the year in which the hospital was started. The age of the institutions selected for the study ranges from 5 to 30 years.

Of the 30 sample units, thirty-three per cent (10) of the hospitals had more than 30 years of service, 30 per cent (9) more than 20 years of service, 23 per cent (7) more than 10 years of service and 13 per cent (4) less than 10 years of service. The details are furnished in Table 4.3.

Table 4.3 : Length of service of hospitals

Year of starting	Number of sample hospitals	Per cent
Before 1975	10	33.3
Between 1975 and 1985	9	30.0
Between 1985 and 1995	7	23.3
After 1995	4	13.3
Total	**30**	**100.0**

Source: Field Survey

Staff Strength in the Sample Units

The staff of the health care institutions consists of management personnel who look after the administrative work, doctors who provide the medical treatment, nurses who take care of peripheral treatment, paramedical staff who provide support services to the medical staff, non- medical staff who render maintenance, ancillary, supportive and other services.

The number of various categories of staff working in the private health care institutions in Kerala selected for the study are given in Table 4.4.

Table 4.4: Distribution of Staff, Category-wise

Type of hospitals	Number of hospital	Number of staff		
		Administrators	Doctors	PTM staff
Small	13	14	132	470
Medium	10	25	297	850
Large	7	21	252	900
Total	**30**	**60**	**681**	**2220**

Source: Field Survey

The total number of Administrators working in the sample hospitals was 60–14 in *small* hospitals, 25 in *medium* hospitals and 21 in *large* hospitals. The number of Doctors working in the sample hospitals was

681–132 in *small* hospitals, 297 in *medium* hospitals and 252 in *large* hospitals. The number of PTM staff in these hospitals was 2,220-470 in *small* hospitals, 850 in *medium* hospitals and 900 in *large* hospitals.

Bed Strength in the Sample Units

The number of beds in the hospital is the main factor deciding the size of the institution, number of doctors and other staff and all other facilities required.

The minimum number of beds in the *small* size hospitals selected for the study was 50 and the maximum 85, in *medium* size hospitals, the minimum number of beds was 100 and the maximum 190 and, in *large* size hospitals, the minimum number of beds was 260 and the maximum 512. On an average, *small* size hospitals had 64 beds, *medium* size hospitals 141 beds, and *large* size hospitals 363 beds.

The number of beds available in the selected hospitals are given in Table 4.5.

Table 4.5: Bed Strength in the Sample Hospitals, Category-wise

Size	Number of beds	Minimum	Maximum	Mean
Small	Up to 99	50	85	64
Medium	100-199	100	190	141
Large	200 and above	260	512	363

Source: Field Survey

PART B

PROFILE OF THE SAMPLE RESPONDENTS

Administrative personnel, doctors, paramedical, technical and ministerial staff represent the respondents for the study. An attempt is made in this section to present a personal profile of the respondents surveyed.

A total of 836 sample respondents from the different categories of employees were selected from among the sample units of 30 private health care intuitions. Under the administrator category 14 from *small* size hospitals, 18 from *medium* size hospitals and 13 from *large* size hospitals (in total ***45***) were selected as sample respondents. Under the Doctors category, 66 Doctors from *small* size hospitals, 149 from *medium* size hospitals and 126 from *large* size hospitals (in total ***341***), were selected as sample respondents. Similarly, 94 PTM staff from *small* size hospitals, 170 from *medium* size hospitals and 186 from *large* size hospitals (in total ***450***) were selected as sample respondents for the purpose of the study. The details are given in Table 4.6.

Table 4.6: Details of Respondents, Category-wise

Type of the hospital	Category			Total
	Administrators	Doctors	PTM staff	
Small	14	66	94	174
Medium	18	149	170	337
Large	13	126	186	325
Total	**45**	**341**	**450**	**836**

Source: Field Survey

Sex of the Respondents

Of the *total* respondents, male and female employees formed 50 per cent each. But the majority of the Administrators and Doctors were male members, while the majority of the PTM staff was female members. Of the Administrators selected, 80 per cent (36) were male and 20 per cent (9) female. Of the Doctors, 75 per cent (255) were male and 25 per cent (86) female. But of the PTM staff (450) selected, only 28 per cent (125) were male and 72 per cent (325) female. The details are given in Table 4.7.

Table 4.7: Sex-wise Distribution of the Respondents

Sex	Category			Total
	Administrators	Doctors	PTM staff	
Male	36 80.0%	255 74.8%	125 27.8%	416 49.8%
Female	9 20.0%	86 25.2%	325 72.2%	420 50.2%
Total	**45** **100.0%**	**341** **100.0%**	**450** **100.0%**	**836** **100.0%**

Source: Field Survey

Age of the Respondents

The age-wise composition of employees as per the data gathered in the survey reveals that of the Administrators, 60 per cent (27) were of the age group '35-55', 31 per cent (14) were of the age group 'above 55' and only 9 per cent (4) were of the age group 'below 35'. Of the Doctors, 59 per cent (202) were in the age group '35-55', 32 per cent (110) in the age group 'below 35' and only 9 per cent (29) were in the age group 'above 55'. 73 per cent (330) of the PTM staff belonged to the age group of 'below 35', 24 per cent (110) to the age group of '35-55', and only 2 per cent (10) to the age group 'above 55'. The age-wise composition of the different categories of employees selected for the study is given in Table 4.8.

Table 4.8 : Age of Respondents, Category-wise

Age	Category			Total
	Administrators	Doctors	PTM staff	
Below 35	4 8.9%	110 32.3%	330 73.3%	444 53.1%
35 to 55	27 60.0%	202 59.2%	110 24.4%	339 40.6%
Above 55	14 31.1%	29 8.5%	10 2.2%	53 6.3%
Total	**45 100.0%**	**341 100.0%**	**450 100.0%**	**836 100.0%**

Source: Field Survey

The analysis shows that the majority of the Administrators 60 percent (27) and Doctors 59 per cent (202) were of the age group '35-55', while the majority of the PTM staff was youngsters of the age group 'below 35'.

Qualification of the Respondents

In a hospital it is necessary that all persons are suitably qualified. Some Administrators and Doctors have specialization in management also. 38 per cent (17), of the Administrators working in the private hospitals were degree holders, 75 per cent (256) of the Doctors were PG Professionals, and 49 per cent (222) belonging to the PTM category were Diploma holders and 30 per cent (135) degree holders. The qualifications of different categories of employees selected as respondents for the study are given in Table 4.9.

Of the Administrators, Doctors, and PTM staff, 19 had some management specializations. Of the 45 sample Administrators, 15 (i.e. one third of them), held MBA Degree, Hospital Administration, or other Management Degrees. Only one Doctor from the sample had Hospital Administration Degree and only one PTM staff had Management qualification. The details are given in Table 4.10.

Experience of the Respondents

In health care institutions, experience is one of the important factors determining the quality of service. The Administrators, Doctors and PTM staff in health care institutions have vast experience to their credit because most of them had experience of working in Government institutions.

Table 4.9 : Qualification of Respondents, Category-wise

Qualification	Category			Total
	Administrators	Doctors	PTM staff	
SSLC, PDC, Certificate Course	0 .0%	0 .0%	40 8.9%	40 4.7%
Diploma	3 6.7%	0 .0%	222 49.3%	225 26.9%
Degree	17 37.8%	0 .0%	135 30.0%	152 18.2%
Degree Professional	6 13.3%	85 24.9%	16 3.6%	107 12.8%
PG	12 26.7%	0 .0%	33 7.3%	45 5.4%
PG Professional	7 15.6%	256 75.1%	4 .9%	267 31.9%
Total	**45 100.0%**	**341 100.0%**	**450 100.0%**	**836 100.0%**

Source: Field Survey

Table 4.10 : Specialised Management Qualifications, Category-wise

Specialization	Category			Total
	Administrators	Doctors	PTM staff	
MBA	4 26.7%	0 .0%	2 66.7%	6 31.6%
Degree/Diploma in HA	7 46.7%	1 100.0%	0 .0%	8 42.1%
Other Management Course	4 26.7%	0 .0%	1 33.3%	5 26.3%
Total	**15 100.0%**	**1 100.0%**	**3 100.0%**	**19 100.0%**

Source: Field Survey

The Administrators had an average experience of 22 years. Among the Doctors, 43 per cent (147) had less than 10 years of service and 35 per cent (120) 10-20 years of service. The majority, 73 per cent (330), of the PTMstaff were youngsters with less than 10 years of service. An almost equal number of Administrators were found in all age groups. The details about the length of service of the respondents in their present hospital and total length of service are given in Table 4.11.

Table 4.11: Length of Service, Category-wise

Specialization	Category			Total
	Administrators	Doctors	PTM staff	
Less than 10 Years	10 22.2%	147 43.1%	330 73.3%	487 58.3%
10 to 20 years	13 28.9%	120 35.2%	85 18.9%	218 26.1%
20 to 30 Years	10 22.2%	51 15.0%	26 5.8%	87 10.4%
30 to 40 years	12 26.7%	18 5.3%	8 1.8%	38 4.5%
Above 40 years	0 .0%	5 1.5%	1 .2%	6 .7%
Total	**45** **100.0%**	**341** **100.0%**	**450** **100.0%**	**836** **100.0%**

Source: Field Survey

Since hospitals form part of service industries, the quality of service depends upon the quality of persons inducted into the organizations and the quality of the efforts put in by the persons to achieve the organizational goals. It is, therefore, obvious that for the hospitals to function more efficiently and to make the employees participate effectively in the management of the hospitals, adequate attention should be given to Human Resource Management practices on a long-term basis.

PART C

HUMAN RESOURCE MANAGEMENT PRACTICES IN THE PRIVATE HEALTH CARE INSTITUTIONS IN KERALA

In this chapter an attempt is made to analyze the Human Resources Management practices followed in the Private Health Care Institutions in the State of Kerala. Human Resource Management being a vast field, this study is concentrated on aspects like communication, motivation, interpersonal relations (especially with superiors and subordinates), co-operation and resistance which are relevant in the context of participative management.

The analysis is based on the primary data obtained by a survey using structured interview schedule. To analyze the data a five-point scale was used. Based on the extent of satisfaction or extent of opportunities or extent of effectiveness, values were assigned, where '1' denoted the lowest and '5' the highest, and thus mean values were computed. Interpretation was done on the following scale.

Mean value	Mean qualified
0-1	very poor
1-2	Poor
2-3	average
3-4	good
4-5	very good

The existing Human Resource Management practices in the health care institutions can be discussed under the following headings.

4.3.1 Job-related factors

4.3.2 Opportunities for Personnel Development

4.3.3 Communication

4.3.4 Motivation

4.3.5 Human relations

- Relationship
- Conflict, Disputes, Discipline and Grievances
- Strikes and unions

Each of the above aspects is now elaborated below to establish its relevance to the study.

Job-related Factors

As in any study regarding Human Resource Management, the primary factors studied here are also those related to the job itself. Though there are numerous factors which can be studied, let us restrict ourselves to a few of them relevant to our study.

The first is the staff selection—which should be fair and transparent, giving the employee a self-esteem regarding the position he is holding. Every organization needs specialized employees and only adequate training can equip an employee to do specialized jobs required of him in a hospital. The single most important factor, in our country, related to any job is salary, which should be in line with one's qualifications, quantum of work, and above all his expectations. Fixation of salary should be scientific and not as per whims and fancy of the management, as salary reflects the status of a particular job more than any other factor, and is also a significant motivating force.

Over and above this come various other factors like flexible workplace rules, good working environment, and adequate welfare facilities, which all help in improving the morale of an employee leading to higher productivity and efficiency on his part.

Personnel management in hospital involves more complexities. Not only must hospital employees be given adequate training in the professional skills necessary to perform their daily tasks, but they must also be trained in the art of getting along with people who are sick and worried[1].

Participation in manpower planning as well as staff postings helps develop a sense of understanding and belonging in the mind of managers. The management can secure commitment of their staff by involving them in human resource planning[2].

The level of satisfaction of employees regarding the job-related factors such as: (*i*) Method of staff selection; (*ii*) Training facilities provided; (*iii*) Salary and other benefits; (*iv*) Workplace rules; (*v*) Working conditions; (*vi*) Welfare facilities provided; (*vii*) Status of job among friends and relatives, were assessed by using a 5-point scale. Mean values were used for analysis. The survey brought out the following results:

With regard to Administrators in *small* hospitals, the level of satisfaction with 'staff selection' was 'very good', with the highest mean score of 4.14. The level of satisfaction was 'good' for 'all other parameters' (mean value between 3.07 and 3.71) with the exception of 'training', for which it was only 'average', the mean value being 2.86. With regard to Administrators in the *medium* hospitals, the level of satisfaction was 'good' for 'all parameters' except 'work place rules,' for which it was 'very good' with the mean value of 4.06. With regard to Administrators in *large* hospitals, their satisfaction was 'good' for 'all the parameters' with the highest mean value of 3.92 for 'status of job among friends and relatives'.

The level of satisfaction of Doctors in the *small* hospitals was 'very good' for 'the method of staff selection' (mean value 4.02) and 'good' for 'all other parameters', with a mean value between 3.33 and 3.91. The level of satisfaction of the Doctors in *medium* hospitals was 'good' for 'all parameters', with a mean value between 3.63 and 3.91. The level of satisfaction of the Doctors of *large* hospitals was 'good' for 'all parameters' (mean value between 3.29 and 3.86) and the mean value was the highest for 'staff selection' (mean value 3.86).

Regarding the level of satisfaction of the *PTM* staff in the *small, medium* and *large* hospitals, it was 'good' for 'all parameters' with the mean value ranging between 3.34 and 3.93.The only exception was the opinion of the PTM staff of *small* hospitals on 'training', for which their satisfaction was only 'average', the mean value being 2.93.

The analysis revealed that the majority of the respondents in *small, medium* and *large* hospitals expressed *higher* level of satisfaction with the 'method of staff selection'. In *small, medium* and *large* hospitals, the Administrators (total mean value 3.27), the Doctors (total mean value 3.50) and PTM staff (total mean value 3.30) expressed the least level satisfaction with 'training facilities' when compared to all other job-related parameters. It is interesting to observe that none of the respondents had reported low level of satisfaction with any of the identified parameters. The survey results are depicted in Table 4.12.

The mean values of *'extent of satisfaction of employees regarding job-related factors' for all the above parameters* were estimated and the differences in the mean level *among different categories, types of hospitals and their interaction* were statistically examined using Two-way ANOVA Test.

Table 4.12: Extent of Satisfaction of Employees Regarding Job-related Factors, Category-wise

Category	Type of hospital	Staff selection	Training facilities	Salary	Work place rules	Working condi-tions	Welfare facilities provided	Status of job
Administrators	Small	4.14	2.86	3.50	3.64	3.71	3.07	3.57
	Medium	3.89	3.64	3.94	4.06	4.00	3.56	3.94
	Large	3.69	3.23	3.85	3.85	3.85	3.38	3.92
	Total	**3.91**	**3.27**	**3.78**	**3.87**	**3.87**	**3.36**	**3.82**
Doctor	Small	4.02	3.52	3.88	3.88	3.91	3.33	3.76
	Medium	3.67	3.63	3.76	3.85	3.88	3.65	3.91
	Large	3.86	3.32	3.78	3.76	3.79	3.29	3.75
	Total	**3.81**	**3.50**	**3.79**	**3.82**	**3.85**	**3.45**	**3.82**
PTM Staff	Small	3.93	2.93	3.72	3.89	3.86	3.34	3.78
	Medium	3.59	3.44	3.45	3.80	3.89	3.51	3.71
	Large	3.92	3.38	3.88	3.85	3.91	3.49	3.82
	Total	**3.80**	**3.30**	**3.68**	**3.84**	**3.90**	**3.47**	**3.77**
ANOVA Test Results [The exact level of significance - P value]								
Mean difference by Category		0.545	0.002	0.035	0.846	0.637	0.683	0.618
Mean difference by Type of hospital		0.001	0.001	0.261	0.269	0.262	0.013	0.071
Their Interaction		0.138	0.008	0.000	0.034	0.152	0.111	0.005

Source: Field Survey

The ANOVA at 5 per cent level of significance revealed that the *mean difference by category was statistically significant* for: (*i*) training facilities provided; and (*ii*) salary and other benefits. For all other parameters, the mean differences were *statistically insignificant.*

Mean difference by *type of hospital* was found *statistically significant* for: (*i*) method of staff selection, (*ii*) training facilities provided; and (*iii*) welfare facilities provided. For all other parameters, the mean differences were found *statistically insignificant.*

At the same time, *their interaction effect* showed *statistically significant differences* in the mean values for some of the parameters like: (*i*) training facilities provided; (*ii*) salary and other benefits; (*iii*) workplace rules; and (*iv*) status of job among friends and relatives among different categories of staff in different types of hospitals. For all other parameters, the *mean differences were found statistically insignificant.*

The analysis leads to the conclusion that almost all categories of employees in all types of hospitals gave a 'good' rating for 'staff selection' because the majority of the highly skilled and qualified and experienced people were mostly inducted into their present job by many offers and incentives by the management and had nothing to complain about. Most of the semi-skilled and unskilled workers, with the existing level of unemployment in the society, were only too happy to have landed in their present job and hence had no reason to complain regarding their selection.

Regarding 'training facility', the informal information gathered from most of the hospitals was that the management was more keen on getting trained personnel from other hospitals than on training people in their own hospital. Real training is imparted only when a new procedure, protocol or equipment is pressed into service about which all staff members have a good opinion.

Regarding 'salary' there is a big monetary divide, with the super-specialists getting monthly salary in lakhs while an unskilled labourer has to be satisfied with a few hundreds. The highly paid employee had nothing to complain while the low paid worker he rather be an employee with a low salary than he an ex-employee who complained about his salary.

Regarding level of satisfaction with the 'workplace rules', 'working conditions' and 'welfare facilities', all the respondents were found to be satisfied and the same was the opinion regarding 'the status of the job'.

Opportunities for Personal Development

By increasing the efficiency, integrity and the intelligence of its personnel an organization will give itself the real means for advancing towards optimum efficiency. The constant improvement of the efficiency of an employee is as much the responsibility of the employee himself as it is of the organization. Improved efficiency resulting in higher productivity is of mutual advantage to both the organization and the staff.

The level of satisfaction of employees regarding the opportunities for personal development was assessed on the basis of the following parameters by using the five point scale: (*i*) Opportunities for promotion; (*ii*) Extent of opportunities to use employees' knowledge and skills; (*iii*) Extent of opportunities to improve employees' knowledge and skills; (*iv*) Extent of opportunities to plan and take decisions about own work; (*v*) Extent of opportunities to influence managerial decisions at higher levels; and (*vi*) Extent of opportunities for personal growth and development in the present job. Mean values were used for analysis.

The survey revealed that the level of satisfaction of the Administrators of *small* hospitals with: (*i*) the extent of opportunities to use their knowledge and skills (mean value 3.93); (*ii*) opportunities to improve their knowledge and skills (mean value 3.97); (*iii*) opportunities to plan and take decisions about employees' own work (mean value 4.00); and (*iv*) opportunities for personal growth and development in the present job (mean value 3.86) was 'good'. But their satisfaction with the extent of opportunities to influence managerial decisions at higher levels was 'average' (mean value 2.50). Their satisfaction with the extent of opportunities for promotion was 'poor' (mean value 1.57).

With regard to the Administrators of *medium* hospitals, the extent of satisfaction with opportunities: (*i*) to use knowledge and skills (mean value 3.44); (*ii*) to improve knowledge and skills (mean value 3.43); (*iii*) to plan and take decisions about own work (mean value 3.83); and (*iv*) for personal growth and development (mean value 3.56) was 'good'. The extent of satisfaction with regard to the 'opportunities to influence managerial decisions' received 'average' satisfaction (mean value 2.50) and the promotion opportunity received 'poor' satisfaction (mean value 1.56).

With regard to the Administrators of *large* hospitals, their satisfaction with 'the opportunities for all the parameters' measured was 'good', with the exception of 'promotion opportunities' with which their satisfaction was 'poor' (mean value 1.62).

The Doctors of *small* hospitals viewed that their level of satisfaction with: (*i*) the extent of opportunities to use their knowledge and skills (mean value 3.88); (*ii*) opportunities to improve their knowledge and skills (mean value 3.95); (*iii*) opportunities to plan and take decisions about their own work (mean value 3.92); and (*iv*) opportunities for personal growth and development in their present job (mean value 3.85) was 'good'. But the 'extent of opportunity to influence managerial decisions' at higher levels received 'average' satisfaction (mean value 2.09). The extent of 'opportunities for promotion' received 'poor' satisfaction (mean value 1.70).

For the Doctors of *medium* hospitals, the extent of satisfaction for 'the opportunities to influence managerial decisions' was 'average' (mean value 2.03), for 'promotion opportunity' was 'poor' (mean value 1.31), and for 'all other parameters', the level of satisfaction was 'good' (mean values between 3.16 and 3.82).

Table 4.13 : Extent of Satisfaction of Employees about Opportunities for Personal Development

Category	Type of hospital	Extent of promotion opportunity	Extent of opportunity to use knowledge and skills	Extent of opportunity to Improve knowledge and skills	Freedom to plan and take decisions about own work	Extent of opportunity to influence managerial decisions	Extent of opportunity for personal growth and deve-lopment
Administrators	Small	1.57	3.93	3.97	4.00	2.50	3.86
	Medium	1.56	3.44	3.43	3.83	2.50	3.56
	Large	1.62	3.85	3.85	3.85	3.00	3.85
	Total	**1.58**	**3.71**	**3.71**	**3.89**	**2.64**	**3.73**
Doctors	Small	1.70	3.88	3.95	3.92	2.09	3.85
	Medium	1.31	3.82	3.70	3.71	2.03	3.16
	Large	1.56	3.81	3.87	3.95	1.89	3.82
	Total	**1.48**	**3.83**	**3.82**	**3.84**	**1.99**	**3.54**
PTM staff	Small	1.80	3.67	3.67	3.52	1.98	3.59
	Medium	1.66	3.64	3.59	3.01	2.26	3.10
	Large	1.94	3.65	3.74	3.54	2.40	3.74
	Total	**1.80**	**3.65**	**3.67**	**3.34**	**2.26**	**3.46**
ANOVA Test Results [The exact level of significance - P value]							
Mean difference by Category		0.000	0.000	0.000	0.000	0.000	0.007
Mean difference by Type of hospital		0.050	0.021	0.000	0.002	0.043	0.000
Their Interaction		0.235	0.156	0.024	0.017	0.000	0.383

Source: Field Survey

The level of satisfaction of the PTM staff of *small* hospitals, with: (*i*) the extent of opportunities 'to use their knowledge and skill'; (*ii*) opportunity 'to improve their knowledge and skills'; (*iii*) opportunities 'to plan and take decisions about their own work'; and (*iv*) opportunities for 'personal growth and development in the present job' was 'good', with mean values between 3.52 and 3.67. They also reported that their satisfaction with the extent of 'opportunity to influence managerial decisions at higher levels' (mean value 1.98) and the extent of 'opportunities for promotion' were 'poor' (mean value 1.80).

The level of satisfaction of the PTM staff of *medium* and *large* hospitals was *good* for the opportunities to: (*i*) use their knowledge and skills; (*ii*) to improve their knowledge and skills; (*iii*) to plan and take decisions about their own work; and (*iv*) for personal growth and development. It was 'average' for the 'opportunity to influence managerial decisions' and was 'poor' for 'opportunities for promotion'. The survey results are furnished in Table 4.13.

The mean values of the *'extent of satisfaction of employees about opportunities for personnel development' for all the above parameters* were estimated and the differences in the mean level *among different categories, types of hospitals and their interaction* were *statistically* examined using Two-way ANOVA test.

The ANOVA at 5 per cent level of significance revealed that the *mean difference by category* and *type of hospital* for all the above parameters was *statistically significant.*

At the same time, *their interaction effect* showed *statistically significant* differences in the mean values of some of the parameters like: (*i*) extent of opportunities to improve employees' knowledge and skills; (*ii*) extent of opportunities to plan and take decision about employees own work; and (*iii*) extent of opportunities to influence managerial decisions at higher levels among different categories of staff in different types of hospitals. But, for all other parameters, mean differences were found statistically *insignificant.*

Of the various parameters studied, irrespective of the category or size of hospital, 'good' rating was received for: (*i*) extent of opportunities to use employees' knowledge and skills; (*ii*) extent of opportunities to improve employees' knowledge and skills; and (*iii*) freedom to take decisions about employees' own work. This is not surprising, considering the fact that each category of employee is qualified to perform in a particular field only, in which he is trained. Regarding 'promotion opportunity', the rating was uniformly 'poor' across all categories of employees in different types of hospitals. This can be explained by the organizational set up of a hospital, where highly skilled to unskilled labourer worked as a congregation with no scope for vertical promotion beyond a particular level. Another interesting finding is the 'poor' rating for the opportunities to influence managerial decisions at higher levels, which makes it clear that many hospitals are run in a totalitarian way with *no effective participation of employees in managerial decisions.*

Communication

Communication is the process of passing messages from one mind to another and is vital to the successful achievement of objectives in hospitals. Better communication network in the hospitals improves the understanding and relations between the staff of different disciplines and levels, which in turn leads to better medical and non-medical staff relationship, staff-patient relationship, and staff-community relationship. This helps in extending spiritual and moral support to the patient's treatment which ultimately reflects in better patient care and early recovery[3]. Effective communication ensures effective participation.

Effectiveness of Communication

The views of different categories of staff about the extent of effectiveness of the communication and information sharing system in the working of the private health care institutions in the State of Kerala were collected.

The survey was made by taking into consideration the following parameters: (*i*) Effectiveness of communication in the working of the hospital; (*ii*) Effectiveness of upward communication; (*iii*) Effectiveness of horizontal communication; (*iv*) Effectiveness of downward communication; (*v*) Communication skills of subordinates; (*vi*) Communication skills of superiors; and (*vii*) Communication skills of peers.

With regard to Administrators in *small, medium* and *large* hospitals, the smoothness as well as effectiveness of the communication system was *good* for 'all identified factors', as the total mean value was between 3.87 and 3.96. It is interesting to observe that the difference between the factors as well as between the sizes of hospitals was narrow.

With regard to Doctors, a similar situation was reported, where for all the identified parameters, the total mean value ranged between 3.81 and 3.89. This was true irrespective of the size of the hospital, and the parameter-wise difference was very narrow.

The PTM staff was also satisfied with the communication system to a 'good' extent. As per their views, the level of satisfaction for the effectiveness and smoothness of the system was between the mean values 3.83 and 3.91. This was true for all the identified parameters, alike in *small, medium and large* hospitals. The survey results are given in Table 4.14.

The mean values of *'the extent of effectiveness of the communication system'* for all the above parameters were estimated and the differences in the mean level *among different categories, types of hospitals and their interaction* were *statistically* examined using Two-way ANOVA test.

The ANOVA at 5 per cent level of significance revealed that the *mean difference by category, type of hospital* and their *interaction effect* on all the above parameters was *statistically insignificant.*

When comparing the views of Administrators, Doctors and the PTM staff, all parties had a ***good rating about the effectiveness of the communication system***. Also, the comparison across *small, medium* and *large* hospitals revealed ***no difference*** and the effectiveness of the communication system received more or less the same rating.

Table 4.14 : Extent of Effectiveness of Communication

Category	Type of hospital	Communication system in general	Upward communication	Horizontal communication	Downward communication	Communication skill of subordinates	Communication skill of superiors	Communicating skill of peers
Administrators	Small	3.93	3.86	3.93	4.00	3.93	4.00	4.00
	Medium	4.00	3.89	3.94	3.94	3.89	4.00	4.00
	Large	3.85	3.85	3.85	3.85	3.85	3.85	3.77
	Total	**3.93**	**3.87**	**3.91**	**3.93**	**3.89**	**3.96**	**3.93**
Doctor	Small	3.88	3.91	3.83	3.80	3.79	3.91	3.89
	Medium	3.89	3.78	3.83	3.90	3.88	3.76	3.86
	Large	3.89	3.87	3.83	3.82	3.75	3.82	3.77
	Total	**3.89**	**3.84**	**3.83**	**3.85**	**3.82**	**3.81**	**3.83**
PTM Staff	Small	3.93	3.93	3.95	3.96	3.85	3.95	3.95
	Medium	3.76	3.71	3.75	3.83	3.88	3.80	3.85
	Large	3.98	3.91	3.85	3.86	3.89	3.95	3.94
	Total	**3.89**	**3.84**	**3.83**	**3.87**	**3.88**	**3.89**	**3.91**
ANOVA Test Results [The exact level of significance - P value]								
Mean difference by Category		0.922	0.989	0.672	0.360	0.194	0.144	0.157
Mean difference by Type of hospital		0.945	0.378	0.663	0.527	0.720	0.382	0.256
Their Interaction		0.127	0.653	0.347	0.198	0.583	0.536	0.180

Source: Field Survey

Two-way Communication

Table 4.14–Column 7 shows the extent of satisfaction of employees regarding the 'communication skill of subordinates' and Table 4.14—Column 8 shows the extent of satisfaction of employees regarding the 'communication skill of superiors' of *small*, *medium* and *large* hospitals.

The extent of satisfaction of Administrators regarding the 'communication skill of subordinates' of *small*, *medium* and *large* hospitals was *good*, with the total mean value of 3.89. Like that, the satisfaction level of Doctors and the PTM staff was also 'good' with total mean values of 3.82 and 3.88 respectively.

The opinion of employees regarding 'the communication skill of superiors' revealed that the level of satisfaction of Administrators was 'good' with the mean value of 3.96 and that of Doctors was also 'good' with the mean value of 3.81. The satisfaction level of PTM staff also remained the same with the mean value of 3.89. This was true irrespective of the size of the hospitals.

The analysis revealed that about three-fourth of the superiors and subordinates were satisfied with their respective communication skills, which lead to the conclusion that there is ***proper two-way communication between superiors and subordinates*** in the functioning of private hospitals.

The fact that a hospital, unlike other industries, ***cannot survive without proper communication*** across all strata of employees, irrespective of its size, stands confirmed by our survey results which show more or less uniformly good rating for inter-personnel communication. This further leads us to conclude that there is at least ***informal participation*** among the peers, immediate superiors and subordinates.

Motivation

Only a properly motivated employee will use his skill, knowledge and ability to the maximum, thereby ensuring the best results. In order to attract talented personnel and to motivate them to work efficiently, an organization should create and maintain such conditions whereby an employee feels like giving his best, gets satisfaction out of his job and is suitably rewarded.

The most important task of the institution must be to give abundant and constant evidence of its belief that the personnel in the health organization are the key to health care services. The tone of an organization is a reflection of the motivation from the top[4].

A man chooses his career on the basis of the salary he expects to receive. It has come tc stay as a status symbol[5]. In modern days, salary cannot be determined on a haphazard basis. A well-designed and properly administered salary system should be one that will not only reward the employees with the material remuneration they think, they deserve, but will also act as a motivating factor.

The managers must motivate the employees through non-financial incentives also, as financial incentives alone have little scope now. Opportunity for better career within the institution will definitely provide the necessary motivation to the employees. This generates a sense of belonging among the employees, both emotionally and morally.

The factors which motivate the employees were measured on the following parameters: (*i*) salary and perquisites; (*ii*) promotion; (*iii*) job security; (*iv*) working conditions; (*v*) freedom to express opinion; (*vi*) non-interference in their work; (*vii*) opportunity to participate in management decisions; and (*viii*) opportunity to participate in decisions connected with the job.

Of these: (*i*) salary and perquisites; (*ii*) promotion; (*iii*) job security; and (*iv*) working conditions can be grouped together as *remuneration package,* as in effect it represents the remuneration for the quantum of work done by the employee in a particular job situation. The factors: (*i*) freedom to express opinion; (*ii*) opportunity to participate in management decision; and (*iii*) opportunity to participate in decisions connected with the job can be grouped together, which motivate employees and indicate the extent of employee participation in management. The third factor included is to what extent 'non-interference in work' motivates an employee.

Data regarding the extent to which these factors motivate the employees of the private hospitals in Kerala were collected. The information received was critically analyzed by using '*Factor Analysis*' technique.

Factor analysis attempts to identify underlying variables, or *factors*, that explain the pattern to correlations within a set of observed variables. It is often used in data reduction to identify a small number of factors that explain most of the variance observed in a much large number of manifest variables.

Through this analysis, the important factors of motivation among different categories of employees in hospitals of Kerala could be identified as follows: the first factor is the *Remuneration Package,* constituted by variables such as, job security, working condition and salary package. The second factor is *Opportunity to participate in the decision-making process,* constituted by variables such as opportunity in managerial decision making, and opportunity in making decision with regard to own job. The third factor of motivation is non-interference in own job by others.

The Factor Analysis statistically revealed that for all categories of employees in all types of hospitals, the *remuneration package is the major motivating factor*.

For the PTM category with so many unemployed but equally qualified hands available, the main motivating factor not surprisingly was the salary, though small in many institutions, combined with the constant fear of losing the job. Only when there is job aplenty and an employee is in a position to choose and change his job at will, will the employee be motivated by factors other than salary package.

In the case of Doctors, the highly qualified ones and specialists are a small number, with so many private hospitals wooing them. They are offered very high remuneration package, and most of them are too busy with their professional work. They either do not have the time or are not much bothered about the administration or management of a hospital, and many maintain the 'I am above all attitude'. Meanwhile the situation of the junior Doctors is not much different from that of the PTM staff.

It is surprising that the Administrators also rated 'remuneration' higher than participative management, which shows lack of practical experience of this concept, the fear of erosion of their authority, or relative insecurity.

All this brings to the fore the stark reality that the finer aspects of motivation like 'non-interference in one's work', 'opportunity to participate in management decision', and 'opportunity to participate in decisions connected with the job' can become determinants only when the basic factors like salary and job security are met. This situation unfortunately leaves a lot to be desired in private hospitals where poor salary (very difficult to ascertain) and long and tedious working schedules and job insecurity are the rule than the exception.

Basically, monetary benefits are the major consideration for all staff and other motivation factors matter much less.

Human Relations

In the majority of private hospitals in India, most of the positions are occupied by personnel, by virtue of merely academic and professional qualifications and seniority, with scant regard for proficiency in managerial ability, inter-personal relations and leadership qualities. As a result, many of them find it difficult to run the health care institutions efficiently. It can be said with certainty that those who understand the socio-psychological make-up of their colleagues prove to be very successful and get most of the work done through them.

The task of human relations in health organizations is basically the integration of people into a work situation. It should, therefore, be the first duty of health-care administrators and personnel managers to see that most of the basic needs of their personnel are met so that their behaviour is one of co-operation and not of aggression at their workplace[6].

(i) Relationship

a. Relationship with Management, Boss and Others

The extent of satisfaction of the employees regarding their relationship with the following parties was measured: (*i*) Relationship with immediate boss; (*ii*) Relationship between management and employees; and (*iii*) Superior-subordinate relationship.

With regard to the Administrators in the *small* hospitals, the level of satisfaction was 'very good' for 'management and employee relationship', (mean value 4.29) and 'superior subordinate relationship' (mean value 4.14), but the satisfaction of relationship with the immediate boss was only 'good' (mean value 3.86). The satisfaction level was 'very good' for 'management and employee relations' (mean value 4.17) and 'good' (mean value 4.00) for, 'relationship with immediate bosses' and 'superior-subordinate relationship' in case of the Administrators of *medium* hospitals. It was 'good' for the Administrators of *large* hospitals for 'management and employee relations' (mean value 3.92) and 'superior-subordinate relations' (mean value 3.92), with the exception of 'the relationship with the immediate boss' for which the rating was 'very good' (mean value 4.08).

Regarding the Doctors of *small*, *medium* and *large* hospitals, it was 'very good' for all parameters except 'superior-subordinate relationship' in *medium* hospitals, for which it was 'good' (mean value 3.96).

The level of satisfaction of the PTM staff of *small*, *medium* and *large* hospitals was 'very good' for all categories of parties except for 'superior-subordinate relationship' in *medium* hospitals, for which the rating was 'good' (mean value 3.97).

When comparing the views of Administrators, Doctors and PTM staff, the total mean values for the Administrators was found to be the highest for 'management and employee relationship' (total mean value 4.13). It was the highest for the PTM staff for 'superior- subordinate relationship' (total mean value 4.03) and was the highest for Doctors for the 'relationship with the immediate boss' (total mean value 4.14). The size-wise comparison revealed that the relationship was 'very good' in almost all categories of respondents. The survey results are furnished in Table 4.15.

This leads us to conclude that there was *good relationship between the employee, and his immediate superior, the management and his subordinates*—which is not surprising, considering the fact that in a work environment where cooperation and coordination is a must, an employee with poor interpersonal or superior-subordinate relationship can adversely affect the functioning of the hospital itself, and in all probability, in private hospitals, may lose his job.

Table 4.15: Relationship with Management, Boss and Others—Category-wise

Category	Type of hospital	Relationship with immediate boss	Relationship between Management and employees	Superior-subordinate relationship
Administrators	Small	3.86	4.29	4.14
	Medium	4.00	4.17	4.00
	Large	4.08	3.92	3.92
	Total	**3.98**	**4.13**	**4.02**
Doctors	Small	4.12	4.02	4.02
	Medium	4.05	4.01	3.96
	Large	4.25	4.07	4.00
	Total	**4.14**	**4.03**	**3.99**
PTM staff	Small	4.11	4.09	4.10
	Medium	4.08	4.02	3.97
	Large	4.15	4.06	4.06
	Total	**4.11**	**4.05**	**4.03**

Source: Field Survey

b. Support and Co-operation

Modern-day health care delivery is so complex that a lone health functionary can never handle it on his own. It requires the cooperation and support of different categories of personnel to achieve the goals of health care, and lack of it not only results in poor delivery of health care but ultimately leads to harassment of patients.

Co-ordination of skills, efforts and services to the patient is regarded as the key function of hospital management. Since the skills and services are highly independent, the work of all associated doctors and different cadres of medical and non-medical staff must come together in the right way and at the right time, if each patient is to receive proper care[7].

Management and workers should look upon each other neither as rivals nor as one homogeneous group but as distinct interest groups who must cooperate and collaborate as equals[8].

The extent of support and cooperation received from the following parties was measured and analyzed: (*i*) from superiors; (*ii*) from colleagues; (*iii*) from others of equal departments; and (*iv*) from subordinates.

With regard to Administrators of *small* hospitals, 'the extent of support and cooperation' was 'very good' from all parties with the highest level of support from subordinates, with the highest mean value of 4.21. The exception was the 'good' rating (mean value 4.00) for the level of 'support from others of equal departments'. Regarding the Administrators of *medium* hospitals, the level of support and cooperation was 'good' from all parties with the highest level of 'support from colleagues' (mean value 3.94). The level of support and cooperation of the Administrators of *large* hospitals was 'good' with an equal mean score of 3.85 from all the categories of respondents.

Doctors of *small* hospitals reported 'good' support and cooperation from all parties with the majority for 'support from colleagues' with the highest mean score of 3.97. With regard to the Doctors of *medium* hospitals, they received 'very good' support from colleagues (mean value 4.05) and 'good' support from all other parties. Like Administrators of *large* hospitals, Doctors of *large* hospitals also reported 'good' support from all parties.

Regarding the *PTM* staff, of *small* hospitals, the level of 'support and cooperation from colleagues' was 'very good' (mean value 4.06), while the level of 'support from superiors' (mean value 3.99) and from 'others of equal departments' (mean value 3.98) was 'good'. In *medium* hospitals, the level of 'support from colleagues' (mean value 4.03) was 'very good', while the level of 'support from superiors' (mean value 3.74) and from 'others of equal departments' (mean value 3.99) was 'good'. In *large* hospitals also, the PTM staff gained 'good' support and co-operation from all with the maximum mean score from 'superiors and colleagues' (mean value 3.98). The survey results are presented in Table 4.16. *(See on next page)*

The analysis revealed that the level of support and cooperation received from superiors, colleagues, others of equal departments, and subordinates was ***good***. The result is in tune with the expected lines, as no hospital without the support and cooperation of its employees can survive in this fiercely competitive field, and the management and the employees are equally aware that it is a matter of survival.

c. *Resistance*

Hospital authorities should make sincere efforts to ensure that all laws which are applicable to hospital are adhered to in letter and spirit and, if possible, should provide more than what is prescribed in the statutes. Then the management must fully accept their responsibility for the education,

Table 4.16: Support and Co-operation from Different Sources, Category-wise

Category	Type of hospital	Level of support from superiors	Level of support from colleagues	Level of support from others of equal departments	Level of support from subordinates
Administrators	Small	4.14	4.14	4.00	4.21
	Medium	3.83	3.94	3.78	3.89
	Large	3.85	3.85	3.85	3.85
	Total	**3.93**	**3.98**	**3.87**	**3.98**
Doctors	Small	3.94	3.97	3.85	3.79
	Medium	3.94	4.05	3.99	3.98
	Large	3.90	3.92	3.70	3.87
	Total	**3.92**	**3.99**	**3.86**	**3.90**
PTM staff	Small	3.99	4.06	3.98	3.99
	Medium	3.74	4.03	3.99	3.98
	Large	3.98	3.98	3.91	3.87
	Total	**3.89**	**4.02**	**3.95**	**3.94**

Source: Field Survey

training, and development of their employees and for providing solutions to their problems.

Resistance seldom arises against workplace rules and is often encountered when new equipment is installed or an innovation in hospital function is implemented, often without employee participation on the decision-making process.

Participation permits a more balanced interaction pattern and, therefore, results in less resistance to innovation. It reduces the negative valence towards the task, and increase motivation for work[9].

When a new scheme is introduced, there may be suspicion and resistance from different parties in the organization. The extent of resistance of the following descriptions was measured: (*i*) Intra-departmental; (*ii*) Inter-departmental; (*iii*) from superiors; and (*iv*) from subordinates.

The extent of resistance shown by different categories of employees in *small*, *medium* and *large* hospital was assessed. The Administrators of *small, medium* and *large* hospitals exhibited 'very poor' extent of resistance, the total mean values ranging between 0.49 and 0.56 for different parties. The resistance from *small*, *medium* and *large* hospitals remained more or less the same with still lower resistance expressed by Administrators of *small* hospitals.

The Doctors of *small, medium* and *large* hospitals reported *very* 'poor' level of resistance, the mean values ranging between 0.66 and 0.72. There was no major difference in the extent of resistance shown by Doctors of *small, medium* and *large* hospitals also. The PTM staff also reported that the extent of resistance from different parties was 'very poor' in *small, medium* and *large* hospitals, with the total mean values ranging between 0.59 and 0.68. The survey results are given in Table 4.17.

Table 4.17 : Extent of Resistance from Different Sources, Category-wise

Category	Type of hospital	Intra-department	Inter-department	Superiors	Subordinates
Administrators	Small	.36	.29	.29	.36
	Medium	.50	.56	.50	.61
	Large	.69	.69	.69	.69
	Total	**.51**	**.51**	**.49**	**.56**
Doctors	Small	.71	.73	.71	.71
	Medium	.64	.65	.65	.67
	Large	.65	.67	.82	.64
	Total	**.66**	**.67**	**.72**	**.67**
PTM staff	Small	.87	.84	.93	.79
	Medium	.43	.54	.55	.56
	Large	.60	.70	.67	.66
	Total	**.59**	**.67**	**.68**	**.65**

Source: Field Survey

The observation revealed that, irrespective of the category of staff or type of hospital or category of personnel from various levels, the extent of resistance exercised was *very low*.

Any one or more of the following can be considered the reason for this:

(*a*) fear of losing job or other repercussions (which is a significant factor as per the informal finding during the survey)

(*b*) There is proper participation of employees in decision-making at managerial level (which is highly unlikely, considering the analysis and finding given in subsequent chapters.)

(*c*) Co-operation of employees- because human lives are involved—is also a significant factor, discussed in subsequent chapters.

Of the three, the third option is the most plausible explanation for this survey finding.

(*ii*) Disputes and Settlement

a. Conflict

Conflict as an active effort by an individual or a group for its own preferred interests at the cost of others is inevitable in any organization despite best efforts and management practices. Conflict can be between the management and the workers or among different cadres of employees or among peers, and can occur in one way or another. Reality demands that this fact should be accepted. More important is to assess *how often conflicts occur,* because a higher frequency can denote a serious flaw in the practices of the management or the attitude of the employees who are the parties involved. This can reflect the quality of co-ordination among different categories of workers, the way disputes are settled, pointing to the strength of human resource management, and the status of the parties involved in settling disputes, which is a pointer to the level of participation in different levels of management.

Frequency of Conflict

Participation is a process whereby the superiors and subordinates in an organization jointly identify its common goals and ensure performance, which will help in reducing conflicts. The management must encourage the development of such concepts among the employees.

The frequency of conflicts in hospitals, involving parties such as: (*i*) the management; (*ii*) other department staff; and (*iii*) colleagues of the same department was assessed.

The observation revealed the following. In the view of Administrators, the frequency of conflicts was *low* with 'other department staff' (total mean value 1.11) and 'colleagues of the same department' (total mean value 1.40), while it was *very low* with the 'management' (total mean value 1.00). The average opinion remains the same in *small*, *medium* and *large* hospitals.

Doctors were also of the opinion that the frequency of conflicts in their hospitals with 'other department staff' (total mean value 1.05) and 'colleagues of the same department' (total mean value 1.10) was *low*, while frequency of conflicts with the 'management' was *very low* (total mean value 1.00). There is no major difference in the opinion of the Doctors of *small*, *medium* and *large* hospital in this regard. The very same opinion was expressed by the PTM staff of *small*, *medium* and *large* hospitals. The survey results are given in Table 4.18.

The analysis revealed that conflicts occurred only ***very rarely*** in hospitals. This result corroborates our findings on previous questions which demonstrated the presence of good two-way communication in hospitals, which will prevent conflicts to a large extent.

Table 4.18 : Frequency of Conflicts in Hospitals

Category	Type of hospital	Conflict with Manage-ment	Other department staff	Colleagues of same department
Administrators	Small	1.00	1.21	1.29
	Medium	1.00	1.11	1.56
	Large	1.00	1.00	1.31
	Total	**1.00**	**1.11**	**1.40**
Doctors	Small	1.00	1.14	1.21
	Medium	1.00	1.03	1.05
	Large	1.00	1.03	1.10
	Total	**1.00**	**1.05**	**1.10**
PTM staff	Small	1.00	1.03	1.04
	Medium	1.00	1.12	1.14
	Large	1.00	1.15	1.34
	Total	**1.00**	**1.12**	**1.20**

Source: Field Survey

b. Settlement of Disputes

In an organization, the methods of resolving conflict depend on the system of management. Although the principles used by the managers are essentially the same in any industry, the specific methods for applying these principles usually differ, depending upon the situation[10].

A conflict cannot be resolved by either trying to defer it indefinitely or by denying the legitimate rights of the workers. The best option would be a settlement by consensus of a receptive management with a responsible workforce, which brings to the fore the concept of participative management.

Satisfaction towards the Steps to Settle Disputes

The level of satisfaction of the employees towards the steps taken by the management to settle disputes was established by the survey.

Regarding the level of satisfaction of the Administrators of *small* and *large* hospitals, it was 'good' with the mean value of 4.00 each; in *medium* hospitals, it was 'very good' with the mean value of 4.17. With regard to Doctors in the *small* hospitals, the level of satisfaction was 'very good' with the mean value of 4.02, and in *medium* and *large* hospitals, it was 'good' with mean values of 3.89 and 3.90 respectively.

The level of satisfaction of the PTM staff, with the steps taken by the management to prevent and settle disputes was 'good' in *small, medium* and *large* hospitals, with the mean values of 3.86, 3.71 and 3.94 respectively. The survey results are given in Table 4.19.

Table 4.19: Satisfaction with the Steps to Prevent and Settle Disputes

Category	Type of hospital	Level of satisfaction with dispute settlement
Administrators	Small	4.00
	Medium	4.17
	Large	4.00
	Total	**4.07**
Doctors	Small	4.02
	Medium	3.89
	Large	3.90
	Total	**3.92**
PTM staff	Small	3.86
	Medium	3.71
	Large	3.94
	Total	**3.84**

Source: Field Survey

The result would reveal a high level of satisfaction regarding settlement of disputes. The prevalence of very low level of conflicts, may naturally lead us to conclude that there is satisfactory level of participative management in the hospitals. But the answers to the next question negate any such conclusion.

Parties Involved in Settling Disputes

In order to avoid disputes getting beyond control, a mature management is always willing to discuss matters and bring a latent conflict to the surface and resolve it. If a conflict cannot be totally eliminated, it can at least bring the suppressed facts to the surface, remove misunderstandings, prevent rumour from spreading, and lead to re-examination of basic issues, assumptions and practices to bring such adjustments which would help not only to resolve conflict but also to improve the organizational effectiveness.

Disputes may be settled at many levels in the hierarchy of a hospital. They may be settled: (*i*) by the top level management; (*ii*) or by a committee consisting of representatives of members from all levels; (*iii*) or by the concerned department.

The extent of satisfaction of the employees regarding the involvement of functionaries at various levels in settling disputes was assessed from responses. The survey results revealed the following:

The extent of satisfaction with regard to the Administrators in *small* hospitals regarding involvement with 'top level management' was 'good', (mean value 4.00), that of the 'concerned department' was 'very good' with the mean value of 4.05, and that of 'committee' was *poor* (mean value 1.00). In the opinion of the Administrators of *medium* hospitals, the extent of satisfaction with involvement of the 'management' and the 'concerned department' in settling disputes was 'very good' with the mean values of 4.11 and 4.10 respectively, while that of the 'committee' in settling disputes was 'average' with the mean value of 2.39. In *large* hospitals, the extent of satisfaction with the involvement of the 'department' was 'very good' with the mean value of 4.02, satisfaction with the involvement of the 'management' was 'good' with the mean value of 3.85, while it was 'poor' (mean value 1.69) with the involvement of the 'committees'.

In the opinion of Doctors in *small*, *medium* and *large* hospitals, the extent of satisfaction regarding 'involvement of management' and 'concerned department' in settling disputes was 'good' with total mean values of 3.76 and 3.87 respectively. It was 'very poor' (mean value 1.00 and 1.52 respectively) regarding the 'involvement of committee' in *small* and *large* hospitals and was '*average*' in *medium* hospitals (mean value 2.99).

The PTM staffs of *small, medium* and *large* hospitals were satisfied to a 'good' extent with the 'involvement of the management' or 'concerned department' in settling disputes (total mean values between 3.74 and 3.94). The 'involvement of committee' in settling disputes in *small* hospitals was rated 'very poor' (mean value 1.00), in *large* hospitals it was 'poor' (mean value 1.61) and in *medium* hospitals it was 'average' (mean value 2.51). The survey results are given in Table 4.20.

The obvious conclusion from the above revelation is that the two levels at which disputes are resolved are at the 'concerned departmental level' and 'top level management'. The good rating for resolution of disputes at department level suggests a reasonable amount of intra-departmental participation.

The faith expressed by employees in the top level management for dispute resolution is quite natural as it is the ultimate authority in the hierarchy. But it can very well be an indication of the high level of control the management has over lower level employees, thereby showing poor delegation of power and very low level of employee participation in higher level management process.

Table 4.20: Level of Satisfaction Regarding the Parties Involved in Settling Disputes

Category	Type of hospital	Top level management	Committee	Concerned Department
Administrators	Small	4.00	1.00	4.05
	Medium	4.11	2.39	4.10
	Large	3.85	1.69	4.02
	Total	**4.00**	**1.76**	**4.07**
Doctors	Small	3.80	1.00	3.80
	Medium	3.77	2.99	3.94
	Large	3.73	1.52	3.90
	Total	**3.76**	**2.06**	**3.87**
PTM staff	Small	3.81	1.00	3.93
	Medium	3.66	2.51	3.94
	Large	3.76	1.61	3.95
	Total	**3.74**	**1.82**	**3.94**

Source: Field Survey

Also the poor rating given to the involvement of committees in dispute settlement denotes very poor level of employee participation in management. Delving deeper into the data, one finds that employees of *medium* sized hospital showed a slightly better satisfaction with committees, probably because of the presence of more committees in such hospitals. For survey results refer Table 5.7 in the chapter V.

c. Discipline

Discipline means orderliness and an orderly behaviour is essential for attaining the organizations' objectives. It is the primary responsibility of the management to maintain discipline by applying standards in a consistent, fair and flexible manner.

Almost every supervisor and executive has to take disciplinary action at one time or another. The procedure for disciplinary action is based on principles of natural justice; an opportunity must be given to the erring employee to show cause. The attitude of the supervisor should be one of counselling and understanding; punishment and disciplinary procedure should be the last resort. Often, disciplinary action has widespread impact on other employees. Negative incentives provided through disciplinary action have, no doubt, a salutary effect. However, for better results, they must be combined with personal leadership, positive incentives and indirect motivation, if a hospital is to be really efficient and dynamic in its operation. Positive incentives provided through motivational activities such as praise, promotion, special increments, incentives in cash or kind, etc., are the best forms of maintaining discipline.

To get a clear idea, about the existing system of discipline, information about: (*i*) the extent of satisfaction of employees about the method of maintaining discipline; and (*ii*) the extent of satisfaction of the employees about the managements' approach towards labourers' indiscipline was collected.

The survey results revealed the following. The level of satisfaction of the Administrators of *small* hospitals was 'very good', in respect of the 'method of maintaining discipline' (mean value 4.21) and 'management's approach to labour indiscipline' (mean value 4.14). Both these aspects were 'good' (mean values 3.67 and 4.00) as per the experience of Administrators of *medium* hospitals. The level of satisfaction of Administrators of *large* hospitals was also 'good' regarding these parameters.

The extent of satisfaction of the Doctors, regarding the 'method of maintaining discipline' and on the 'management's approach towards labourers indiscipline' was 'good' with the total mean value of 3.87 each. There was no major difference in the extent of satisfaction of the Doctors in *small*, *medium* and *large* hospitals, regarding these factors.

The level of satisfaction of the PTM staff in *small*, *medium* and *large* hospitals regarding the 'method of maintaining discipline' and 'management's approach towards labourers' indiscipline' also remained 'good' with total mean values of 3.95 and 3.94 respectively. The survey results are given in Table 4.21.

The analysis revealed that there was no major difference in the opinions of different categories of staff in different types of hospitals. Also, from the available data, we can safely conclude that the level of discipline was quite good and employees at all levels understood the importance of it in health care.

Table 4.21: Extent of Satisfaction about Discipline

Category	Type of hospital	Method of maintaining discipline	Management's approach to indiscipline
Administrators	Small	4.21	4.14
	Medium	3.67	4.00
	Large	3.85	3.85
	Total	**3.89**	**4.00**
Doctors	Small	3.91	3.94
	Medium	3.78	3.80
	Large	3.94	3.90
	Total	**3.87**	**3.87**
PTM staff	Small	3.99	3.98
	Medium	3.88	3.89
	Large	3.99	3.95
	Total	**3.95**	**3.94**

Source: Field Survey

d. Grievance

In any industrial organization where workers work together for achieving a common objective, there is a likelihood of friction and misunderstanding. Furthermore, the working condition, the workplace rules, or even personal likes and dislikes, may lead to unhappiness and dissatisfaction among the workers. The dissatisfaction of the workers is very often manifested in their behaviour at the workplace. If the conditions causing dissatisfaction of the workers are not corrected, the irritation is likely to increase and can in the long run adversely affect the efficiency of the organization.

The procedure for the settlement of grievances is sometimes established pursuant to legislation or perhaps through general agreements between the management and trade unions or workers[11].

The extent of satisfaction of the various categories of employees about parameters such as: (*i*) the mode of presenting grievances, (*ii*) the mode of settling grievances, and (*iii*) the time taken for redress of grievances in the private health care institutions was estimated.

For the Administrators of *small* hospitals, the level of satisfaction for all parameters like 'mode of presenting grievances', 'mode of settling grievances' and 'time taken for redress of grievances' was 'very good' with the mean value of 4.07 each. For the Administrators of *medium* hospitals, the level of satisfaction was 'good' for 'all parameters' like 'mode of presenting grievances' (mean value 3.78), 'mode of setting grievances' (mean value 3.94) and 'time taken for redress of grievances' (mean value 3.89). The response remained more or less the same in the case of Administrators of *large* hospitals also.

With regard to Doctors of *small* hospitals, the extent of satisfaction about the 'mode of presenting grievances', 'mode of settling grievances' and the 'time taken for the redress of grievances' was 'good' with mean values 3.88, 3.85 and 3.85 respectively. The Doctors of *medium* hospitals also opined that the extent of satisfaction in respect of all these parameters was 'good', with *mean* values ranging between 3.69 and 3.74. The extent of satisfaction expressed by the Doctors of *large* hospitals also was 'good' with mean values ranging between 3.79 and 3.83.

Regarding the opinion of the PTM staff of *small*, *medium* and *large* hospitals, the extent of satisfaction was 'good' for all the parameters like 'mode of presenting grievances' (total mean value 3,83), 'mode of setting grievances' (total mean value 3.88) and 'time taken for redress of grievances' (total mean value 3.83). The survey results are given in Table 4.22.

The findings of the survey revealed that irrespective of the size of hospitals, the Administrators, Doctors and the PTM staff were satisfied with all the parameters regarding redress of grievances. This leads to the

Table 4.22: Satisfactions about Grievance Redress Procedure

Category	Type of hospital	Mode of presenting grievances	Mode of setting grievances	Time Taken for redress of grievances
Administrators	Small	4.07	4.07	4.07
	Medium	3.78	3.94	3.89
	Large	3.85	3.85	3.92
	Total	**3.89**	**3.96**	**3.96**
Doctors	Small	3.88	3.85	3.85
	Medium	3.69	3.71	3.74
	Large	3.83	3.79	3.83
	Total	**3.78**	**3.77**	**3.79**
PTM staff	Small	3.81	3.89	3.81
	Medium	3.74	3.74	3.67
	Large	3.92	3.99	3.98
	Total	**3.83**	**3.88**	**3.83**

Source: Field Survey

conclusion that in the private hospitals, complaints and grievances are expressed and dealt with immediately so that they do not persist as a disturbing factor affecting the functioning of the hospital.

(*iii*) Strikes and Unions

a. Strike

Strikes, demonstrations and picketing in hospitals, unlike in other industries, can harm both the patient and the employee profoundly. For the patient, the treatment cost goes up and their lives can be endangered. Strikes lower the public image of a hospital, which is a sure recipe for loss of revenue and failure, which ultimately will leave the employee in the lurch.

Justification of Strikes

Table 4.23: Justification of Strikes

Category	Type of hospital	Justification of occurrence of strikes		Total
		Yes	No	
Administrators	Small	0 .0%	14 100.0%	14 100.0%
	Medium	0 .0%	18 100.0%	18 100.0%
	Large	0 .0%	13 100.0%	13 100.0%
	Total	**0 .0%**	**45 100.0%**	**45 100.0%**
Doctors	Small	0 .0%	66 100.0%	66 100.0%
	Medium	0 .0%	149 100.0%	149 100.0%
	Large	0 .0%	126 100.0%	126 100.0%
	Total	**0 .0%**	**341 100.0%**	**341 100.0%**
PTM staff	Small	0 .0%	94 100.0%	94 100.0%
	Medium	0 .0%	170 100.0%	170 100.0%
	Large	0 .0%	186 100.0%	186 100.0%
	Total	**0 .0%**	**450 100.0%**	**450 100.0%**

Source: Field Survey

The opinions of different categories of employees in different types of hospitals regarding the justification of strikes in the hospitals were collected.

The survey results revealed that 'none' of the Administrators, Doctors and PTM staff from *small, medium* and *large* hospitals justified the occurrence of strikes in private hospitals. All the respondents reported that strikes in hospitals were unjustified. The survey results are given in Table 4.23.

This leads to the conclusion that the employees of hospitals do not see strikes as a justifiable means of achieving their goals in a hospital setting, as lives of patients are at stake.

Occurrence of Strikes

Table 4.24: Occurrence of Strikes

Category	Type of hospital	Justification of occurrence of strikes		Total
		Yes	No	
Administrators	Small	0 .0%	14 100.0%	14 100.0%
	Medium	0 .0%	18 100.0%	18 100.0%
	Large	0 .0%	13 100.0%	13 100.0%
	Total	**0 .0%**	**45 100.0%**	**45 100.0%**
Doctors	Small	0 .0%	66 100.0%	66 100.0%
	Medium	0 .0%	149 100.0%	149 100.0%
	Large	0 .0%	126 100.0%	126 100.0%
	Total	**0 .0%**	**341 100.0%**	**341 100.0%**
PTM staff	Small	0 .0%	94 100.0%	94 100.0%
	Medium	0 .0%	170 100.0%	170 100.0%
	Large	0 .0%	186 100.0%	186 100.0%
	Total	**0 .0%**	**450 100.0%**	**450 100.0%**

Source: Field Survey

The employees of hospitals are generally found to consider strikes unjustifiable. Even then, exceptional situations might induce hospital employees to go on strike. Hence the details about (i) the occurrence or (ii) non-occurrence of strikes in the private hospitals in Kerala were collected.

It was observed that none of the employees, whether Administrators (45) or Doctors (341) or PTM staff (450) from *small, medium* and *large* hospitals experienced strikes during their service. The survey results are given in Table 4.24.

The data show total absence of strikes in private hospitals, which goes hand in gloves with the opinion that strikes are not justified in hospitals. Even though many hospital authorities feel that the recognition of the union is a direct invitation to strike, in the two hospitals in our sample where union was functioning, there was no instance of strike. It is against this scenario, where strikes and other disruptive forms of protest are not considered justifiable, that participative management, which is mutually beneficial for the employee and the management, becomes all the more important.

b. Union

Development of a positive relationship between management and employees is important for strategic management of human resources in the sector. It is when groups of employees feel that management is not interested in their welfare that they may opt to have a union to represent them and bargain for them[12].

The hospital personnel also being emotional human beings, low emoluments and unsatisfactory service conditions agitate their minds as intensely as in the case of any other employee, and lead them to organize themselves into unions to safeguard their rights.

Presence or Absence of Unions

Information about the presence or absence of unions in the private hospitals of Kerala was collected ***hospital- wise***. Of the 30 private hospitals selected as sample units, only 7 per cent (2) hospitals had unions, one *small*-size hospital and only one *medium* size hospital. The results show very low prevalence of unions in private hospitals. The survey results are given in Table 4.25.

One of the strongest means by which an employee can influence the management decision, or participate in management function, is through a truly representative, responsible union, the lack of which calls for strong organized systems for employees where they feel secure and involved in managerial processes.

Table 4.25: Presence of Unions in Private Hospitals

Type of hospital	Presence of Trade Union		Total
	Yes	No	
Small	1 7.7%	12 92.3%	13 100.0%
Medium	1 10.0%	9 90.0%	10 100.0%
Large	0 .0%	7 100.0%	7 100.0%
Total	**2** **6.7%**	**28** **93.3%**	**30** **100.0%**

Source: Field Survey

Another point that needs mention is the difficulty in forming an effective single union or association, as the hospital personnel belong to different cadres, classes and professions.

Seen in a different perspective, the very nature of the medical profession, where good human relations are part of every employee's daily duties, certainly will go a long way in establishing good relation with superiors and subordinates, thereby leading to an environment in private hospitals where union is not of much relevance.

Working of Union

Unions usually fight for better pay, improved fringe benefits, more promotional avenues and setting up of grievance redress procedures. Recently, unions themselves have become concerned with broader managerial issues such as labour participative management at the top, middle and lower levels. They want their say in all the issues concerning the hospitals.

If hospital authorities and union leaders want to ensure the operation of collective agreements in a true spirit, there should be a sharing of information and joint consultation, because such efforts will lead to full co-operation to provide better health services, reduce costs, maintain discipline and create a congenial atmosphere, which are the prime concerns of hospital administrators.

Even though union was present in only 2 hospitals in our sample, an attempt was made to assess its functions and effectiveness. The extent of satisfaction of the members of the union in *small* hospitals and *medium* hospitals **(where there were unions)** about: (*i*) functioning of trade unions; (*ii*) union-management relations; (*iii*) employees' participation in trade unions; (*iv*) unions' support to management in solving disputes; (*v*) trade unions' participation in settling grievances; (*vi*) trade unions' approach towards labour problems; and (*vii*) unions' influence on the decisions of the top level management, was assessed. The survey results are given in Table 4.26.

Table 4.26: Satisfaction about Working of Union

Category	Type of hospital	functioning of trade union	Union-Manage-ment relation-ship	Employees' partici-pation in Trade Union	Union's support to mana-gement in solving disputes	Trade union's partici-pation in settling grie-vances	Trade union's approach toward labour problems	Union's influence on the decision of top level manage-ment
Administrators	Small	1.00	1.00	1.00	1.00	2.00	4.00	2.00
	Medium	4.00	3.00	1.00	2.00	3.00	1.00	4.00
	Total	**3.00**	**2.33**	**1.00**	**1.67**	**2.67**	**2.00**	**3.33**
Doctors	Small	1.33	4.67	1.83	2.83	2.33	3.00	1.67
	Medium	1.32	2.48	1.29	1.77	1.84	1.94	1.32
	Total	**1.32**	**2.84**	**1.38**	**1.95**	**1.92**	**2.11**	**1.38**
PTM staff	Small	1.71	4.43	2.43	2.00	2.00	3.14	1.29
	Medium	2.18	2.71	1.82	1.57	1.50	1.93	1.25
	Total	**2.09**	**3.06**	**1.94**	**1.66**	**1.60**	**2.17**	**1.26**

Source: Field Survey

With regard to Administrators of *small* hospitals, the level of satisfaction was 'good' for 'unions' approach towards labour problems' (mean value 4.00). It was 'poor' for 'participation in settling grievances' (mean value 2.00) and 'its influence on the decision of top level management' (mean value 2.00). Regarding all other parameters, their level of satisfaction, was 'very poor' (mean value 1.00). The satisfaction level of administrators of *medium* hospitals was 'good' (mean value 4.00) for 'functioning of trade union', and its 'influence on top level management' (mean value 4.00). It was 'average' for 'union-management relations' (mean value 3.00) and 'union's participations in settling grievances' (mean value 3.00). Their level of satisfaction was 'poor' (mean value 2.00) for 'its support to management in solving disputes'. It was 'very poor' (mean value 1.00) for 'employees' participation in trade union' and its 'approach toward labour problems'.

Regarding the level of satisfaction of Doctors in the *small* hospitals, it was 'very good' (mean value 4.67) for 'union-management relationship'. It was 'average' for 'its support to management in solving disputes' (mean value 2.83), 'its participation in settling grievances' (mean value 2.33), and 'its approach toward labour problems' (mean value 3.00). It was 'poor' for its 'general functioning' (mean value 1.33), 'members' participation in trade union' (mean value 1.83), and its influence on the decision of top level management (mean value 1.67). In the *medium* sector, it was 'poor' (mean values between 1.29 and 1.94) for all parameters except 'union management relations' (mean value 2.48), for which it was 'average'.

The level of satisfaction of the PTM staff in the *small* hospitals was 'very good' (mean value 4.43) for 'union-management relations'. It was 'good' (mean value 3.14) for 'union's approach toward labour problems'. The satisfaction level was 'average' for 'employees' participation in trade union' (mean value 2.43). It was 'poor' for 'support to management in solving disputes' (mean value 2.00), 'union's participation in settling grievances' (mean value 2.00), 'functioning of trade union' (mean value 1.71), and 'union's influence on the decision of top level management (mean value 1.29). In the *medium* sector, it was 'average' for 'functioning of trade union' (mean value 2.18) and 'union-management relations' (mean value 2.71). The satisfaction level was 'poor' (mean values between 1.25 and 1.93) for 'all other parameters'.

The analysis revealed that only 7 per cent (2) of the sample units had unions and that the satisfaction of the employees about the working of the unions was 'poor' only. The survey results are presented in Table 4.26.

Though various parameters regarding the functioning of unions are analyzed, the fact that the data is from only two hospitals, which had unions, makes it very difficult to draw concrete conclusions.

Even then, the available data, except for very few positive ratings, show uniformly low rating for the various parameters, thereby indicating that though a union was present, its functioning was unsatisfactory. This leads us to believe that just the presence of unions does not lead to participation in management.

The analysis of the existing *Human Resource Management practices* revealed that almost all categories of employees in all types of hospitals had given a 'good' rating for the different job related factors analysed. All parties recorded a *good rating about the effectiveness of the communication system.* The important factors of *motivation* among different categories of employees in hospitals of Kerala can be identified as Remuneration Package constituted by variables such as job security, working condition and salary package. There has existed *good relationship between the employee, his immediate superior, the management and his subordinates.* The survey shows total absence of strikes and very low prevalence of unions in private hospitals, which goes hand in gloves with the opinion that strikes are not justified in hospitals.

REFERENCES

1. Sudhir Dawra, *Hospital Administration and Management*, Delhi: Mohit Publications, 2002, p. 579.
2. Ramesh Bhat and Sunil Kumar Maheswari, 'Human Resource Issues, Implications for Health Sector Reforms', *Journal of Health Management*, Vol. 7, No. 1, Jan-June 2005, pp. 1–36.
3. Mohammed Akbar Ali Khan, *Hospital Management*, Delhi: A.P.H Publishing Corporation, 1999, pp. 208, 209.
4. Goyel, S. L., *Health Care Management and Administration*, Delhi: Deep and Deep Publications Private Ltd., 2004, p. 290.
5. Radrabasavarj, M. N., *Dynamic Personnel Administration—Management of Human Resources*, Bombay: Himalaya Publishing Company, 1979, p. 295.
6. Sudir Dawra, *Hospital Administration and Management,* Delhi: Mohit Publications, 2002, p. 578.
7. Mohammed Akbar Ali Khan, *Hospital Management*, Delhi: A.P.H. Publishing Corporation, 1999, p. 208.
8. Sheth, N. R., *The Joint Management Council: Problems and Prospects*, Delhi: Sri Ram Centre for Industrial Relations and Human Resources, 1972, p. 135.
9. Alexander, K. C., *Participative Management: The Indian Experience*, Delhi: Sri Ram Centre for Industrial Relations and human Resources, 1972, pp. 5, 6.
10. Lallan Prasad, A. M., Bannerjee, *Management of Human Resources*, Delhi: Sterling Publishers Pvt. Ltd., 1985, p. 55-57.
11. Jacob, K. K., Giri, V. V., 'Grievance Redressal Procedure and Labour Management Relations in State Level Public Enterprises', *Labour and Development,* International Labour Institute, Vol.11, No.1, June 2001, p. 230-240.
12. Savitha Sharma K' Cherry, *Hospital Management*, Delhi: Common Wealth Publishers, 1996, p. 43.

Existing System of Participation

The service industries give prominence to the people who deliver services as they are the ones who shape the destiny of the business, and not the structures, systems and processes that are effectively formulated in the organizations. Since hospitals are part of the service sector, the quality of service depends upon the quality of persons inducted into the organizations and the quality of the efforts put in by them to achieve the organizational goals.

It can be argued that non-remuneration factors can also play an important role against wholehearted effort on the part of an employee in an organization. Though delegation and job enrichment may make an employee feel that he is important in the organization, participation by an employee in management goes a step further in motivating him to give his best for the organization.

To determine to what extent each individual is helping, coordinating and participating in the management of day-to-day running of private hospitals, different categories of employees in private health care institutions in Kerala were interviewed and information so collected was analysed under the following heads:

- Forms of Participation
- Levels of Participation
- Informal Participation
- Concept of Team Work
- Employees' Participation through Committees
- Control and Participation

FORMS OF PARTICIPATION

There are many types of participation like: (*i*) Informative participation; (*ii*) Consultative participation; (*iii*) Joint decision making; and (*iv*) Collective bargaining. Forms of participation vary from organization to organization depending upon the level of power or authority enjoyed by employees at different levels and also from situation to situation.

Data regarding the various forms of participation existing in the private hospitals of Kerala were collected and analysed ***hospital-wise***. The analysis revealed that 92 per cent (12) of *small* size hospitals had 'informative participation' and only 8 per cent (1) of the *small* hospital had 'consultative participation'. In *medium* size hospitals there were 'informative participation' in 70 per cent (7) of hospitals and 'consultative participation' in 30 per cent (3) of hospitals. Among the *large* size hospitals 'consultative participation' was prevalent in 57 per cent (4) and 'informative participation' in (43) per cent (3) of hospitals.

The study revealed that of the total hospitals studied, there was only 'informative participation' in 73 per cent (22), and 'consultative participation' in 27 per cent (8) of hospitals. 'Informative participation' was dominant among *small* hospitals and *medium* hospitals while 'consultative participation' was dominant in the *large* size hospitals. There was no 'joint decision making' or 'consultative participation' in any of the *small*, *medium* and *large* hospitals. The survey results are given in Table 5.1.

Using chi-square test, the association between 'form of participation' and 'different types of hospitals' was statistically examined.

Table 5.1: Form of Participation Existing in Hospitals

Type of hospital	Form of participation in hospital functioning				Total
	Informative participation	Consultative participation	Joint decision	Collective bargaining	
Small	12 92.3%	1 7.7%	0 .0%	0 .0%	13 100.0%
Medium	7 70.0%	3 30.0%	0 .0%	0 .0%	10 100.0%
Large	3 42.9%	4 57.1%	0 .0%	0 .0%	7 100.0%
Total	**22** **73.3%**	**8** **26.7%**	**0** **.0%**	**0** **.0%**	**30** **100.0%**

Source: Field Survey

Table 5.1(a): Chi-Square Test - Form of Participation Existing in Hospitals

	Value	df	Asymp. Sig. (2-sided)
Pearson Chi-Square	5.775(a)	2	.056
Likelihood Ratio	5.966	2	.050
Linear-by-Linear Association	5.564	1	.018
N of Valid Cases	30		

Source: Computed

3 cells (50.0 per cent) have expected count less than 5. The minimum expected count is 1.87.

Note : For analysis, if more than 20 per cent of the cells have expected count less than 5, it is more appropriate to use Likelihood ratio.

If the significance level of chi-square value/ Likelihood ratio is equal or less than 0.05, the chi-square test indicates a significant association between the two variables. In this study, all the chi-square test analysis is made considering these points.

Table5.1(a) revealed that there is *statistically significant association* between 'form of participation' and 'different types of hospitals'.

The analysis leads to the conclusion that ***informative participation**, the least effective among all forms of participation, **was widely prevalent** in hospitals* irrespective of their size. However, its presence was more prevalent in the *small* and *medium* scale sector. Even though the prevalence of **'consultative participation'**, which is slightly better than informative participation, **was more in *large*-sized hospitals**, the difference was not statistically significant. The most noteworthy point is the ***total absence of joint decision making or collective bargaining,** which is a true indicator of effective participative management, in any of the small, medium or large hospitals.*

LEVELS OF PARTICIPATION

A management may be considered participative if it gives scope for workers to influence its decision making process at any level or sphere, or if it shares with workers some of its managerial prerogatives.

Participation may be:

Participation at higher level /Ascending participation

Participation at lower level/Descending participation

In *ascending participation,* workers may be given an opportunity to influence managerial decision at higher levels, through their elected representatives to works councils or the board of the enterprise. In *descending participation,* they may be given more power to plan and make decisions about their own works[1].

Participation at Higher Level/Ascending Participation

If the workers are given an opportunity to influence managerial decisions at higher levels either directly or through their elected representatives, it is *Ascending Participation.*

The extent of existence of higher level participation was analysed on the basis of the rating given by the various employees on the extent of opportunity existing in the hospital for an employee to influence managerial decisions at higher levels.

It was measured on the basis of the views of Administrators, Doctors and the PTM staff by using a five-point scale as 'very low', 'low', 'moderate', 'high', and 'very high'. Based on the extent of opportunities, values were assigned, where '1' denoted the lowest and '5' the highest, and thus mean values were computed. Interpretation was done on the scale of '0-1' as 'very poor', '1-2' as 'poor', '2-3' as 'average', '3-4' as 'good' and '4-5' as 'very good'.

On examining the opinion of Administrators-71 per cent (10) from *small* hospitals, 61 per cent (11) from *medium* hospitals and 100 per cent (13) from *large* hospitals, it was found that the extent of opportunity they got to influence managerial decisions at higher levels was *moderate.*

The majority, i.e., 39 per cent (26) *Doctors* of *small* hospitals reported having 'low' opportunity to influence managerial decisions at the higher levels, while 35 per cent (23) reported having 'moderate' opportunity and 26 per cent (17) reported having 'very low' opportunity to influence managerial decisions at the higher levels. The majority, i.e., 54 per cent (80) of the Doctors of *medium* hospitals reported having 'low opportunity' to influence managerial decisions. Like that majority, 44 per cent (56) Doctors of *large* hospitals also reported having 'low opportunity', to influence managerial decisions. This shows that the majority of the Doctors had *low opportunity* to participate in management decisions.

With regard to the *PTM* staff of *small* hospitals, while 38 per cent (36) had 'low' opportunity to influence managerial decisions at the higher levels, 32 per cent (30) had 'very low' opportunity and 30 per cent (28) had only 'moderate' opportunity to influence managerial decisions. 54 per cent (91) of the PTM staff of *medium* hospitals had 'low' opportunity to influence managerial decisions at the higher levels, while 37 per cent (62) had 'moderate' opportunity. 47 per cent (87) of the PTM staff of *large* hospitals reported having 'low' opportunity while another 47 per cent (87) reported having 'moderate' opportunity to influence managerial decisions at the higher levels.

The analysis revealed that 76 per cent (34) of the Administrators had 'moderate' opportunity, 48 per cent (162) of Doctors and 48 per cent (214) of the PTM category reported having 'low' opportunity to influence managerial decisions at the higher levels. Moreover, 27 per cent (91) of Doctors and 13 per cent (59) of the PTM staff reported having 'very low' opportunity to influence managerial decisions at the higher levels. None of the Administrators, Doctors or PTM staff reported having 'high' or 'very high' opportunity to influence managerial decisions at the higher levels. The survey results are given in Table 5.2.

Here using chi square test, the association between 'extent of opportunity to influence managerial decisions' and different categories of staff in different types of hospitals was statistically examined [(Table 5.2(a)].

Table 5.2: Extent of Opportunity to Influence Managerial Decisions

Category	Type of hospital	Extent of opportunity to influence managerial decisions					Total
		Very low	Low	Moderate	High	Very high	
Administrators	Small	3 21.4%	1 7.1%	10 71.4%	0 .0%	0 .0%	14 100.0%
	Medium	2 11.1%	5 27.8%	11 61.1%	0 .0%	0 .0%	18 100.0%
	Large	0 .0%	0 .0%	13 100.0%	0 .0%	0 .0%	13 100.0%
	Total	**5 11.1%**	**6 13.3%**	**34 75.6%**	**0 .0%**	**0 .0%**	**45 100.0%**
Doctors	Small	17 25.8%	26 39.4%	23 34.8%	0 .0%	0 .0%	66 100.0%
	Medium	32 21.5%	80 53.7%	37 24.8%	0 .0%	0 .0%	149 100.0%
	Large	42 33.3%	56 44.4%	28 22.2%	0 .0%	0 .0%	126 100.0%
	Total	**91 26.7%**	**162 47.5%**	**88 25.8%**	**0 .0%**	**0 .0%**	**341 100.0%**
PTM staff	Small	30 31.9%	36 38.3%	28 29.8%	0 .0%	0 .0%	94 100.0%
	Medium	17 10.0%	91 53.5%	62 36.5%	0 .0%	0 .0%	170 100.0%
	Large	12 6.5%	87 46.8%	87 46.8%	0 .0%	0 .0%	186 100.0%
	Total	**59 13.1%**	**214 47.6%**	**177 39.3%**	**0 .0%**	**0 .0%**	**450 100.0%**

Source: Field Survey.

The chi square test at 5 per cent level of significance revealed that there was *statistically significant* association between the opinion on 'extent of opportunity to influence managerial decisions' and the Administrators and the PTM staff in different types of hospitals. For Doctors, the association was found *statistically insignificant.*

This leads to the conclusion that managerial decisions were mostly taken by the *investors. Administrators had limited opportunity while the Doctors and the PTM staff had low or very low opportunity to participate in managerial decisions.* The fact that even the Doctor, who plays the key role in making decisions regarding patient care, starting from diagnosis, investigations and treatment, did not have much say in the management is quite surprising and does not augur well for these organizations.

Table 5.2(a): Chi-Square Test - Extent of Opportunity to Influence Managerial Decisions

Category		Value	Df	Asymp. Sig. (2-sided)
Administrators	Pearson Chi-Square	9.295(a)	4	.054
	Likelihood Ratio	11.529	4	.021
	Linear-by-Linear Association	3.545	1	.060
	N of Valid Cases	45		
Doctors	Pearson Chi-Square	8.759(b)	4	.067
	Likelihood Ratio	8.551	4	.073
	Linear-by-Linear Association	3.970	1	.046
	N of Valid Cases	341		
PTM staff	Pearson Chi-Square	41.040(c)	4	.000
	Likelihood Ratio	35.423	4	.000
	Linear-by-Linear Association	23.438	1	.000
	N of Valid Cases	450		

Source : Computed

[a] 6 cells (66.7 per cent) had expected count less than 5. The minimum expected count was 1.44.

[b] 0 cells (.0 per cent) had expected count less than 5. The minimum expected count was 17.03.

[c] 0 cells (.0 per cent) had expected count less than 5. The minimum expected count was 12.32.

On the whole, the results indicate that there existed little opportunity for employees to influence managerial decisions, thereby making it amply clear that there was ***no effective ascending participation in managerial decisions***.

Participation at Lower Level/Descending Participation

In hospitals, professionals are often assigned to guide non-professionals; each one functions according to his ability. There is team work at the lower level.

For proper participation at the lower level, job descriptions must be unambiguous and allow scope for staff to control their work and participate in decision making. Besides, there should be a minimum of standing committees and rules and an emphasis on flexibility and innovation[2].

The extent of opportunities of the employees to plan and take decisions about their own work was assessed on the basis of the views of Administrators, Doctors and the PTM staff by using five-point scales. Based on the extent of opportunities, values were assigned, where '1' denoted the lowest and '5' the highest, and thus mean values were computed. Interpretation was done on the following scale as '0-1' as 'very poor', '1-2' as 'poor', '2-3' as 'average', '3-4' as 'good' and '4-5' as 'very good'.

The survey result revealed the following. The majority of the *Administrators* comprising 64 per cent (9) of *small* hospitals, 61 per cent (11) of *medium* hospitals and 85 per cent (11) of *large* hospitals reported that they had 'high' opportunity to plan and take decisions about their own work. With regard to Doctors, 74 per cent (49) of *small* hospitals, 71 per cent (106) of *medium* hospitals and 75 per cent (94) of *large* hospitals expressed the same view. The opinions of the PTM staff also revealed that 56 per cent (53) from *small* hospitals, 34 per cent (57) from *medium* hospitals and 61 per cent (114) from *large* hospitals had 'high' opportunity to plan and take decisions about their own work.

Thus, the majority of the staff—69 per cent (31) of Administrators, 73 per cent (249) of Doctors and 50 per cent (224) of the PTM staff had high opportunity to take decisions connected with their job. Even though the Administrators, Doctors and the PTM staff gave a high rating regarding the opportunity to take decisions connected with their job, the rating given by the PTM staff was less when compared to the other two categories of staff, irrespective of the size of the hospital. The survey results are presented in Table 5.3.

Table 5.3: Freedom to Plan and Take Decisions Connected with Their Job

Category	Type of hospital	Freedom to plan and take decision about own work					Total
		Very low	Low	Moderate	High	Very high	
Administrators	Small	0 .0%	1 7.1%	1 7.1%	9 64.3%	3 21.4%	14 100.0%
	Medium	0 .0%	0 .0%	5 27.8%	11 61.1%	2 11.1%	18 100.0%
	Large	0 .0%	0 .0%	2 15.4%	11 84.6%	0 .0%	13 100.0%
	Total	**0 .0%**	**1 2.2%**	**8 17.8%**	**31 68.9%**	**5 11.1%**	**45 100.0%**
Doctors	Small	0 .0%	0 .0%	11 16.7%	49 74.2%	6 9.1%	66 100.0%
	Medium	4 2.7%	0 .0%	35 23.5%	106 71.1%	4 2.7%	149 100.0%
	Large	0 .0%	0 .0%	19 15.1%	94 74.6%	13 10.3%	126 100.0%
	Total	**4 1.2%**	**0 .0%**	**65 19.1%**	**249 73.0%**	**23 6.7%**	**341 100.0%**
PTM staff	Small	2 2.1%	2 2.1%	36 38.3%	53 56.4%	1 1.1%	94 100.0%
	Medium	15 8.8%	38 22.4%	55 32.4%	57 33.5%	5 2.9%	170 100.0%
	Large	1 .5%	8 4.3%	63 33.9%	114 61.3%	0 .0%	186 100.0%
	Total	**18 4.0%**	**48 10.7%**	**154 34.2%**	**224 49.8%**	**6 1.3%**	**450 100.0%**

Source: Field Survey

Using chi-square test the association between 'Freedom to plan and take decisions about your work' and different categories of staff in different types of hospitals was statistically examined [Table 5.3(a)].

The chi-square at 5 per cent level of significance revealed that there was no statistically significant association between 'Freedom to plan and take decisions about own work' in the case of Administrators in different types of hospitals. But with regard to Doctors and the PTM staff, the association was found statistically significant.

From this we can conclude that the Administrators and Doctors had freedom to plan their work, irrespective of size, and the PTM staff did not enjoy the same freedom. It was there for them in *large*-sized hospitals but not in the *medium* size and not so much in the *small* size hospitals.

Table 5.3(a): Chi-Square Test- Freedom to Plan and take Decisions Connected with their Job

Category		Value	Df	Asymp. Sig. (2-sided)
Administrators	Pearson Chi-Square	7.613(a)	6	.268
	Likelihood Ratio	8.980	6	.175
	Linear-by-Linear Association	.442	1	.506
	N of Valid Cases	45		
Doctors	Pearson Chi-Square	14.628(b)	6	.023
	Likelihood Ratio	16.780	6	.010
	Linear-by-Linear Association	16.780	1	.279
	N of Valid	341		
PTM staff	Pearson Chi-Square	72.800(c)	8	.000
	Likelihood Ratio	76.121	8	.000
	Linear-by-Linear Association	3.107	1	.078
	N of Valid Cases	450		

Source : Computed

[a]9 cells (75.0 per cent) had expected count less than 5. The minimum expected count was .29.

[b]4 cells (33.3 per cent) had expected count less than 5. The minimum expected count was .77.

[c]4 cells (26.7 per cent) had expected count less than 5. The minimum expected count was 1.25.

Considering ascending and descending participation together, it is obvious that the *Administrators had moderate participation at the higher level and high level of influence over the lower level,* which need not necessarily be due to descending participation, as the *PTM* staff *had expressed low ability to influence management decisions. Doctors had expressed poor ascending participation with high level of descending participation,* which could be explained by their unique professional authority. The PTM staff had low level of ascending and relatively low descending participation. Taken together, all these factors indicated ***poor employee participation in management activities in private hospitals***.

INFORMAL PARTICIPATION

Workers participate in management either through formal mechanisms or through informal procedures, and both can be considered instances of participative management. In some organizations, there may not be any formal way of participation, but informally, the higher level managers may allow the employees to participate in management. For the success of any institution, both formal and informal forms of participation are necessary. In other words, both institutional and interpersonal forms of participation are necessary; actually the two are interdependent. Yet, the former may become ritualistic without the latter; interpersonal participation can occur even without the 'structures' and may even yield the desired outcomes.[3]

Existence of Informal Participation

The presence or absence of informal participation in private health care institutions in Kerala was examined on the basis of the experience of Administrators, Doctors and PTM staff in different types of hospitals.

A good number-64 per cent (9) of the Administrators of *small* hospitals, 72 per cent (13) of *medium* hospitals, and 54 per cent (7) of *large* hospitals-reported that they were informally consulted before taking decisions. Doctors also held more or less the same view. 55 per cent (36) of the Doctors in *small* hospitals, 77 per cent (115) in *medium* hospitals, and 60 per cent (76) in *large* hospitals also reported that they were informally consulted before taking decisions. Only 53 per cent (50) of the PTM staff from *small* hospitals, 64 per cent (108) from *medium* hospitals, and 38 per cent (71) from *large* hospitals reported that they were informally consulted before making decisions.

A comparison of the opinions of the three categories of employees reveals that 64 per cent (29) of the Administrators, 67 per cent (227) of the Doctors and 51 per cent (229) of the PTM staff were consulted informally by the management before taking decisions. Relevant details are furnished in Table 5.4.

Informal consultation was there among all employees, but its degree was low with the PTM category. When comparing *small* hospitals, *medium* hospitals and *large* hospitals, informal consultation was present in all the three types of hospitals; however, it was more in *medium* hospitals than in *small* and *large* hospitals.

From the results the obvious conclusion is that ***informal consultation***, the least effective form of participative management, ***was prevalent*** in hospitals. In the hospital settings, as time is an important factor, it is very difficult and cumbersome to arrange formal meetings and take decisions regarding issues which require immediate solution. So, depending on situations, whenever necessary, the persons actually in the field will be consulted informally and decisions taken. Such being the situation in any hospital, it is quite natural that so many of the employees acknowledge the fact that there is informal consultation. But more important is to what extent these consultations influence the managerial decisions, which aspect is examined below.

Table 5.4: Presence of Informal Discussion Before Decision-making

Category	Type of hospital	Presence of Informal discussion before decision making		Total
		Yes	No	
Administrators	Small	9 64.3%	5 35.7%	14 100.0%
	Medium	13 72.2%	5 27.8%	18 100.0%
	Large	7 53.8%	6 46.2%	13 100.0%
	Total	**29** **64.4%**	**16** **35.6%**	**45** **100.0%**
Doctors	Small	36 54.5%	30 45.5%	66 100.0%
	Medium	115 77.2%	34 22.8%	149 100.0%
	Large	76 60.3%	50 39.7%	126 100.0%
	Total	**227** **66.6%**	**114** **33.4%**	**341** **100.0%**
PTM staff	Small	50 53.2%	44 46.8%	94 100.0%
	Medium	108 63.5%	62 36.5%	170 100.0%
	Large	71 38.2%	115 61.8%	186 100.0%
	Total	**229** **50.9%**	**221** **49.1%**	**450** **100.0%**

Source: Field Survey.

Influence of Informal Consultation

The extent of influence of informal consultation depends on a number of factors like management-employee relationship, the available time, the subject matter and others.

It was found that only a consistently democratic style created a climate conducive to participation, leading to relatively stress-free interpersonal relations, higher job satisfaction and work efficiency. Later researchers opine that a climate for mere discussion would only lead to pseudo-participation. A perceived sense of being able to influence decision making is more important.[4]

To what extent the views of the employees of the private health care institutions in Kerala, expressed in this informal consulting influenced the managerial decisions was gathered and analysed in the survey.

The study revealed that the majority of the *Administrators*- 67 per cent (6) of *small* hospitals, 31 per cent (4) of *medium* hospitals, and 57 per cent (4) of *large* hospitals-opined that informal consultation with them influenced the managerial decisions 'moderately'. It is worth observing that 11 per cent (1) of the *Administrators* of *small* hospitals, 54 per cent (7) of *medium* hospitals and 29 per cent (2) of *large* hospitals opined that the influence of informal consultation with them in managerial decisions was 'high'.

The majority, 61 per cent (22) of the *Doctors* of *small* hospitals, 65 per cent (75) of *medium* hospitals, and 43 per cent (33) of *large* hospitals reported that informal consultation with them influenced the managerial decisions 'moderately'.

The opinion of the PTM staff was almost identical to that of the Doctors. 58 per cent each of the PTM category from *small* hospitals (29) and *medium* hospitals (63), and 55 per cent (39) from *large* hospitals reported that their influence in decision making was 'moderate'.

The analysis revealed that 48 per cent (14) of the Administrators, 57 per cent (130) of the Doctors and 57 per cent (131) of the PTM staff believed that the informal consultations influenced the decisions of the management 'moderately' only. In addition to this, 35 per cent (10) of the Administrators, 26 per cent (58) of the Doctors and 21 per cent (48) of the PTM staff reported that informal consultation with them had 'high' influence in decision making. The relevant survey results are furnished in Table 5.5.

Regarding administrative matters of a hospital, the majority of the Administrators gave a 'good' rating about their influence in managerial decisions through informal discussions, while both Doctors and PTM staff gave 'average' to 'low' rating regarding their influence in management decisions. This naturally leads one to believe that the high rating given by the Administrators would suggest a good level of participative management practices in hospitals, but the relatively low rating given by the Doctors and the PTM staff would indicate that the Administrators, by virtue of their position or proximity to the owners, are imposing decisions on other staff rather than making a joint decision. Hence, it may be inferred that though there is good amount of informal consultations in hospitals, it

cannot be counted as a true manifestation of participative management.

Table 5.5: Extent of Influence of Informal Discussion

Category	Type of hospital	Extent of influence					Total
		Very low	Low	Mode-rate	High	Very high	
Administrators	Small	0 .0%	0 .0%	6 66.7%	1 11.1%	2 22.2%	9 100.0%
	Medium	0 .0%	0 .0%	4 30.8%	7 53.8%	2 15.4%	13 100.0%
	Large	0 .0%	0 .0%	4 57.1%	2 28.6%	1 14.3%	7 100.0%
	Total	**0 .0%**	**0 .0%**	**14 48.3%**	**10 34.5%**	**5 17.2%**	**29 100.0%**
Doctors	Small	0 .0%	10 27.8%	22 61.1%	4 11.1%	0 .0%	36 100.0%
	Medium	4 3.5%	12 10.4%	75 65.2%	24 20.9%	0 .0%	115 100.0%
	Large	4 5.3%	9 11.8%	33 43.4%	30 39.5%	0 .0%	76 100.0%
	Total	**8 3.5%**	**31 13.7%**	**130 57.3%**	**58 25.6%**	**0 .0%**	**227 100.0%**
PTM staff	Small	1 2.0%	11 22.0%	29 58.0%	9 18.0%	0 .0%	50 100.0%
	Medium	2 1.9%	19 17.6%	63 58.3%	24 22.2%	0 .0%	108 100.0%
	Large	1 1.4%	16 22.6%	39 55.0%	15 21.1%	0 .0%	71 100.0%
	Total	**4 1.75%**	**46 20.1%**	**131 57.2%**	**48 20.9%**	**0 .0%**	**229 100.0%**

Source: Field Survey

CONCEPT OF TEAM WORK

United, we stand; divided, we fall. All over the world, the most successful managements always develop a team for efficient organization of their work. One member customarily presides over the team, but all are equal.

In hospitals, the lower levels of employees are usually not taken into serious consideration by the hospital authorities at any stage. The present-day employees expect to be treated with dignity. Therefore, all the concerned hospital executives must stop working from above or pushing from behind. They should, instead, start leading from the front and work together with other categories of employees, enlisting their whole-hearted co-operation for the hospitals to achieve its goal.[5]

The Griffiths NHS Management Inquiry 1983 also emphasized that responsibility should be pushed as far down the line as possible to the point where action can be taken efficiently. [6]

The delivery of health services to individuals and to groups of individuals is inherently an administrative process dependent upon planning, allocation of scarce resources, evaluation of performance and other tasks basic to management. This is not to say that administrator can carry out the task alone. Obviously, team efforts are required, which involve physicians, nurses and other health professionals as well as administrators, and it is important to note that responsibility for effective administration is shared by all members of this team.

A hospital is a place where diversified professionals and non-professionals interact in rendering services to the patients. The interactional process builds up team spirit and a sense of participation in the functionaries[7].

Team work as a variable was measured by taking into consideration the extent of superiors' ability to promote team work and the extent of team work actually existing in the hospitals.

Mean value was used for analysis. The five-point scale was used for this purpose. Based on the superiors' ability to promote team work, values were assigned, where '1' denoted the lowest extent of team work and '5' the highest. Interpretation was done with '0-1' as 'very poor', '1-2' as 'poor', '2-3' as 'average', '3-4' as 'good', and '4-5' as 'very good'.

According to the Administrators, the extent of superiors' 'ability to promote team work' as well as 'the extent of team work' existing in the hospitals was 'good' for *small* hospitals (mean value 4.00 each), *medium* hospitals (mean values 3.67 and 3.83) *and large* hospitals (mean values 3.69 and 3.85).

In the opinion of Doctors of *small* hospitals, the extent of superiors' 'ability to promote team work' as well as 'the extent of team work' existing in the hospitals was also *good* with mean values 3.77 and 3.92 respectively, those of Doctors of *medium* hospitals were 3.86 and 3.89 respectively, and those of Doctors of *large* hospitals were 3.71 and 3.82 respectively.

In the view of the PTM staff of *small* hospitals, the superiors' 'ability to promote team work' as well as 'the level of team work' existing in the hospital was *good* with mean values 3.70 and 4.00 respectively; those of the PTM staff of *medium* hospitals were 3.81 and 4.03 respectively, and those of the PTM staff of *large* hospitals were 3.88 and 3.93 respectively. The survey results are given in Table 5.6.

A comparison of the views of the Administrators, Doctors and PTM staff in *small* hospitals, *medium* hospitals and *large* hospitals revealed that 'the extent of superiors' ability to promote team work' as well as 'the extent of team work' existing in the private hospitals in Kerala was *good*.

Table 5.6: Existing Concept of Team Work

Category	Type of hospital	Superiors ability to promote team work	Existing level of team work
Administrators	Small	4.00	4.00
	Medium	3.67	3.83
	Large	3.69	3.85
	Total	**3.78**	**3.89**
Doctors	Small	3.77	3.92
	Medium	3.86	3.89
	Large	3.71	3.82
	Total	**3.79**	**3.87**
PTM staff	Small	3.70	4.00
	Medium	3.81	4.03
	Large	3.88	3.93
	Total	**3.81**	**3.98**

Source: Field Survey

Hospitals, unlike other industries, where whole unit can be considered as a team, are run by multiple task-centred teams. Each patient care activity is carried out by a team comprising a limited category of workers only, and the satisfaction level expressed by an employee can only be taken as that of this task-oriented small team. This sort of teams, even though limited to a few categories of employees, lead to cross-category involvement of employees in a task. This is inevitable in each and every patient care activity, and, as such, there is no task or platform other than celebrations or events which can bring all the staff in a hospital together as a team. Participation cutting across categories as a concept in the true sense is far different from this task-oriented team approach. Hence, we can safely conclude that the satisfaction expressed by employers in team work is ***not an indicator of the presence of participative management.***

EMPLOYEES' PARTICIPATION THROUGH COMMITTEES

A committee may be defined as a group of persons in an organization, who function collectively on an organized basis to perform some administrative activity. No absolute figure can be given as the optimum size of a committee. The size of the group should be small enough to permit discussion. On the other hand, it should be large enough to represent various interest groups.

Committee members, whether volunteer, appointed or elected, should possess certain personal qualities; they should be able to

- express themselves in a group
- keep to the point
- discuss issues in a practical rather than theoretical way
- give information that advances the thinking of the group about the topic rather than about themselves
- discuss the topic in an orderly yet flexible way
- suppress the natural desire to speak for the sake of being heard or of saying what they think the leader or some powerful member wants to hear. The members should also have sufficient authority to commit the unit or group that they represent to the course of action adopted by the committee. Committee members should be of approximately equal rank and status in the organization, in order to permit the free exchange of ideas[8].

Committees permit wide participation in decision making. Persons who take part in planning a program or making a decision usually feel more enthusiastic about accepting and executing it. Even limited participation can be helpful. The use of committees to motivate subordinates to support a program or decision requires skilled handling. It is by no means certain that deliberations of this kind will kindle enthusiastic support, for they can also result in the deepening of existing divisions among participants[9].

Committees in Health Care System

In a health care system, decision making involves different specializations; therefore, group decision-making would enhance its value.

Health care organizations need committees to help consolidate the dual authority tracks within the medical authority structure and the administrative/support structure[10]. Committees and the working of the committees in hospitals were analysed on the basis of the following factors:

(*i*) Presence of committees

(*ii*) Mode of selection of members of the committee

(*iii*) Tenure of office of the members of the committee

(*iv*) Frequency of committee meetings

(*v*) Satisfaction regarding working of committees

(*vi*) Effectiveness of committee meetings

Presence of Committees

The presence or absence of Committees in the private hospitals of Kerala was surveyed *hospital-wise,* and the result revealed the following. The majority of the hospitals-70 per cent (21)—did not have committees of any form. There were only 30 per cent (9) of hospitals in the sample which had committees of some form.

A comparison among *small, medium* and *large* hospitals revealed that none of the *small* hospitals had committees; among the *large* hospitals, 43 per cent (3) had committees. There was a striking difference in the *medium* size hospitals, where 60 per cent (6) of the units had committees of some form. It is worth observing that 100 per cent (13) of *small* hospitals, 40 per cent (4) of *medium* hospitals and 57 per cent (4) of *large* hospitals had no committees. The survey results are given in Table 5.7.

Table 5.7: Presence of Formal Organizational Committee

Type	Presence of formal organizational committees		Total
	Yes	No	
Small	0 .0%	13 100.0%	13 100.0%
Medium	6 60.0%	4 40.0%	10 100.0%
Large	3 42.9%	4 57.1%	7 100.0%
Total	**9** **30%**	**21** **70%**	**30** **100.0%**

Source: Field Survey.

The employees of the hospital vary from highly specialized medical professionals to uneducated sweepers. As they belong to different cadres, classes and professions, there will not be free exchange of ideas among the employees normally. Specialized segmented group involvement through Committees is not possible in *small* hospitals. Hence, committees with representatives from all sections of employees is the only forum in which exchange of creative ideas and innovations about hospital management can come up, and compliance to those can be assured at least to a reasonable extent.

In other words, in hospitals, joint committees can be considered as the single most effective mechanism by which participative management can at least be attempted. From the total absence of committees in any form in *small* hospitals and very small percentage of hospitals in the *medium* and *large* sectors having committees, it is apparent that there is ***no effective participative management***.

Even though only a small number of *medium* and *large* hospitals had committees, a sincere attempt was made to assess the nature, functions, effectiveness and acceptance of these committees.

Mode of Selection of the Members of the Committees

The members of the committees should be selected with utmost care, ensuring that all the categories of employees are represented adequately, giving weightage based on the functional importance of each category of employees for the effective functioning of an organization and not merely based on numbers.

If a committee is to be successful, the members must be representative of the interests they are expected to serve. They must also possess the required authority and be able to perform well as a group. Finally, the members should have the capacity for communicating well and reaching group decisions by integrated group thinking rather than by inappropriate compromise.

The selection of members may be by: (*a*) nomination by management; (*b*) nomination by trade union; (*c*) election by secret ballot; (*d*) election by open ballot; and (*e*) consensus, of which (*c*) is considered to be optimal.

The analysis is made on the basis of the information collected from ***the hospitals where there were committees***. The surprising result was that in all hospitals where there were committees, the members were ***nominated by the management*** and there was ***not even a single elected representative.***

Hence the members of such committees cannot be considered as true employee representative and their views and decisions will in all probability be in line with those of the management rather than those of the employees. So, the obvious conclusion is that even in hospitals where committees are present the mode of selection of members ***negates the true concept of participative management.***

Table 5.8 gives the *hospital-wise* details about the 'mode of selection of members of the committee' in *medium* and *large* hospitals

Table 5.8: Existing Mode of Selection

Type of hospital	Existing mode of selection					Totals
	Nomination by the management	Nomination by trade union	Election by secret ballot	Election by open ballot	Consensu	
Medium	8 100.0%	0 .0%	0 .0%	0 .0%	0 .0%	8 100.0%
Large	3 100.0%	0 .0%	0 .0%	0 .0%	0 .0%	3 100.0%
Total	**11** **100.0%**	**0** **.0%**	**0** **.0%**	**0** **.0%**	**0** **.0%**	**11** **100.0%**

Source: Field Survey

Existing Tenure of Office of Members of the Committee

The tenure of office of members of the committee may be fixed according to the requirements and convenience of the organization. This is analysed *hospital-wise* on the basis of the alternatives such as: (*i*) not more than one year; (*ii*) not more than three years; (*iii*) until transfer, retirement or death whichever is earlier; (*iv*) representation according to position.

The survey result revealed the following. In 38 per cent (3) of the *medium* hospitals, 'until transfer or retirement whichever is earlier', in 25 per cent (2) of the hospitals 'not more than one year', and in another 25 per cent (2) of the hospitals 'not more than three years' were the terms of tenure of office of members of the committee. The tenure of office of the members of the committee in 67 per cent (2) of the *large* hospitals was 'until transfer, retirement or death whichever is earlier', and in 33 per cent (1) of the hospitals, it was 'not more than three years'. The survey results are given in Table 5.9.

Using chi-square test, the association between 'tenure of office of the members of the committee' and 'different types of hospitals' was statistically examined [Table 5.9(a)].

The chi- square at 5 per cent level of significance revealed that there was *no statistically significant association* between tenure of office of the members of the committee and different types of hospitals.

The analysis revealed that in 46 per cent (5) of the hospitals the existing tenure of office of members of committees was unlimited 'until transfer or retirements whichever is earlier'. When the same person is representing a group of employees permanently, the following deficiencies creep in.

(*i*) He may not be effective in conveying the true problems of the employees as he is not accountable to them.

Table 5.9: Existing Tenure of Members of the Committee

Type of hospital	Existing tenure of members				Total
	Not more than one year	Not more than three years	Until transfer or retirement whichever is earlier	Repre-sentation according to position	
Medium	2 25.0%	2 25.0%	3 37.5%	1 12.5%	8 100.0%
Large	0 .0%	1 33.3%	2 66.7%	0 .0%	3 100.0%
Total	**2** **18.2%**	**3** **27.3%**	**5** **45.5%**	**1** **9.1%**	**11** **100.0%**

Source: Field Survey

Table 5.9(a): Chi-Square Test - Existing Tenure of Members of the Committee

	Value	df	Asymp. Sig. (2-sided)
Pearson Chi-Square	1.589(a)	3	.662
Likelihood Ratio	2.342	3	.505
Linear-by-Linear Association	.213	1	.645
N of Valid Cases	11		

Source : Computed

8 cells (100.0%) had expected count less than 5. The minimum expected count was .27.

(*ii*) He may become more of management personnel than employee representative;

(*iii*) He may impose on subordinates;

(*iv*) His effectiveness as a member in a committee, if inadequate, will adversely affect the prospects of the department he represents; and

(*v*) The situation can lead to corruption.

This ***unlimited tenure*** coupled with the ***undemocratic selection*** of the members ***leads to near total absence of true employee participation*** in committee meetings.

One of the major avenues for participation in management is through committees, the absence of which in small hospitals denotes near total lack of participation of employees in management decisions. Even though a small number of medium and large hospitals have committees, ***the management's nomination of its members and permanent tenure of members are factors effectively annulling the concept of true participative management.***

Frequency of Committee Meetings

Committees which held meetings regularly were effective in giving chance to all the staff to air their opinions, clarify their doubts, review important decisions and formulate short and long-term plans.

In those hospitals where there were committees, the frequency of the committee meetings was analysed. In order to analyze the frequency the following standards were formulated:

very rarely—less than once in a month

rarely—once in a month

once in a while—2-3 times a month

often—more than 3 times a month

The survey results revealed the following. With regard to Administrators in the *medium* sector, 47 per cent (7) reported having meetings 'often' and 33 per cent (5) had them 'once in a while' only. In *large* hospitals, 40 per cent (2) reported having meetings 'rarely' and another 40 per cent (2) had them 'often'.

41 per cent (55) of the Doctors of *medium* hospitals reported having meetings 'often', while 33 per cent (45) reported having meetings 'once in a while' only. But a good number of the Doctors i.e., 49 per cent (16) in *large* hospitals reported having meetings 'once in a while', and 30 per cent (10) had them 'often'.

A large section of the PTM staff of *medium* hospitals, i.e., 37 per cent (50) reported having meetings 'often' while 32 per cent (43) had them 'once in a while', and 31 per cent (42) held them 'rarely'. In *large* hospitals, a higher percentage, i.e., 46 per cent (30) had meetings 'once in a while', while 36 per cent (24) had them 'often' only.

A comparison between *medium* with *large* hospitals revealed that the majority of the Doctors and the PTM staff in *large* hospitals had meetings 'once in a while', while the same categories of respondents of *medium* hospitals reported of having meetings 'often'. The survey results are presented in Table 5.10.

The analysis revealed that meetings were held when required. The frequency was slightly better for *medium* size hospitals. But these frequent meetings of the committee members *nominated by the management with unlimited tenure* were only ***going to further the cause of the controlling authority at the expense of employees benefits.***

Table 5.10: Frequency of Committee Meetings

Category	Type of hospital	Frequency of meetings				Total
		Very rarely	Rarely	Once in a while	Often	
Administrators	Medium	0 .0%	3 20.0%	5 33.3%	7 46.7%	15 100.0%
	Large	0 .0%	2 40.0%	1 20.0%	2 40.0%	5 100.0%
	Total	**0 .0%**	**5 25.0%**	**6 30.0%**	**9 45.0%**	**20 100.0%**
Doctors	Medium	1 .7%	34 25.2%	45 33.3%	55 40.7%	135 100.0%
	Large	0 .0%	7 21.2%	16 48.5%	10 30.3%	33 100.0%
	Total	**1 .6%**	**41 24.4%**	**61 36.3%**	**65 38.7%**	**168 100.0%**
PTM staff	Medium	1 .7%	42 30.9%	43 31.6%	50 36.8%	136 100.0%
	Large	0 .0%	12 18.2%	30 45.5%	24 36.4%	66 100.0%
	Total	**1 .5%**	**54 26.7%**	**73 36.1%**	**74 36.6%**	**202 100.0%**

Source: Field Survey

Satisfaction Regarding Working of the Committees

Members of a committee play a variety of roles. Some seek information; others give information; some try to engage others to contribute; others are followers. Some try to coordinate the group's effort or to achieve a compromise when disagreements occur, while others take a more aggressive role. Committee's work should be limited to subject matter that can be handled in group discussions. Certain kinds of subjects lend themselves to committee action, while others do not. Jurisdictional disputes and strategy formulation, for example, may be suitable for group deliberation, while certain isolated, technical problems may be better solved by an expert in the specialized field[11].

The level of satisfaction of employees regarding the working of committees was measured on the following parameters:

(*a*) advance circulation of notice and agenda for the meeting;

(*b*) attendance of members at the meeting;

(*c*) freedom of members to express their opinion in the meeting;

(*d*) communication of minutes of the meeting;

(*e*) members' representation in the committee; and

(*f*) representatives' involvement in the committee.

Mean value was used for analysis. *Mean* was computed by putting *level of satisfaction* on the working of committees on a five-point scale, where the lowest satisfaction was represented by 1 and the highest level of satisfaction by 5. Analysis was made on the basis of the following parameters: 0-1 for 'very poor', 1-2 for 'poor', 2-3 for 'average', 3-4 for 'good', and 4-5 for 'very good'.

Regarding the level of satisfaction of Administrators in *medium* hospitals, it was 'good' for 'all parameters' with the highest level for 'their representations in committee' (mean value 3.73) 'freedom to express opinion in the committee' (mean value 3.73), and the lowest for 'their representatives' involvement in the committee' (mean value 3.07). With regard to Administrators in *large* hospitals, it was observed that it was 'good' for 'all parameters' except 'their representatives' involvement' in the committee (mean value 2.80), for which it was 'average'.

The level of satisfaction of Doctors in *medium* hospitals was 'good' for 'all parameters' with the highest level of satisfaction for 'freedom to express opinion' (mean value 3.76) and the lowest for 'representatives' involvement in the committee' (mean value 3.20). Regarding the Doctors of *large* hospitals, the satisfaction level was 'good' for 'all parameters' with the exception of 'average' level of satisfaction with 'attendance in committee meetings' (mean value 3.00).

The level of satisfaction of the PTM staff in *medium* hospitals was also the highest for 'freedom to express opinion' (3.76) and the lowest for 'representatives' involvement in the committee' (mean value 2.74). The *large* hospital PTM staff showed the highest level of satisfaction with 'circulation of minutes' (mean value 3.68) and the lowest with 'their representatives' involvement in the committee' (mean value 2.52). The survey results are furnished in Table 5.11.

Using two-way ANOVA test, the differences in the mean values in the different parameters affecting the working of committees, among different categories, types of hospitals and their interaction were tested.

The ANOVA at 5 per cent level of significance revealed that the mean differences by categories were found statistically *significant*, regarding 'the attendance in committees', 'circulation of minutes' and 'representatives' involvement' in the committee. But the mean differences by types were found statistically *insignificant for all parameters.* At the same time, their interaction effect also showed *statistically insignificant difference* in the mean values of all the different parameters of the working of committees.

Table 5.11: Satisfaction Regarding Working of Committees

Category	Type of hospital	Notice in advance and agenda for the meeting	Attendance of members in committee	Freedom to express opinion	Circulation of minutes	Members representation in committee	Representatives involvement
Administrators	Medium	3.67	3.67	3.73	3.47	3.73	3.07
	Large	4.00	4.00	4.00	4.00	4.00	2.80
	Total	**3.75**	**3.75**	**3.80**	**3.60**	**3.80**	**3.00**
Doctors	Medium	3.69	3.63	3.76	3.37	3.44	3.20
	Large	3.24	3.00	3.18	3.15	3.06	3.21
	Total	**3.60**	**3.51**	**3.64**	**3.33**	**3.37**	**3.20**
PTM staff	Medium	3.66	3.65	3.76	3.48	3.51	2.74
	Large	3.58	3.48	3.64	3.68	3.26	2.52
	Total	**3.63**	**3.60**	**3.72**	**3.54**	**3.43**	**2.67**
ANOVA test result (The exact level of significance-P value)							
1. Mean difference by category		.251	.034	.098	.027	.098	.004
2. Mean difference by type of hospital		.720	.391	.441	.383	.535	.546
3. Intraction of 1 and 2		.179	.059	.092	.172	.526	.772

Source: Field Survey

When comparing the mean values regarding the views of Administrators, Doctors and PTM staff, 'freedom to express opinion' for all was high and 'representation in committee' was high for Administrators.

The analysis revealed that all categories of employees from the different types of hospitals had expressed a 'good' level of satisfaction regarding 'circulation of notice in advance and with proper agenda' regarding committee meetings. Also, the level of 'attendance in committee meetings' was satisfactory. Even though committees were present in only a small number of hospitals, the 'committee meetings' were conducted in a proper manner in those hospitals where there were committees.

The 'freedom of members of the committee to express their opinion in meetings' was also given a 'good' rating, which was not surprising considering the fact that all committee members could in effect be considered as part of the controlling authority since all of them were nominated by the management.

The next point considered was the effectiveness of the 'communication of minutes of the meeting' to all strata of employees, for which also a *good* rating was given by all sections of employees. These tallies with our finding in the previous chapter which demonstrated a high level of informative participation.

The representation of each employee in the committee through a committee member from his cadre was also given a good rating. This can be explained by the observations made at the field survey which revealed that the management usually involved the *heads of departments or those in charge of each department* for the committee meeting. Even though an employee may not be satisfied with his representative in the committee, in effect he is represented.

The final point considered was with regard to the satisfaction, the involvement and functioning of each employee representative in the committee meeting, for which, not surprisingly, a lower rating was given, when compared with all the other parameters regarding the working of committees considered so far. This can easily be explained by the proven fact that none of the employee representatives in committees was democratically elected.

Effectiveness of Existing Committees

The Committee must be worth its cost. It may be difficult to count the benefits. Properly conducted committee meetings, used for the right purpose, can result in a greater motivation, improved problem-solving and increased output.

Committees may help solving problems and development of new ideas. Such group interactions have been found to be especially enlightening in policy matters. Indeed, at times, group deliberations may be superior to individual judgment.

The respondents were asked to measure the effectiveness of the working of the committee on the following parameters: (*a*) improving patient care; (*b*) reducing the cost of treatment; (*c*) eliminating waste; (*d*) improving communication; and (*e*) improving labour management relations.

Mean value was used for analysis. Mean was computed by giving the rate of effectiveness of the working of the committee on a five-point scale, where the lowest level was represented by 1 and the highest by 5. The mean values were 0-1 for 'very poor' , 1-2 for 'poor', 2-3 for 'average', 3-4 for 'good' and 4-5 for 'very good'.

The analysis revealed that the ratings of Administrators in *medium* hospitals, were 'good' for the involvement of the committee on 'improving patient care' (mean value 3.67), 'eliminating waste' (mean value 3.20) and improving labour management relations (mean value 3.27). It was *average* on 'reducing the cost of treatment' (mean value 3.00). The Administrators in *large* hospitals reported that the involvement of the committee was 'very good' (mean value 4.20) for 'improving patient care' and 'good' (mean value 4.00) for all other parameters.

With regard to Doctors in *medium* hospitals, the effectiveness of the committee was 'good' for all parameters with the highest level of efficiency for 'improving patient care' and 'disposal of waste' (mean value 3.86 each). Doctors of *large* hospitals also reported that the extent of effectiveness was 'good' for all parameters, with the highest rate for 'improving communication' and 'improving labour management relations' (mean value 3.45 each).

The PTM staff of *medium* hospitals also stated that the effectiveness of the committee was 'good' for all parameters with the highest rate for 'involvement in patient care' (mean value 3.85). The PTM staff of *large* hospitals revealed that the extent of efficiency of the committee was 'good' for all parameters with the highest level of efficiency for its involvement in 'improving labour management relations' (mean value 3.82). The survey results are depicted in Table 5.12.

Table 5.12: The Extent of Effectiveness of Committees

Category	Type of hospital	Involvement of committee in				
		Improving patient care	Reducing the treatment cost	Eliminating waste	Improving communi-cation	Labour manage-ment relations
Administrators	Medium	3.67	3.00	3.20	3.00	3.27
	Large	4.20	4.00	4.00	4.00	4.00
	Total	**3.80**	**3.25**	**3.40**	**3.25**	**3.45**
Doctors	Medium	3.86	3.52	3.86	3.78	3.71
	Large	3.33	3.24	3.42	3.45	3.45
	Total	**3.76**	**3.46**	**3.77**	**3.71**	**3.66**
PTM staff	Medium	3.85	3.40	3.74	3.79	3.71
	Large	3.70	3.62	3.68	3.71	3.82
	Total	**3.80**	**3.48**	**3.72**	**3.76**	**3.75**
ANOVA test result (Exact level of significance – P value)						
Mean difference by category		.141	.497	.761	.358	.296
Mean difference by Type of hospital		.760	.074	.522	.254	.293
Category x Type of hospital		.039	.013	.017	.032	.104

Source: Field Survey

Using two-way ANOVA test, the significant difference in the mean values of the effectiveness of the existing committee among different categories, types of hospitals and their interaction were tested.

The ANOVA at 5 per cent level of significance revealed *no statistically significant difference* in the views of different categories of staff in different types of hospitals regarding the 'extent of effectiveness of committees' in private hospitals. At the same time, their interaction effect showed *statistically significant differences* in the mean values of the extent of effectiveness of the committee for all factors except 'improving labour management relations'.

A detailed analysis of the results revealed that the efficiency of the committee was 'good' for 'all parameters' with the highest mean value for 'involvement of committee in patient care' with regard to Administrators, Doctors and the PTM staff of *medium* hospitals and Administrators of *large* hospitals.

The analysis apparently leads us to the conclusion that the committees, wherever they are present, seemed to be effective in all the parameters studied. It seemed highly unlikely that this positive response was actually due to effective employee participation in management through committees. The nomination of committee members by management and unlimited tenure of office of members of the committee annul the true concept of participative management. Hence, it is concluded that *the high rating of effectiveness of committees can only be due rather to overt or covert coercion by the management* than to employee participation in management.

The observations made in the field survey revealed that the management called the 'Heads of Departments' or 'In-charge of Departments' for committee meetings and the committee meetings in many institutions were just a ritual with no meaningful discussion or decision. A management-nominated committee was usually biased and the true problems of lower level employees were not taken up earnestly. Furthermore, the HOD being a member of the committee which was close to the controlling authority, the subordinate staff was naturally forced to toe the line with the HOD.

CONTROL AND PARTICIPATION

In the hospital, authority does not emanate from a single source and does not flow along a single line of command as it does in most formal organizations. Each of the different groups, the trustees, the medical staff, and the administrators has a basis for the exercise of legitimate authority.

The Griffiths report recommended the need to involve clinicians more closely in the management process. General practitioners can involve in the Trust's decision making and can influence the major decisions taken.

Among the major factors influencing the effectiveness of health service management structures, the organization believes in devolving considerable management responsibility to clinical or locality groups, and value and encourage staff participation in making decisions[12].

The analysis regarding control system in hospitals was made on the basis of the following parameters:

(*i*) Existing system of hospital control; and

(*ii*) Existing system of Doctors' control over others.

Existing System of Hospital Control

The private hospitals may be controlled by: (*a*) the investor, (*b*) a non-medical professional administrator; (*c*) a medical and non-medical administrator; (*d*) a committee consisting of only medically qualified personnel; or (*e*) a committee consisting of representatives from all cadres.

Hospital-wise details about the parties who are controlling the hospitals were collected. The survey revealed the following. 100 per cent (13) of the *small* hospitals and 100 per cent (7) of the *large* hospitals covered by the study were controlled by the 'the investor'. Of the *medium* hospitals, 80 per cent (8) were controlled solely by 'the investor', 10 per cent (1) by 'a medical and non-medical administrator and another 10 per cent (1) by 'a committee consisting of medically qualified personnel'.

A great majority, i.e., 93 per cent (28) of the hospitals were controlled by 'the investor only'. The survey results are given in Table 5.13.

Table 5.13: Existing System of Hospital Control

Type of hospital	Existing system of hospital control					Total
	The investor only	A non medical profe-ssional admini-strator	A medical and non medical admini-strator	A Committee consisting of medically qualified personnel	A Committee consisting of repres-entatives from all cadre	
Small	13 100.0%	0 .0%	0 .0%	0 .0%	0 .0%	13 100.0%
Medium	8 80.0%	0 .0%	1 10.0%	1 10.0%	0 .0%	10 100.0%
Large	7 100.0%	0 .0%	0 .0%	0 .0%	0 .0%	7 100.0%
Total	**28** **93.3%**	**0** **.0%**	**1** **3.3%**	**1** **3.3%**	**0** **.0%**	**30** **100.0%**

Source: Field Survey

Using chi-square test, the statistical significance of association between 'the parties controlling the hospital' and 'different types of hospitals' were tested [Table 5.13(a)].

Table 5.13(a): Chi-square Test- Existing System of Hospital Control

	Value	Df	Asymp. Sig. (2-sided)
Pearson Chi-Square	4.286(a)	4	.369
Likelihood Ratio	4.688	4	.321
Linear-by-Linear Association	.129	1	.719
N of Valid Cases	30		

Source : Computed

6 cells (66.7 per cent) had expected count less than 5. The minimum expected count was 23.

The chi-square test at 5 per cent level of significance revealed that there was *no statistically significant association* between the parties controlling the hospital and the different types of hospitals.

This leads to the conclusion that irrespective of the size of the hospitals, the private hospitals in Kerala were controlled by the investors only. Of the 30 hospitals studied, only one hospital was run by a committee of medically qualified persons. Even in that hospital, the committee consisted only of Doctors, thereby showing that there was not much participation by lower grade employees. Almost all other hospitals were ***controlled by the investors only***.

Existing System of Doctors' Control Over Others

Doctors, being the primary controllers and users of the new technology, have an important responsibility to assist in the formulation of policy at all levels in a hospital. They should strive for consensus with colleagues and most importantly with other professional groups.

The medical staff has a high status within the hospital organization. Legally, they are the only ones who can prescribe therapeutic care and treatment. Physicians have the knowledge for task performance based upon intensive training and specialization[13].

Adequate control over Para-medical, Technical and Ministerial staff by a treating physician in a hospital can help to a large extent in improving the quality of services provided to the patient.

The extent of control the doctors of private health care institutions in Kerala had over: (*a*) Para-medical; (*b*) Technical; and (*c*) Ministerial staff was analysed. The views of employees were collected on a five-point scale as 'very low', 'low', 'average' 'high' and 'very high'.

Mean value was used for analysis. Mean was computed by putting level of control on a five-point scale, where the lowest level of control was represented by 1 and the highest by 5. Mean values were qualified as follows: 0-1 as 'very low'; 1-2 as 'low'; 2-3 as 'average'; 3-4 as 'high' and 4-5 as 'very high'.

The extent of control the *small* hospital Doctors had on Para-medical, Technical and Ministerial staff was 'good' with mean value 3.41, 3.36 and 3.38 respectively. The control the *medium* hospital Doctors had on Para-medical, Technical and Ministerial staff was also 'good' (but mean value less than that of *small* hospitals) with mean values 3.34, 3.19 and 3.13 respectively. The extent of control the *large* hospital Doctors had on the Para-medical, Technical and Ministerial staff was 'good', with mean values of 3.56, 3.53 and 3.26 respectively.

When comparing the degree of control over para-medical, technical and ministerial staff, Doctors had more control over para-medical staff (total mean value 3.43) than over technical (total mean value 3.35) and ministerial staff (total mean value 3.23). The survey results are furnished in Table 5.14.

Table 5.14: Doctors' Administrative Control Over Para-medical, Technical and Ministerial Staff

Type of hospital	Para medical	Technical	Ministerial staff
Small	3.41	3.36	3.38
Medium	3.34	3.19	3.13
Large	3.56	3.53	3.26
Total	**3.43**	**3.35**	**3.23**

Source: Field Survey

This leads to the conclusion that Doctors, who had high status in the hospital and were the actual decision makers regarding patient care, had ***good control over the PTM staff***. Doctors, though not promoting participative management, directly or indirectly did control or coordinate the activities of others to provide better patient care.

The analysis of the existing system of participation revealed that 'informative participation', *the least effective among all forms of participation,* was dominant among *small* hospitals and among *medium* hospitals, while 'consultative participation' was dominant in the *large* hospitals. The private hospitals in Kerala are controlled by the 'investors' only. *Doctors had expressed poor ascending participation with high level of descending participation,* which can be explained by their unique professional authority. The PTM staff had low level of ascending and relatively low descending participation. *Informal consultation*, the least effective form of participative management, was found *prevalent* in hospitals. 'The extent of superiors' ability to promote team work' as well as 'the extent of team work' existing in the private hospitals was *good*. There was total absence of committees in any form in *small* hospitals, and only a small percentage of the *medium* and *large* hospitals had committees. In all hospitals where there were committees, the members were nominated by the management and they held the office for an unlimited period 'until transfer or retirement whichever is earlier'. Taken together, all these factors indicate the existence of *poor employee participation in management activities in the private hospitals of Kerala.*

REFERENCES

1. Clerk, J. M., 'Workers Participation in Management—Some Preliminary Considerations' in W. Albeda Erasmus (Ed), *Participative Management,* Rotherdam: University Press, 1973, p. 10.
2. Jenny Cowpe, 'Managing Within the Organization' in David M. Hanselll and Brian Salter (Eds), *The Management of Health Care—The Clinicians Management Hand Book,* London : WB Saunders Company Ltd, 1995.
3. Roy, S.K., 'Participative Management in Public Industry: Organizational Groundwork Necessary' in Thakur, C. P., Sethi, K. C. (Eds), *Industrial Democracy: Some Issues and Experiences*, Delhi : Sri Ram Centre for Industrial Relations and Human Resources, 1973, p. 60.
4. Mrityunjay Athreya, 'Organizational Determinants of Participation' in Thakur, C. P., Sethi, K. C. (Eds), *Industrial Democracy: Some Issues and Experiences,* Delhi: Sri.Ram Centre for Industrial Relations and Human Resources, 1973, p. 76.
5. Sudhir Dawra, 'Hospital Administrative and Management', Delhi : Mohit Publications, 2002, p. 580.
6. Ron Parker, 'The Management Challenge' in David M. Hansell and Brian Salter (Eds), *The Management of Health Care: The Clinicians Management Hand Book,* London : WB Saunders Company Ltd, 1995, p. 3.
7. Sankara Rao, M., *Hospital Organization and Administration*, Delhi : Deep and Deep Publications, 1992, p. 8.
8. John Gratto Liebler, Charles R. McConnell, *Management Principles for Health Professionals*, Mary Land : An Aspen Publication, 1999, pp. 329-331.
9. Heinz Weihrich, Harold Koontz, *'Management' A Global Perspective,* Singapore : Mc. Graw-Hill Book Co, 1994, p. 520.
10. John Gratto Liebler, Charles R. Mc Connell, *Op. cit.,* p. 318.
11. Heinz Weihrich, Harold Knoontz, *Op.cit.,* pp. 515-527.
12. Jenny Cowpe, 'Managing within the Organization' in David M Hansell and Brian Salter (Eds), *The Management of Health Care: The Civilians Management Hand Book,* London : W.B Saunders Company Ltd, 1973, p. 76.
13. Fremont E. Kast, James E. Resenzweig, A., *Systems Approach*, New York : McGrew Hill Book Company, 1970, pp. 538-546.

CHAPTER 6

Feasibility of Participative Management in Private Health Care Industry

Participative management is recognized as particularly pertinent to organizations dealing with complex, knowledge-based problems. Extensive research conducted as early as the 1950s and 1960s demonstrated that participative management is particularly well suited to science-based organizations like hospitals, whose key staff are noted for their creatively intensive motivation for work that interests them, stronger affiliation with their discipline than their organization, and sensitivity to directive management.

The next step in our study, as we have already concluded that there is no effective participative management in private hospitals, is to study the feasibility of participative management in private health care institutions in Kerala.

The opinions of different categories of employees regarding participative management, their true attitude towards the concept and their genuine views regarding its implementation in the private health care industry in Kerala, were collected. The responses received have been classified and analysed under the following heads:

- Managing Personnel
- Concept of Participative Management
- Forms of Participation
- Degrees of Participation
- Sharing of Equal Powers
- Extent of Participation

- Committees and Participation
- For and Against of Implementing Participative Management
- Statutory Participation
- Participative Management in Kerala
- Hurdles to Successful Participative Management.

MANAGING PERSONNEL

The hospital, for its efficient functioning, relies on an extensive division of labour among its members, upon a complex organizational structure which encompasses many different departments, staff, officers and positions, and upon an elaborate system of coordination of tasks, function and social interaction.

The opinions of various categories of employees about: (*i*) Control and responsibility expected; (*ii*) Efficiency of managing personnel; (*iii*) Satisfaction about managing personnel; (*iv*) Doctors controlling others; (*v*) Professional relationship between Doctors and PTM staff; and (*vi*) Coordination and control, were studied and analysed here.

Control and Responsibility Expected

The hospital may be controlled by a group or a person who is legally responsible and is the prime authority formulating the policy matters of a hospital. The controlling authority can be any one of the following.

(*i*) the investor; or

(*ii*) a non-medical professional administrator; or

(*iii*) a medical and non-medical administrator; or

(*iv*) a committee consisting of medically qualified personnel; or

(*v*) a committee consisting of representatives from all cadres.

An opinion survey was conducted among employees regarding this. The result revealed that 79 per cent (11) of the Administrators of *small* hospitals, 72 per cent (13) of *medium* hospitals, and 85 per cent (11) of *large* hospitals opined that the control should be with 'the investor' only.

The majority of the Doctors were of the same opinion. 89 per cent (59) of the Doctors of *small* hospitals, 71 per cent (106) of *medium* hospitals, and 72 per cent (91) of *large* hospitals favoured control by 'the investor' only.

The majority of the PTM staff, i.e., 71 per cent (67) of *small* hospitals, 68 per cent (116) of *medium* hospitals, and 70 per cent (130) of *large* hospitals also favoured control by 'the investor' only.

The analysis revealed that majority of the employees, i.e., 78 per cent (35) of the Administrators, 75 per cent (256) of the Doctors, and 70 per cent (313) of the PTM staff wanted hospitals to be controlled by 'the investor' only.

Only 20 per cent (9) of the Administrators, 21 per cent (73) of the Doctors, and 28 per cent (128) of the PTM staff were of the view that the hospital should be controlled by 'a committee consisting of representatives of employees from all cadres'.

None of the Administrators, Doctors and PTM staff from *small, medium* and *large* hospitals suggested control by 'a committee consisting of medically qualified personnel'. Only 6 per cent (1) of the Administrators of *medium* hospitals and 1 per cent (2) of the Doctors from *medium* hospitals suggested control by 'a non-medical professional administrator'. The survey results are given in Table 6.1. *(See on next page)*

If more than 20% of the cells have expected count less than 5, it is more appropriate to use Likelihood ratio chi-square test.

If the significance value of the chi-square value is equal or less than 0.05, we can conclude that the chi-square test indicates a significant association between the two variables. In this study, all the chi-square test analysis was made by considering these two points.

Using Chi-square test, the association between the opinions on parties controlling the hospitals and different categories of staff in different types of hospitals were statistically examined [Table 6.1(a)]. *(See on next page)*

The chi-square test at 5 per cent level of significance revealed that there is significant association between the opinions of parties controlling the hospital and the Doctors in different types of hospitals. But with regard to the Administrators and the PTM staff, the association was found insignificant.

From the analysis we can conclude that about three quarters of the employees from all categories feel that the controlling authority should be a single source, i.e., 'the investors' only. This observation tallies with the existing practice as shown in Chapter V, Table 5.13, and the natural conclusion is that the employees accept the existing system. The primary stakeholder in the management is still believed to be the investor alone and other stakeholders' interest is yet to find place in the management system.

The next point studied was the verdict regarding the managing personnel, by the non-managerial employees in the hospitals. The Administrators themselves in various hospitals were of varying categories like investor, professionally qualified non-medical administrators,

Table 6.1: Expected System of Hospital Control

Category	Type of hospital	System of hospital control					Total
		The investor only	Non-medical profess-ional adminis-trator	Medical and non-medical adminis-trator	Committee consisting of medically qualified personnel	Committee consisting of repre-sentatives from all cadres	
Administrators	Small	11 78.6%	0 .0%	0 .0%	0 .0%	3 21.4%	14 100.0%
	Medium	13 72.2%	1 5.6%	0 .0%	0 .0%	4 22.2%	18 100.0%
	Large	11 84.6%	0 .0%	0 .0%	0 .0%	2 15.4%	13 100.0%
	Total	**35** **77.8%**	**1** **2.2%**	**0** **.0%**	**0** **.0%**	**9** **20.0%**	**45** **100.0%**
Doctors	Small	59 89.4%	0 .0%	0 .0%	0 .0%	7 10.6%	66 100.0%
	Medium	106 71.1%	2 1.3%	6 4.0%	0 .0%	35 23.5%	149 100.0%
	Large	91 72.2%	0 .0%	4 3.2%	0 .0%	31 24.6%	126 100.0%
	Total	**256** **75.1%**	**2** **.6%**	**10** **2.9%**	**0** **.0%**	**73** **21.4%**	**341** **100.0%**
PTM staff	Small	67 71.3%	0 .0%	2 2.1%	0 .0%	25 26.6%	94 100.0%
	Medium	116 68.2%	0 .0%	3 1.8%	0 .0%	51 30.0%	170 100.0%
	Large	130 69.9%	0 .0%	4 2.2%	0 .0%	52 28.0%	186 100.0%
	Total	**313** **69.6%**	**0** **.0%**	**9** **2.0%**	**0** **.0%**	**128** **28.4%**	**450** **100.0%**

Source: Field Survey

professionally unqualified non-medical administrators, and Doctors without professional qualification in management. Hence, the opinion expressed by each of these categories of Administrators regarding efficiency of managing personnel, satisfaction about managing personnel, and opinion regarding coordination and control were biased.

Hence the *opinions of Doctors and the PTM staff* regarding the management personnel were sought and analysed as follows:

Table 6.1(a): Chi-Square Test— Expected System of Hospital Control

Category		Value	df	Asymp. Sig. (2-sided)
Administrators	Pearson Chi-Square	1.848(a)	4	.764
	Likelihood Ratio	2.190	4	.701
	Linear-by-Linear Association	.142	1	.706
	N of Valid Cases	45		
Doctors	Pearson Chi-Square	11.892(b)	6	.064
	Likelihood Ratio	15.191	6	.019
	Linear-by-Linear Association	5.114	1	.024
	N of Valid Cases	341		
PTM staff	Pearson Chi-Square	.435(c)	4	.980
	Likelihood Ratio	.436	4	.979
	Linear-by-Linear Association	.017	1	.896
	N of Valid Cases	450		

Source: Computed

[a]6 cells (66.7%) have expected count less than 5. The minimum expected count is .29.

[b]6 cells (50.0%) have expected count less than 5. The minimum expected count is .39.

[c]3 cells (33.3%) have expected count less than 5. The minimum expected count is 1.88.

Opinion Regarding Efficiency of Managing Personnel

The management system is difficult to define. The hospital has a complex psycho-social system. Although the likes of the various participants, such as physicians, administrative staff, nurses, and paramedical personnel are rather well defined, there are substantial conflicts. The psycho-social system is strongly influenced by the norms and values of professionalism, with which various participants are indoctrinated.

The hospital may be managed by an individual or a group of persons belonging to medical profession or a non-medical profession. He may or may not be a management professional. The efficiency of management by these parties may differ according to their ability, experience, professional knowledge, and capacity to create inter-personal relations.

On the basis of the opinions of Doctors and the PTM staff, the efficiency of management by the following parties was measured. To analyze the data, a five-point scale was used. Based on the extent of satisfaction about the efficiency of the managing personnel, values were assigned where '1' denoted the lowest and '5' the highest, and thus mean values were computed. Interpretation was done by taking '0-1' as 'very poor', '1-2' as 'poor', '2-3' as 'average', '3-4' as 'good', and '4-5' as 'very good'.

The efficiency of management by the following choice of personnel was measured:

(*a*) a non-medical professional administrator without first-hand knowledge of patient care;

(*b*) doctor without professional training in management;

(*c*) doctor with professional training in management;

(*d*) jointly by non-medical professional administrator and doctors;

(*e*) a committee consisting of representatives from all cadres.

Doctors of *small* hospitals opined that the efficiency of management would be 'good' if the hospital was managed by 'Doctor with professional training in management' (mean value 3.88), or 'non-medical professional administrator and Doctors' (mean value 3.65) or a 'committee consisting of representatives from all cadres.' (mean value 3.08). It would be 'average' (mean value 2.35) if managed by 'doctor without professional training in management,' and 'bad' (mean value 1.94) if managed by 'non-medical professional administrator'.

Doctors of *medium* hospitals also viewed that the efficiency of management would be 'good' if the hospital was managed by 'doctors with professional training in management' (mean value 3.72), 'jointly by non-medical professional administrator and doctors' (mean value 3.85), and 'a committee consisting of representatives from all cadres' (mean value 3.15). Doctors also stated that the efficiency of management would be 'average' if the hospital was managed by 'doctors without professional training in management' (mean value 2.42) and 'bad' if managed by 'a non-medical professional administrator without firsthand knowledge of patient care' (mean value 1.83). The opinion of Doctors of *large* hospitals also was more or less the same.

The PTM staff of *small* hospitals also opined that the efficiency of management would be 'very good' if the hospital was managed by 'Doctor with professional training in management' (mean value 4.05). It would be 'good' if the hospital was managed by a 'non-medical professional administrator and Doctors' (mean value 3.95) and a 'committee consisting of representatives from all cadres' (mean value 3.28) and also by 'doctor without professional training in management' (mean value 3.17). It would be 'average' (mean value 2.19) if managed by 'non-medical professional administrator'.

The PTM staff of *medium* and *large* hospitals opined that the efficiency of management would be 'good' if the hospital was managed by 'Doctors with professional training in management' (mean values 3.95 and 4.00 respectively), 'Non-medical professional administrator and Doctors' (mean values 3.71 and 3.86 respectively) and 'a committee with representatives from all cadres' (mean values 3.36 and 3.39 respectively). The PTM staff of *medium* and *large* hospitals opined that the efficiency of management would be 'average' if the hospital was managed by 'non-medical professional administrator' (mean values 2.31 and 2.20 respectively) and 'Doctors without professional training in management' (mean value 2.94 each). The survey results are given in Table 6.2.

Table 6.2: Opinion Regarding Efficiency of Managing Personnel

Category	Type of hospital	Non-medical professional Adminis-trator	Doctor without professional training in management	Doctor with professional training in management	Non-medical professional Administrator and Doctors	A committee consisting of repre-sentatives from all cadres
Doctors	Small	1.94	2.35	3.88	3.65	3.08
	Medium	1.83	2.42	3.72	3.85	3.15
	Large	1.89	2.51	3.91	3.71	3.19
	Total	**1.87**	**2.44**	**3.82**	**3.76**	**3.15**
PTM staff	Small	2.19	3.17	4.05	3.95	3.28
	Medium	2.31	2.94	3.95	3.71	3.36
	Large	2.20	2.94	4.00	3.86	3.39
	Total	**2.24**	**2.98**	**3.99**	**3.83**	**3.35**

Source: Field Survey

Doctors and the PTM staff were unanimous in their opinion that 'non-medical professional administrator' would not be efficient in managing a hospital. A 'Doctor without professional training in management' also was considered to be 'average' in his capacity to run a hospital efficiently. Good rating was given for: (*i*) 'Doctor with professional training in management'; (*ii*) jointly by non-medical professional administrator and doctors; and (*iii*) a committee consisting of representatives from all cadres. Of the three choices with good rating, 'Doctor with professional training in management' was the most preferred and a 'committee consisting of representatives of all cadres' came only third.

Hence it is concluded that, as per the opinion of Doctors and the PTM staff, the highest level of efficiency in managing a hospital would be achieved when it was managed by *Doctors with professional training in management*. Here, the belief that knowledge of medication and management ought to be combined was found present.

Clinicians are the people responsible for initiating the expenditure. It is, therefore, important for some clinicians to accept responsibility for management and to be prepared to play a leading role in managing the affairs of the hospital. A pertinent point here is to what extent the doctor who is burdened with the patient care activities would be able to devote his time for administrative duties.

Satisfaction about Managing Personnel

Employees may be satisfied with working under a person of the same profession. The managerial control of professional members by non-members is excluded at a certain stage. This is because the latter can no longer judge the competence of such professionals or assess the technical problems encountered. Only monitoring and coordinating role relationships are possible in this context. The leadership style varies from person to person. Some may be democratic or some may be autocratic. Employees may be satisfied with working under them, depending upon their ability and style of leadership.

As the professionals have discretion to adjust the work to the situation and have independence of action, much of the works of the hospitals are carried out by professionals largely working on their own or in very small teams. This independence may lead to a certain degree of isolation and it does not encourage a wider team approach within a profession or control by others.

The extent of satisfaction of Doctors and the PTM staff, if working under different categories of managers like: (*i*) Non-medical manager; (*ii*) Doctor manager; (*iii*) Doctor with professional training in management; (*iv*) Non-medical professional administrator and Doctors; and (*v*) A committee consisting of representatives from all cadres, was analysed by collecting the information on a five-point scale, where '1' denoted the lowest and '5' the highest, and thus mean values were computed. Interpretation was done for '0-1' as 'very poor', '1-2' as 'poor', '2-3' as 'average', '3-4' as 'good' and '4-5' as 'very good'.

With regard to the satisfaction with working under different categories of employees, Doctors of *small, medium* and *large* hospitals opined that it was 'good' to work under 'doctors with professional training in management (mean values 3.88, 3.56 and 3.90 respectively), and under 'non-medical professional administrators and doctors' (mean values 3.59, 3.84and 3.72 respectively), as well as under a 'committee consisting of representatives from all cadres' (mean values between 3.05, 3.24 and 3.35 respectively).

Doctors of *small*, *medium* and *large* hospitals, however, felt that the satisfaction was 'poor' when working under 'non-medical professional administrators without first-hand experience in actual patient care' (mean values 2.00, 1.97 and 1.90 respectively). When managed by Doctors 'without professional training in management', the satisfaction was 'average' to 'good' (mean values 2.95, 2.53, and 3.08 respectively). The size-wise difference was also very narrow.

The PTM staff of *small* hospitals expressed exceptionally 'very good' level of satisfaction with working under 'Doctors with professional training in management' (mean value 4.05). The PTM staff of *medium* and *large* hospitals also gave the same (mean values 3.95 and 4.00) opinion. The PTM staff of *small, medium* and *large* hospitals opined that it would be 'good' if working under 'non-medical professional administrators and doctors' (mean values 3.95, 3.71 and 3.86 respectively) as well as under a 'committee consisting of representatives from all cadres' (mean values 3.28, 3.36 and 3.39 respectively).The PTM staff, however, felt that the satisfaction was 'average' when working under 'non-medical professional administrators without first-hand experience in actual patient care' (mean value 2.19, 2.31 and 2.20 respectively). When managed by Doctors 'without professional training in management', the satisfaction was 'average' to 'good' (mean values 3.17, 2.94 and 2.94 respectively). The survey results are furnished in Table 6.3.

Table 6.3: Satisfaction of Doctors about Managing Parties

Category	Type of hospital	Non-medical manager	Doctor manager	Doctor with professional training in management	Non-medical professional Administrators and Doctors	A committee consisting of represen-tatives from all cadres
Doctors	Small	2.00	2.95	3.88	3.59	3.05
	Medium	1.97	2.53	3.56	3.84	3.24
	Large	1.90	3.08	3.90	3.72	3.35
	Total	**1.95**	**2.82**	**3.75**	**3.75**	**3.24**
PTM staff	Small	2.19	3.17	4.05	3.95	3.28
	Medium	2.31	2.94	3.95	3.71	3.36
	Large	2.20	2.94	4.00	3.86	3.39
	Total	**2.24**	**2.98**	**3.99**	**3.84**	**3.34**

Source: Field Survey

Irrespective of the size of the hospital, the satisfaction of the Doctors and the PTM staff was 'good' if working under any of the following parties in the order of their preference:

(*a*) Doctor with professional training in management; or

(*b*) Non-medical professional Administrator and Doctors; or

(*c*) A committee consisting of representatives from all cadres.

According to them, the highest level of satisfaction comes when hospitals are managed by *Doctors with professional experience in management.*

A notable point in the five sets of analyses given above is the good rating given to 'a committee consisting of representatives from all cadres' which, although third in position, is only marginally less rated than the first rated choice.

As it is clear from the above analysis that a 'Doctor with professional training in management' is the preferred choice for hospital management, the opinions of doctors and the PTM staff about control relations and such factors were studied next.

Doctors' Opinions about Controlling Others

The importance of doctors in management can be expressed as follows. If doctors do not get involved in managing their own affairs, they will be subject to external control by others who perhaps lack personal insight into the problems of caring for patients. The doctor-manager has the potential for being a more effective performer than the traditionally trained manager. They are the appropriate persons to interact with various interest groups and orchestrate the management of the medical industrial complex.

Experts have stated that 'whether they know it or not, or wish to admit it or not, doctors are managers of health care resources, both financial and human. Individual doctors allocate resources and decide on priorities. On a daily basis they take umpteen management decisions[1]. In most of the hospitals there is dual control over the PTM staff, which led to conflict of interests.

The opinions of Doctors about the extent to which their direct control of the PTM staff will help in providing proper patient care were obtained and analysed by collecting the information on a five-point scale where '1' denotes the lowest and '5' the highest and thus mean values were computed. Interpretation was done by treating '0-1' as 'very poor', '1-2' as 'poor', '2-3' as 'average', '3-4' as 'good' and '4-5' as 'very good'.

Doctors of *small* hospitals opined that if they had direct control over the Para-medical staff (mean value 3.44), technical (mean value 3.45) and ministerial staff (mean value 3.55) that will help in providing proper patient care to a 'good' extent. Doctors of *medium* hospitals and *large* hospitals also hold the same view. The survey results are provided in Table 6.4.

Table 6.4: Doctors' Control over Other Staff

Type of hospital	Para medical staff	Technical staff	Ministerial staff
Small	3.44	3.45	3.55
Medium	3.61	3.54	3.54
Large	3.79	3.78	3.64
Total	**3.64**	**3.61**	**3.58**

Source: Field Survey

This picture of the opinions of doctors leads to the conclusion that their direct control over the PTM staff was felt essential for providing proper patient care. In other words, the doctors felt that the control of the PTM staff should be with them and not with a Non-medical Administrator.

Professional Relationship between PTM Staff and Doctors Regarding Patient Care

Another important aspect to be studied in this context is the level of satisfaction the PTM staff had in their professional relationship with the Doctors in the matter of patient care. Patient care activities can be effectively carried out only when there is a cordial professional relationship between the PTM staff and Doctors—whether a treating physician or a Doctor-manager. The data regarding the level of satisfaction expressed by the PTM staff regarding their professional relationship with treating physician/ Doctor-manager were collected and analysed.

The PTM staff of *small* hospitals opined that their professional relationship with the treating physician was 'good' with the mean value of 3.88. The PTM staff of *medium* hospitals also had the same idea with mean value of 3.85 and the PTM staff of *large* hospitals also reported that their professional relationship with the treating Doctor was good with the mean value of 3.97. The survey results are furnished in Table 6.5.

Table 6.5: Professional Relationship between Doctors and PTM Staff

Type of hospital	Mean values
Small	3.88
Medium	3.85
Large	3.97
Total	**3.91**

Source: Field Survey

The presence of good professional relationship between the PTM staff and Doctors enables us to conclude that the PTM staffs feel comfortable to work under Doctor-managers.

Co-ordination and Control

In the modern health care institutions, the medical staffs obviously are the primary source of technology. Physicians have the knowledge required for task performance, based upon intensive training and specialization. Nurses also represent a source of knowledge and carry out many of the technical functions in the hospital. There are also a growing number of specialists who are not part of the medical or nursing staff. The chemist, bacteriologist, physical therapist, recreational director, dietician, social worker, and many other participants are highly trained and are applying their technical knowledge in the hospital setting. The increased number of these specialists has created a more complex organizational structure. With increased complexities, there has been a growing need for improved techniques of organization and management. In the modern hospital, more sophisticated approaches for the coordination of activities are necessary[2].

In the present-day complex hospital set up, the Doctors and managers have started feeling the necessity for absolute coordination among the various specialists and staff for proper patient care delivery. Hence, the emphasis is slowly shifting from the concept of control to coordination. At this juncture, the importance of coordination as realized by the Doctors, Para-medical, Technical and Ministerial staff of the private health care institutions was analysed.

The observation revealed the following. The Doctors from *small* hospitals opined that coordination was a better option than control, to a 'good' (mean value 3.88) extent. The Doctors from *medium* and *large* hospitals also opined that coordination was a better option than control, to a 'good' or nearly 'very good' extent (mean value 3.98).

The PTM staff from *small* (mean value 3.90), *medium* (mean value 3.91) and *large* hospitals (mean value 3.95) also reported that coordination was a better option than control, to a 'good' or nearly 'very good' extent. The survey results are presented in Table 6.6.

From this we can conclude that the Doctors, the treating physician or Doctor-manager, have understood and accepted the present-day reality of managing the subordinate staff by coordinated cooperative team work which is more fruitful than imposed controls. The PTM staff also sees coordination as better than control in day-to-day patient care activities. For proper coordination among various categories of staff, satisfied, confident and motivated employees are a must. It is in this context that employee participation becomes all the more important.

Table 6.6: Co-ordination and Control

Category	Type of hospital	Mean values
Doctors	Small	3.88
	Medium	3.98
	Large	3.98
	Total	**3.96**
PTM staff	Small	3.90
	Medium	3.91
	Large	3.95
	Total	**3.90**

Source: Field Survey

CONCEPT OF PARTICIPATIVE MANAGEMENT

A management is considered participative if it provides scope for workers to influence its decisions or to share in some of the managerial functions and prerogatives.

The concept of participation means sharing of decision-making power through proper representatives at all levels of management in the entire range of managerial action[3].

Different employees had different opinions on the concept of participative management. They were: (*i*) Equal powers to management and employees both in ownership and in management; (*ii*) Employees' participation in all management functions but not in ownership; (*iii*) Employees' participation limited to certain parameters in management (for example, excluding selected administrative matters like policy, finance and /or others from its ambit); (*iv*) Participation in the form of informal consultation only in all managerial functions. The opinions of the employees of the private hospitals of Kerala on the above-mentioned aspects were collected and analysed.

The survey results revealed that the majority of the Administrators - 64 per cent (9) of *small* hospitals, 67 per cent (12) of *medium* hospitals and 92 per cent (12) of *large* hospitals viewed participation as 'employees' participation in all management functions but not in ownership'.

The majority of the Doctors—58 per cent (38) of *small* hospitals, 58 per cent (86) of *medium* hospitals and 48 per cent (61) of *large* hospitals favoured 'employees' participation in all management functions but not in ownership'.

The PTM staff also had the same opinion- 48 per cent (45) of *small* hospitals, 65 per cent (110) of *medium* hospitals and 62 per cent (116) of *large* hospitals also supported 'employee's participation in all management functions but not in ownership'.

Thus the majority of the respondents, i.e., 73 per cent (33) of the Administrators, 54 per cent (185) of the Doctors and 60 per cent (271) of the PTM staff opined that the concept of participation means 'employees'

Table 6.7: Concept of Participative Management

Category	Type of hospital	Concept of participative management				No response	Total
		Equal powers to management and employees in both ownership and management	Employees' participation in all management functions but not in ownership	Employees' participation limited to certain parameters in management	Participation in the form of informal consultation only in all managerial functions		
Administrators	Small	0 .0%	9 64.3%	1 7.1%	2 14.3%	2 14.3%	14 100.0%
	Medium	2 11.1%	12 66.7%	3 16.7%	1 5.6%	0 .0%	18 100.0%
	Large	0 .0%	12 92.3%	1 7.7%	0 .0%	0 .0%	13 100.0%
	Total	**2 4.4%**	**33 73.3%**	**5 11.1%**	**3 6.7%**	**2 4.4%**	**45 100.0%**
Doctors	Small	3 4.5%	38 57.6%	10 15.2%	10 15.2%	5 7.6%	66 100.0%
	Medium	28 18.8%	86 57.7%	29 19.5%	5 3.4%	1 .7%	149 100.0%
	Large	3 2.4%	61 48.4%	24 19.0%	36 28.6%	2 1.6%	126 100.0%
	Total	**34 10.0%**	**185 54.3%**	**63 18.5%**	**51 15.0%**	**8 2.3%**	**341 100.0%**
PTM staff	Small	3 3.2%	45 47.9%	21 22.3%	18 19.1%	7 7.4%	94 100.0%
	Medium	14 8.2%	110 64.7%	26 15.3%	20 11.8%	0 .0%	170 100.0%
	Large	10 5.4%	116 62.4%	45 24.2%	13 7.0%	2 1.1%	186 100.0%
	Total	**27 6.0%**	**271 60.2%**	**92 20.4%**	**51 11.3%**	**9 2.0%**	**450 100.0%**

Source: Field Survey.

participation in all management functions but not in ownership'. The survey results are given in Table 6.7.

Using chi-square test, the association between opinions about 'the concept of participation' in different categories of staff in different types of hospitals was statistically examined and shown in Table 6.7(a).

Table 6.7(a): Chi-Square Tests—Concept of Participative Management

Category		Value	df	Asymp. Sig. (2-sided)
Administrators	Pearson Chi-Square	11.286(a)	8	.186
	Likelihood Ratio	12.698	8	.123
	Linear-by-Linear Association	.001	1	.978
	N of Valid Cases	45		
Doctors	Pearson Chi-Square	61.419(b)	8	.000
	Likelihood Ratio	63.560	8	.000
	Linear-by-Linear Association	17.067	1	.000
	N of Valid Cases	341		
PTM staff	Pearson Chi-Square	35.842(c)	8	.000
	Likelihood Ratio	33.658	8	.000
	Linear-by-Linear Association	1.006	1	.316
	N of Valid Cases	450		

Source: Computed

[a]12 cells (80.0%) have expected count less than 5. The minimum expected count is .58.

[b]3 cells (20.0%) have expected count less than 5. The minimum expected count is 1.55.

[c]*3 cells (20.0%) have expected count less than 5. The minimum expected count is 1.88.*

The chi-square test at 5 per cent level of significance revealed statistically significant association between the opinions on 'the concept of participation' and the Doctors and the PTM staff in different types of hospitals. For administrators, the association was found statistically insignificant.

From the analysis it may be concluded that all categories of employees, irrespective of the size of the hospital, have a uniform concept regarding participative management, i.e., 'participation in all management functions but not in ownership'. It is interesting to note that all categories of employees have in-depth understanding regarding participative management as revealed by the low rating given to informal consultation and limited extent participation in management. ***Everyone perceives participation in all***

managerial functions as true participative management. Also, the employees are practical in their outlook as they don't conceptualize participation in ownership.

FORMS OF PARTICIPATION

If the employees participate in management, either through formal or through informal procedures, it should be considered as an instance of participative management.

In many organizations, top level managers set the basic stone for planning, determine overall goals for the organization, and give direction on the context of policies and similar planning documents. This is not done in isolation but is based on information provided through the feedback cycle, through reports and special studies and through the direct participation of personnel in each department or division[4].

The opinions of the respondents about the form of participation expected by them in their hospitals: (*i*) informative participation; (*ii*) consultative participation; (*iii*) joint decision; (*iv*) collective bargaining were collected.

The survey results revealed that majority of the Administrators—43 per cent (6) of *small* hospitals, 50 per cent (9) of *medium* hospitals and 77 per cent (10) of *large* hospitals opted for 'consultative participation' as the best form of participation. The majority of the Doctors—39 per cent (26) of *small* hospitals, 79 per cent (117) of *medium* hospitals and 79 per cent (99) of *large* hospitals—also suggested 'consultative participation' as the best one. 'Consultative participation' was suggested as the best from of participation by the PTM staff- 52 per cent (49) of *small* hospitals, 77 per cent (130) of *medium* hospitals and 69 per cent (129) of *large* hospitals.

It is worth noting that 27 per cent (12) of the Administrators, 13 per cent (45) of the Doctors and 16 per cent (72) of the PTM staff reported that 'informative participation' was the best form of participation.

Another 18 per cent (8) of the Administrators, 16 per cent (54) of the Doctors and 15 per cent (67) of the PTM staff suggested 'joint decision' as the best expected form of participation.

None of the Administrators, Doctors and PTM staff from all the different types of hospitals, with the exception of 2 per cent (3) of the PTM staff from *large* hospitals suggested 'collective bargaining' as the best form of participation.

The analysis revealed that the majority of the respondents, Administrators—56 per cent (25), Doctors—71 per cent (242) and PTM staff—68 per cent (308) suggested 'consultative participation' as the best form of participation. The survey results are given in Table 6.8.

Table 6.8: Expected Form of Participation

Category	Type of hospital	Form of participation				Total
		Informative Participation	Consultative participation	Joint Decision making	Collective Bargaining	
Administrators	Small	7 50.0%	6 42.9%	1 7.1%	0 .0%	14 100.0%
	Medium	2 11.1%	9 50.0%	7 38.9%	0 .0%	18 100.0%
	Large	3 23.1%	10 76.9%	0 .0%	0 .0%	13 100.0%
	Total	**12** **26.7%**	**25** **55.6%**	**8** **17.8%**	**0** **.0%**	**45** **100.0%**
Doctors	Small	34 51.5%	26 39.4%	6 9.1%	0 .0%	66 100.0%
	Medium	2 1.3%	117 78.5%	30 20.1%	0 .0%	149 100.0%
	Large	9 7.1%	99 78.6%	18 14.3%	0 .0%	126 100.0%
	Total	**45** **13.2%**	**242** **71.0%**	**54** **15.8%**	**0** **.0%**	**341** **100.0%**
PTM staff	Small	31 33.0%	49 52.1%	14 14.9%	0 .0%	94 100.0%
	Medium	4 2.4%	130 76.5%	36 21.2%	0 .0%	170 100.0%
	Large	37 19.9%	129 69.4%	17 9.1%	3 1.6%	186 100.0%
	Total	**72** **16.0%**	**308** **68.4%**	**67** **14.9%**	**3** **.7%**	**450** **100.0%**

Source: Field Survey

Using chi-square test, the association between opinions on 'form of participation in the hospital' and different categories of staff in different types of hospitals was statistically examined [Table 6.8(a)].

The chi-square test at 5 per cent level of significance revealed statistically significant association between the 'form of participation' and different categories of staff in different types of hospitals.

The analysis revealed that, as a whole, the majority of the employees opined 'consultative participation' as the best form of participation. There could be many reasons for employees not opting for higher level participation, such as:

- absence of elected committees rules out more efficient form of participation like joint decision making and collective bargaining;
- reluctance on the part of employees to shoulder responsibility, which comes with deeper level of participation in management;
- lack of knowledge or skills in administration for employees who are skilled in other specialized jobs.

Table 6.8(a): Chi-Square Tests - Expected Form of Participation

Category		Value	df	Asymp. Sig. (2-sided)
Administrators	Pearson Chi-Square	13.843(a)	4	.008
	Likelihood Ratio	15.064	4	.005
	Linear-by-Linear Association	.704	1	.402
	N of Valid Cases	45		
Doctors	Pearson Chi-Square	108.123(b)	4	.000
	Likelihood Ratio	89.680	4	.000
	Linear-by-Linear Association	23.799	1	.000
	N of Valid Cases	341		
PT M staff	Pearson Chi-Square	56.666(c)	6	.000
	Likelihood Ratio	65.255	6	.000
	Linear-by-Linear Association	.089	1	.765
	N of Valid Cases	450		

Source: Computed

[a] 6 cells (66.7%) have expected count less than 5. The minimum expected count is 2.31.

[b] 0 cells (.0%) have expected count less than 5. The minimum expected count is 8.71.

[c] 3 cells (25.0%) have expected count less than 5. The minimum expected count is .63.

Even though the employees do not want joint decision making and collective bargaining, they want to be consulted in all management activities. This could be due to the fact that each employee trained in a particular field could only give authentic suggestion regarding that field or do not want any management decision to affect him adversely.

Often, we are forced to conclude that the age-old mindset of management and employees lead to distrust between them and any extent of participation beyond consultative participation is beyond the realms of their imagination.

Another point noticed in the findings from small hospitals is that the Administrators and Doctors (who are part of the ownership) reported that informative participation, the least effective form of participation, is enough. While the PTM staff expected consultative participation, thereby making it apparent that many small-sized hospitals are run in a totalitarian way.

Having concluded that 'consultative participation' is desired by the majority of the employees, it is high time that the power sharing aspects of participative management were considered.

DEGREES OF PARTICIPATION

By degree of participation is meant how far workers influence managerial decisions, on a scale extending from complete unilateral control by management at one end, to complete unilateral control by workers at the other. Participation is possible at all levels of management[5]. The interdependence of scientific research and hence of scientific organizations, requires participation at multiple levels[6].

Participation may be: (*i*) at the Director Board level; (*ii*) at the administrative level; (*iii*) at the department level; (*iv*) at all the three levels simultaneously; and (*v*) to begin at the bottom and to rise gradually upward. The suggestions of the three different categories of employees of the private health care institutions in Kerala regarding the levels at which they suggested participation were collected and analysed.

Participative management meant 'participation at the administrative level' to 50 per cent (7) of the *small* hospital, 17 per cent (3) of the *medium* hospital, and 46 per cent (6) of the *large* hospital Administrators. In addition to this, 21 per cent (3) of the Administrators from *small* hospitals, 33 per cent (6) from *medium* hospitals and 46 per cent (6) from *large* hospitals opined that their concept of participative management was 'participation to begin at the bottom and to rise gradually upward'.

The Doctors had different opinions—5 per cent (3) of *small,* 40 per cent (59) of the *medium* and 24 per cent (30) of the *large* hospitals explained their concept of participation as 'participation at the administrative level', while another 53 per cent (35) of *small,* 24 per cent (36) of *medium,* and 17 per cent (21) of *large* hospitals suggested 'participation at the department level'. In addition to this, 20 per cent (13) of *small,* 10 per cent (15) of *medium,* and 37 per cent (46) of *large* hospitals opined that their concept of participative management was 'participation to begin at the bottom and to rise gradually upward'.

The majority of the PTM staff—49 per cent (46) of *small,* 57 per cent (97) of *medium,* and 58 per cent (107) of *large* hospitals opined that their concept of participative management was 'participation to begin at the bottom and to rise gradually upward'.

The analysis revealed that there was no equality in the opinions of Administrators, Doctors and PTM staff regarding the level of hierarchy at which the concept of participative management should operate. While 36 per cent (16) of Administrators suggested participation 'at the administrative

Table 6. 9: Expected Degree of Participation

Category	Type of hospital	Level of hierarchy and participation					Total
		At the director board level	At the administrative level	At the department level	At the three levels simulta-neously	Participation to begin at the bottom and to rise gradually upwards	
Administrators	Small	3 21.4%	7 50.0%	0 .0%	1 7.1%	3 21.4%	14 100.0%
	Medium	2 11.1%	3 16.7%	5 27.8%	2 11.1%	6 33.3%	18 100.0%
	Large	0 .0%	6 46.2%	1 7.7%	0 .0%	6 46.2%	13 100.0%
	Total	**5** **11.1%**	**16** **35.6%**	**6** **13.3%**	**3** **6.7%**	**15** **33.3%**	**45** **100.0%**
Doctors	Small	5 7.6%	3 4.5%	35 53.0%	10 15.2%	13 19.7%	66 100.0%
	Medium	21 14.1%	59 39.6%	36 24.2%	18 12.1%	15 10.1%	149 100.0%
	Large	5 4.0%	30 23.8%	21 16.7%	24 19.0%	46 36.5%	126 100.0%
	Total	**31** **9.1%**	**92** **27.0%**	**92** **27.0%**	**52** **15.2%**	**74** **21.7%**	**341** **100.0%**
PTM staff	Small	8 8.5%	6 6.4%	8 8.5%	26 27.7%	46 48.9%	94 100.0%
	Medium	13 7.6%	19 11.2%	11 6.5%	30 17.6%	97 57.1%	170 100.0%
	Large	15 8.1%	21 11.3%	35 18.8%	8 4.3%	107 57.5%	186 100.0%
	Total	**36** **8.0%**	**46** **10.2%**	**54** **12.0%**	**64** **14.2%**	**250** **55.6%**	**450** **100.0%**

Source: Field Survey

level', 33 per cent (15) suggested participation 'to begin at the bottom and to rise gradually upward'. 27 per cent (92) each of Doctors suggested participation at the 'administrative level' and 'department level' respectively and 22 per cent (74) suggested 'participation to begin at the bottom and to rise gradually upward'. 56 per cent (250) of the PTM staff from *small*, *medium* and *large* hospitals with a clear majority suggested 'participation to begin at the bottom and to rise gradually upward'. Only a limited percentage was interested in participation at the Director Board level, administrative level or department level. The survey results are given in Table 6.9.

Using chi-square test, the association between 'opinion about expected extent of participation' and 'different categories of staff in different types of hospitals' was statistically and presented in Table 6.9(a).

The chi-square test at 5 per cent level of significance revealed statistically significant association between opinions on expected extent of participation and different categories of staff in different types of hospitals.

Table 6.9(a): Chi-Square Tests—Expected Degree of Participation

Category		Value	df	Asymp. Sig. (2-sided)
Administrators	Pearson Chi-Square	13.459(a)	8	.097
	Likelihood Ratio	16.973	8	.030
	Linear-by-Linear Association	2.461	1	.117
	N of Valid Cases	45		
Doctors	Pearson Chi-Square	75.806(b)	8	.000
	Likelihood Ratio	78.980	8	.000
	Linear-by-Linear Association	6.774	1	.009
	N of Valid Cases	341		
PTM staff	Pearson Chi-Square	41.411(c)	8	.000
	Likelihood Ratio	43.746	8	.000
	Linear-by-Linear Association	.554	1	.457
	N of Valid Cases	450		

Source: Computed

[a]13 cells (86.7%) have expected count less than 5. The minimum expected count is .87.

[b]0 cells (.0%) have expected count less than 5. The minimum expected count is 6.00.

[c]0 cells (.0%) have expected count less than 5. The minimum expected count is 7.52.

The analysis led to some intriguing observation. As already discussed, there is no effective participative management in private hospitals and when introduced for the first time it is ideal 'to start from the bottom and then rise', rather than starting simultaneously at all levels.

The results showed that only few respondents favoured starting at 'all levels simultaneously'. But thc PTM staff was the only group that gave the highest rating for starting from the bottom and then to rise. This apparently was not a reflection of their in-depth knowledge of the concept but more of a wish of the PTM staff for participation, thereby leading to freedom in work at least at their level, which, as per the previous analysis, was relatively low.

The Doctors' responses were divided as between administrative level, departmental level and starting from below, from which no special conclusions could be drawn.

The Administrators' opinions were more or less evenly distributed between administrative level and starting at bottom, which denoted reasonable understanding and willingness to accept the concept.

Sharing of Equal Powers

The concept of participation means sharing of decision-making power through proper representatives, at all levels of management in the entire range of managerial action. Participation is a situation where workers' representatives are, to some extent, involved in the process of management decision-making, but where the ultimate power is in the hands of the management.

Opinions about Granting of Equal Powers to Manager and Employees' Representatives

The opinions of employees regarding giving or not giving equal powers to manager and employee representatives of the private health care institutions in Kerala, for effective participation in management, were collected and analysed.

The majority, i.e., 64 per cent (9) of *small* hospitals, 61 per cent (11) of *medium* hospitals and 85 per cent (11) of *large* hospitals were 'not in favour of giving equal powers to employee and manager representatives'. More than three-fourth of the Doctors—79 per cent (52) from *small* hospitals, 75 per cent (111) from *medium* hospitals, and 78 per cent (98) from *large* hospitals were 'not in favour of giving equal powers to employee and manager representatives'. The majority of the PTM staff—67 per cent (63) from *small* hospitals, 71 per cent (121) from *medium* hospitals, and 77 per cent (143) from *large* hospitals also opined that equal powers should not be given to manager and employee representative.

A comparison of the views of Administrators, Doctors and the PTM staff revealed that the majority of all of them, i.e., 69 per cent (31) of the Administrators, 77 per cent (261) of the Doctors, and 73 per cent (327) of the PTM staff 'did not favour the idea of giving equal powers to employee and manager representatives'. Only 31 per cent (14) of the Administrators, 24 per cent (80) of the Doctors, and 27 per cent (123) of the PTM staff favoured the idea of giving equal powers to employee and manager representatives. The survey results are shown in Table 6.10.

Table 6.10: Opinions about Equal Powers to Manager and Employees' Representatives

Category	Type of hospital	Yes	No	Total
Administrators	Small	5 35.7%	9 64.3%	14 100.0%
	Medium	7 38.9%	11 61.1%	18 100.0%
	Large	2 15.4%	11 84.6%	13 100.0%
	Total	**14 31.1%**	**31 68.9%**	**45 100.0%**
Doctors	Small	14 21.2%	52 78.8%	66 100.0%
	Medium	38 25.5%	111 74.5%	149 100.0%
	Large	28 22.2%	98 77.8%	126 100.0%
	Total	**80 23.5%**	**261 76.5%**	**341 100.0%**
PTM staff	Small	31 33.0%	63 67.0%	94 100.0%
	Medium	49 28.8%	121 71.2%	170 100.0%
	Large	43 23.1%	143 76.9%	186 100.0%
	Total	**123 27.3%**	**327 72.7%**	**450 100.0%**

Source: Field Survey

By using chi square test, the association between 'opinion about granting of the same powers to employee and manager representatives' and 'different categories of staff in different types of hospitals' was statistically examined and shown in Table 6.10(a).

Table 6.10(a): Chi-Square Tests - Opinions about Equal Powers to Manager and Employees' Representatives

Category		Value	df	Asymp. Sig. (2-sided)
Administrators	Pearson Chi-Square	2.147(a)	2	.342
	Likelihood Ratio	2.330	2	.312
	Linear-by-Linear Association	1.223	1	.269
	N of Valid Cases	45		
Doctors	Pearson Chi-Square	.640(b)	2	.726
	Likelihood Ratio	.639	2	.727
	Linear-by-Linear Association	.000	1	.989
	N of Valid Cases	341		
PTM staff	Pearson Chi-Square	3.362(c)	2	.186
	Likelihood Ratio	3.362	2	.186
	Linear-by-Linear Association	3.324	1	.068
	N of Valid Cases	450		

Source: Computed

[a] 2 cells (33.3%) have expected count less than 5. The minimum expected count is 4.04.

[b] 0 cells (.0%) have expected count less than 5. The minimum expected count is 15.48.

[c] 0 cells (.0%) have expected count less than 5. The minimum expected count is 25.69.

The chi-square test at 5 per cent level of significance revealed no statistically significant association between the opinions about granting of equal powers to employee and manager representatives and the different categories of staff in different types of hospitals.

Even though only 217 of the respondents (Administrators-14, Doctors-80, PTM staff-123) favoured giving equal power to employee and manager representatives, it is worthwhile at this point to examine the points put forward by them regarding the choice they choose.

The interesting aspect is that the PTM staff, who are the most likely category of employees to opt for equal power, themselves had preferred more power for the management. But they had made it clear in the previous discussion that they should be consulted at all managerial levels, thereby backing a non-confrontationist and mutually beneficial form of participative management. Hence the hospital employees could be considered to be having a matured outlook and flexible approach.

Reasons for Favouring Equal Powers to Manager and Employees' Representative

The researcher observed that sharing of power was not widely advocated, and so the reasons were analysed. Of the total respondents, only 217 (Administrators-14, Doctors-80 and PTM-123) were in favour of giving equal powers to manager and employees' representative as per the Table 6.10. The reason for favouring this concept was arrived at by suggesting the following reasons and analyzing the responses obtained:

(*i*) Without equal powers, the employees' representatives will be subordinated to the management representative;

(*ii*) Without equal powers, employees' representative will not be able to participate effectively in the management process;

(*iii*) Without equal powers, the very intention behind the scheme will be defeated.

From 217 respondents, 131 percentage (284) multiple responses were received (Table 6.11). The analysis was made with the help of *percentage*

Table 6.11: Reasons Favouring Granting of Equal Powers to Managers' and Employees' Representatives—Total Multiple Responses

Reasons	Code	Count	Percentage of responses	Percentage of cases
Without equal powers the employee representatives will be subordinated to the management representative	1	55	19.4	25.3
Without equal powers employee representative will not be able to participative effectively in the management process	2	49	17.3	22.6
Without equal powers the very intention behind the scheme will be defeated	3	180	63.4	82.9
Total responses		**284**	**100.00**	**130.9**

Source: Field Survey

Note: 217 valid cases (respondents), 284 responses

on the responses received, as *multiple responses* were received from some respondents.

The majority of the responses of the Administrators - 57 per cent (4) from *small* hospitals, 55 per cent (6) from *medium* hospitals, and 100 per cent (2) from *large* hospitals opined that equal powers should be given to employee and manager representatives because 'without equal powers the very intention behind the scheme will be defeated'.

The majority of the responses of the Doctors-75 per cent (12) from *small* hospitals, 72 per cent (34) from *medium* hospitals, and 45 per cent (19) from *large* hospitals also opined that equal powers should be given to employee and manager representatives because 'without equal powers the very intention behind the scheme will be defeated'.

The same opinion was given by the PTM staff also. The majority of the PTM staff- 66 per cent (29) from *small* hospitals, 80 per cent (43) from *medium* hospitals, and 51 per cent (31) from *large* hospitals opined that equal powers should be given to employee and manager representatives because 'without equal powers the very intention behind the scheme will be defeated'.

Thus, the majority of the Administrators—60 per cent (12), Doctors—62 per cent (65) and PTM staff—65 per cent (103) viewed that *equal powers should be given to manager and employee representatives because 'without equal powers the very intention behind the scheme will be defeated'.* The survey results are given in Tables 6.11(a). *(See on next page)*

This leads to the conclusion that to get the full meaning of participation and to achieve the very intention behind the scheme, equal powers should be given to employee and manager representatives.

Next, the reasons for not favouring equal powers to employee and management representatives were studied in detail.

Reasons for Not Favouring Equal Powers to Employees' and Managers' Representatives

The majority of the respondents, i.e., 619 (Administrators- 31, Doctors—261 and PTM staff—327), were not in favour of giving equal powers to manager and employee representatives, as per Table 6.10. The reasons suggested by employees during the pilot study, too, were considered and given to respondents, and the survey results received were analysed. The following reasons were suggested:

(*i*) The employee representatives might become manager-representatives, trade unions becoming managerial organizations;

(*ii*) The joint forum might degenerate into a collective bargaining counter or an arena for ego clash;

Table 6.11(a): Favouring Equal Powers to Managers' and Employees' Representatives—Reasons

Category	Type of hospital	Without equal powers employee representative will be subordinated to the management representative	Without equal powers employees will not be able to participate effectively in the management process	Without equal powers the very intention behind the scheme will be defeated	Total
Administrators	Small	1 14.3%	2 28.6%	4 57.1%	7 35.0%
	Medium	2 18.2%	3 27.3%	6 54.5%	11 55.0%
	Large	0 .0%	0 .0%	2 100.0%	2 10.0%
	Total	**3** **15.0%**	**5** **25.0%**	**12** **60.0%**	**20** **100.0%**
Doctors	Small	3 18.8%	1 6.3%	12 75.0%	16 15.2%
	Medium	6 12.8%	7 14.9%	34 72.3%	47 44.8%
	Large	12 28.6%	11 26.2%	19 45.2%	42 40.0%
	Total	**21** **20.0%**	**19** **18.1%**	**65** **61.9%**	**105** **100.0%**
PTM staff	Small	8 18.2%	7 15.9%	29 65.9%	44 27.7%
	Medium	6 11.1%	5 9.3%	43 79.6%	54 34.0%
	Large	17 27.9%	13 21.3%	31 50.8%	61 38.4%
	Total	**31** **19.5%**	**25** **15.7%**	**103** **64.8%**	**159** **100.0%**

Source: Field Survey
Note: Percentages and totals based on responses

(*iii*) Employee representatives might develop hunger for power and cease to represent employees;

(*iv*) Employee representatives might be lacking in managerial competence and executive capacity.

From the 619 respondents, 151 per cent (932) multiple responses were received (Table 6.12). The analysis was made with the help of percentage on the responses received, as multiple responses were received from some respondents.

Table 6.12: Reasons for Not Favouring Equal Powers to Manager and Employee Representatives—Total Multiple Responses

Reasons	Code	Count	Per cent of responses	Per cent of cases
Employee representative will become manager representatives	1	202	21.7	32.6
Committee will become a collective bargaining counter	2	302	32.4	48.8
Employee representative will develop hunger for power	3	233	25.0	37.6
Employee representative lack managerial competence and executive capacityexecutive capacity	4	195	20.9	31.5
Total responses		**932**	**100.0**	**150.6**

Source: Field Survey

Note: 619 valid cases (respondents), 932 responses

The survey result revealed the following: The majority of the Administrators– 44 per cent (4) from *small* hospitals, 50 per cent (7) from *medium* hospitals, and 14 per cent (2) from *large* hospitals viewed that equal powers should not be given to the manager and employee representatives because 'employees lack managerial ability'. Another group of the Administrators – 11 per cent (1) from *small* hospitals, 7 per cent (1) from *medium* hospitals, and 64 per cent (9) from *large* hospitals opined that equal powers should not be given because the 'joint forum will become a collective bargaining counter'.

The majority of the Doctors—31 per cent (21) from *small* hospitals, 34 per cent (68) from *medium* hospitals, and 28 per cent (35) from *large* hospitals also opined that equal powers should not be given because 'the joint forum will become a collective bargaining counter'. Another group of the Doctors-33 per cent (22) from *small* hospitals, 38 per cent (77) from *medium* hospitals, and 13 per cent (17) from *large* hospitals opined that if equal power was given, the employees would develop hunger for power.

The majority of the PTM staff, 33 per cent (29) from *small* hospitals, 35 per cent (74) from *medium* hospitals and 33 per cent (64) from *large* hospitals also opined that equal powers should not be given because the 'joint forum will become a collective bargaining counter'.

Thus, the majority of the respondents, 31 per cent (124) of Doctors and 34 per cent (167) of the PTM staff opined that equal powers should not be given to manager and employee representative because the 'joint forum will degenerate into a collective bargaining counter'. 30 per cent (11) of the Administrators also agreed to this opinion. A large number of the Administrators i.e., 35 per cent (13) opined that 'the employees lack managerial ability'. The survey results are shown in Tables 6.12(a). *(See on next page)*

The analysis revealed that, as per the opinion of the respondents, the main reason for not granting equal powers to manager and employee representatives was that 'if equal powers were given, the joint forum will become a collective bargaining counter'. In addition to this, a reasonably equal number of respondents suggested other reasons such as: (*i*) The employee representatives will become manager- representatives, trade unions becoming managerial organizations; (*ii*) Employee representatives will develop hunger for power and cease to represent employees; and (*iii*) Employee representatives lack managerial competence and executive capacity.

The analysis revealed that all categories of the employees in all types of hospitals were of the view that the power should be in the hands of the management only. Employees felt that they should be given freedom to express their opinion and that all reasonable suggestions from them should be considered before taking important managerial decisions.

After discussion of the sharing of power, the issues of the extent, degree and committee for participation were taken up for consideration.

EXTENT OF PARTICIPATION

The number of employees participating in the management of the hospital represents the extent of participation. Full staff participation is important both as a means of tapping the practical and intellectual resources of all the health personnel for the benefit of the health organization and as a way of making work in the organization more meaningful for everyone.

The proportion of workers take part represents the extent of participation and this may vary widely from a few workers to the whole work force. Indirect participation through representatives involves less participation by individuals than could occur in direct participation[7].

Table 6.12(a): Reasons for Not Favouring Equal Powers to Manager and Employee Representatives

Category	Type of hospital	Employee representative will become manager representatives	Committee will become a collective bargaining counter	Employee representative will develop hunger for power	Employee representative lack managerial competence and executive capacity	Total
Administrators	Small	3 33.3%	1 11.1%	1 11.1%	4 44.4%	9 24.3%
	Medium	3 21.4%	1 7.1%	3 21.4%	7 50.0%	14 37.8%
	Large	1 7.1%	9 64.3%	2 14.3%	2 14.3%	14 37.8%
	Total	**7** **18.9%**	**11** **29.7%**	**6** **16.2%**	**13** **35.1%**	**37** **100.0%**
Doctors	Small	14 20.9%	21 31.3%	22 32.8%	10 14.9%	67 16.9%
	Medium	32 15.8%	68 33.5%	77 37.9%	26 12.8%	203 51.1%
	Large	32 25.2%	35 27.6%	17 13.4%	43 33.9%	127 32.0%
	Total	**78** **19.6%**	**124** **31.2%**	**116** **29.2%**	**79** **19.9%**	**397** **100.0%**
PTM staff	Small	19 21.6%	29 33.0%	19 21.6%	21 23.9%	88 17.7%
	Medium	29 13.6%	74 34.7%	60 28.2%	50 23.5%	213 42.8%
	Large	69 35.0%	64 32.5%	32 16.2%	32 16.2%	197 39.6%
	Total	**117** **23.5%**	**167** **33.5%**	**111** **22.3%**	**103** **20.7%**	**498** **100.0%**

Source: Field Survey

Note: Percentages and totals based on responses

More participation is characterized by a higher percentage, greater breadth, higher proportion, and earlier entrance into the decision-making process[8]. To increase the extent of participation, the primary requirement is the availability of employees who are competent to participate in management either directly or as employee representatives.

Table 6.13: Percentage of Employees Competent to be Employee Representatives

Category	Type of hospital	Employees competent to be employee representatives (in percentage)				Total
		0-25	25-50	50-75	75-100	
Administrators	Small	8 57.1%	2 14.3%	4 28.6%	0 .0%	14 100.0%
	Medium	10 55.6%	3 16.7%	5 27.8%	0 .0%	18 100.0%
	Large	7 53.8%	0 .0%	6 46.2%	0 .0%	13 100.0%
	Total	**25** **55.6%**	**5** **11.1%**	**15** **33.3%**	**0** **.0%**	**45** **100.0%**
Doctors	Small	34 51.5%	22 33.3%	10 15.2%	0 .0%	66 100.0%
	Medium	87 58.4%	32 21.5%	26 17.4%	4 2.7%	149 100.0%
	Large	88 69.8%	24 19.0%	12 9.5%	2 1.6%	126 100.0%
	Total	**209** **61.3%**	**78** **22.9%**	**48** **14.1%**	**6** **1.8%**	**341** **100.0%**
PTM staff	Small	51 54.3%	28 29.8%	14 14.9%	1 1.1%	94 100.0%
	Medium	85 50.0%	53 31.2%	29 17.1%	3 1.8%	170 100.0%
	Large	103 55.4%	54 29.0%	27 14.5%	2 1.1%	186 100.0%
	Total	**239** **53.1%**	**135** **30.0%**	**70** **15.6%**	**6** **1.3%**	**450** **100.0%**

Source: Field Survey

Hence, percentages of each category of employees who are in their own opinion, were competent to be employee representatives for effective participation in management in the private health care institutions, Kerala, were collected. For convenience the data were collected in different ranges of 0-25%, 25-50%, 50-75%, 75-100% and analysed.

The survey revealed the following: The majority of the Administrators-57 per cent (8) from *small* hospitals, 56 per cent (10) from *medium* hospitals, and 54 per cent (7) from *large* hospitals opined that only less than 25 per cent of the employees in a hospital were competent to be employee representatives for effective participation in management.

The majority of the Doctors also were of the same opinion- 52 per cent (34) of the *small* hospitals, 58 per cent (87) of the *medium* hospitals, and 70 per cent (88) of the *large* hospitals opined that only less than 25 per cent of the employees were competent for this.

The majority of the PTM staff—54 per cent (51) from small hospitals, 50 per cent (85) from medium hospitals, and 55 per cent (103) from large hospitals opined that only 0-25 per cent of employees were competent to participate in management.

The analysis revealed that in the opinion of 56 per cent (25) of the Administrators, 61 per cent (209) of the Doctors and 53 per cent (239) of the PTM staff the percentage of employees competent to be employee representatives for effective participation in management was 0-25 per cent only. The survey results are presented in Table 6.13.

By using chi-square test, the association between the number of employees competent to be employee representatives and different categories of staff in different types of hospitals was statistically examined in Table 6.13(a).

The chi-square at 5 per cent level of significance revealed that there was no statistically significant association between the number of employees competent to be employee representatives and the views of the Administrators and the PTM staff in different types of hospitals. But, with regard to the Doctors, the association was found statistically significant.

The survey reveals that only a limited number of employees were competent to take managerial responsibility. They believed that, an institution dealing with human lives, where experience is very important, control should not be disbursed to the incapable and inexperienced persons.

From these results, it may be concluded that there is not much scope for increasing the extent of participation of employees in management to higher levels. But the important point is that, as per the survey, the employees who are competent to participate in management can effectively represent the other employees. Lack of competence to participate, is the belief behind centralized control and unwillingness to share power.

Table 6.13(a): Chi-Square Tests - Percentage of Employees Competent to be Employee Representatives

Category		Value	df	Asymp. Sig. (2-sided)
Administrators	Pearson Chi-Square	2.988(a)	4	.560
	Likelihood Ratio	4.300	4	.367
	Linear-by-Linear Association	.333	1	.564
	N of Valid Cases	45		
Doctors	Pearson Chi-Square	11.848(b)	6	.065
	Likelihood Ratio	12.716	6	.048
	Linear-by-Linear Association	4.118	1	.042
	N of Valid Cases	341		
PTM staff	Pearson Chi-Square	1.435(c)	6	.964
	Likelihood Ratio	1.422	6	.965
	Linear-by-Linear Association	.148	1	.700
	N of Valid Cases	450		

Source: Computed

[a] 5 cells (55.6%) have expected count less than 5. The minimum expected count is 1.44.

[b] 3 cells (25.0%) have expected count less than 5. The minimum expected count is 1.16.

[c] 3 cells (25.0%) have expected count less than 5. The minimum expected count is 1.25.

COMMITTEES AND PARTICIPATION

A committee may be defined as a group of persons in an organization, who function collectively on an organized basis to perform some administrative activity.

Health care organizations need committees to help consolidate the dual authority tracks within the medical authority structure and the administrative/support structure. The joint conference committee, consisting of representatives from the medical staff, the board of trustees and the administrator is commonly used for this purpose. Functions of health care organizations are typically monitored and assessed by committees including pharmacy and therapeutics, infection control, patient care evaluation, surgical case review, medical records, quality assurance and utilization review[9].

The employees' opinions regarding the method of selection of members and tenure of office of committee members were collected and analysed.

Mode of Selection of Members Suggested for the Committee

The committee members must be selected with due care, ensuring adequate representation from each category of staff. The method of selection should be transparent and not biased. So, the opinions of all the respondents, *irrespective of whether committees were present or not* in their hospital, regarding their expected mode of selection of members, on the basis of the various alternatives, were obtained and analysed. The alternatives suggested were: (*a*) nomination by management; (*b*) nomination by trade union; (*c*) election by secret ballot; (*d*) election by open ballot; and (*e*) consensus.

The survey result revealed the following: The majority of the Administrators—43 per cent (6) from *small* hospitals, 56 per cent (10) from *medium* hospitals, and 69 per cent (9) from *large* hospitals suggested 'nomination by management' as the best mode of selection of members for the committee.

The majority of the Doctors - 44 per cent (29) from *small* hospitals, 58 per cent (86) from *medium* hospitals, and 52 per cent (66) from *large* hospitals—also opined that 'management should nominate' the members for the committee.

A major segment of the PTM staff - 46 per cent (43) of *small* hospitals, 61 per cent (103) of *medium* hospitals, and 38 per cent (70) of *large* hospitals supported 'nomination by management'.

Another large number of the respondents viewed 'consensus' as the best method of selection of members for the committee. 43 per cent (6) Administrators of *small* hospitals, 39 per cent (7) of *medium* hospitals, and 31 per cent (4) of *large* hospitals opted for 'consensus' as the best method of selection of members of the committee. 46 per cent (30) of the Doctors of *small* hospitals, 37 per cent (55) of *medium* hospitals and 21 per cent (26) of *large* hospitals also viewed 'consensus' as the best method. A large section of the PTM staff—45 per cent (42) of *small* hospitals, 34 per cent (57) of *medium* hospitals, and 20 per cent (38) of *large* hospitals also favoured 'consensus' as the best method of selection of members for the committee.

In short, a good majority of the respondents—56 per cent (25) of the Administrators, 53 per cent (181) of the Doctors and 48 per cent (216) of the PTM staff suggested nomination by management' as the best method. A slightly lesser percentage of respondents—38 per cent (17) of the Administrators, 33 per cent (111) of the Doctors and 30 per cent (137) of the PTM staff reported 'censensus' as the best method. None of the Administrators suggested nomination by the trade union. Only a negligible percentage suggested the other methods. There was no major difference among the opinions of respondents of *small*, *medium* and *large* hospitals. The survey results are given in Table 6.14.

The results of the study threw up some surprising findings: The majority opinion of all categories of employees regarding mode of selection was to retain the existing system, i.e., through 'nomination by management'; the second best option expressed was through 'consensus'. Regarding Administrators and Doctors, this result is understandable, as by both nomination and consensus the employee representative most likely would be a person who toes the management's line. Furthermore, this would reflect the innate distrust of the management towards lower level employees, what was quite unexpected was the response of the PTM staff who also favoured nomination by management. This was because of many factors like:

Table 6.14: Suggestion to Improve the Mode of Selection of Members of the Committee

Category	Type of hospital	Mode of selection of members of the committee					Total
		Nomination by management	Nomination by the Trade Union	Election by secret ballot	Election by open ballot	Consensus	
Administrators	Small	6 42.9%	0 .0%	1 7.1%	1 7.1%	6 42.9%	14 100.0%
	Medium	10 55.6%	0 .0%	0 .0%	1 5.6%	7 38.9%	18 100.0%
	Large	9 69.2%	0 .0%	0 .0%	0 .0%	4 30.8%	13 100.0%
	Total	**25 55.6%**	**0 .0%**	**1 2.2%**	**2 4.4%**	**17 37.8%**	**45 100.0%**
Doctors	Small	29 43.9%	0 .0%	5 7.6%	2 3.0%	30 45.5%	66 100.0%
	Medium	86 57.7%	0 .0%	5 3.4%	3 2.0%	55 36.9%	149 100.0%
	Large	66 52.4%	3 2.4%	22 17.5%	9 7.1%	26 20.6%	126 100.0%
	Total	**181 53.1%**	**3 .9%**	**32 9.4%**	**14 4.1%**	**111 32.6%**	**341 100.0%**
PTM staff	Small	43 45.7%	0 .0%	7 7.4%	2 2.1%	42 44.7%	94 100.0%
	Medium	103 60.6%	0 .0%	8 4.7%	2 1.2%	57 33.5%	170 100.0%
	Large	70 37.6%	14 7.5%	54 29.0%	10 5.4%	38 20.4%	186 100.0%
	Total	**216 48.0%**	**14 3.1%**	**69 15.3%**	**14 3.1%**	**137 30.4%**	**450 100.0%**

Source: Field Survey

(*i*) Absence of committees in a majority of hospitals, leading to lack of proper knowledge about their functioning;

(*ii*) The PTM staffs are subordinated to such an extent that they are afraid to demand an election;

(*iii*) HODs or in-charges are nominated by the management in committees, and as the PTM staffs have to work under the HODs and in-charges at departmental level, they don't want to antagonize them by speaking against their nomination.

The fact that a very low percentage opted for election can be explained by the near total absence of unions in hospitals.

Another mode of selection which got good rating was by 'consensus'. This can be easily explained by the work culture of the hospital where cooperation rather than confrontation is the rule.

Tenure of Office of Members Suggested for the Committee

Suggestions of the respondents as regards the tenure of office of the members of the committee were collected by giving choices such as: (*i*) not more than one year; (*ii*) not more than three years; (*iii*) until transfer or retirement whichever is earlier; and (*iv*) representation according to position.

In the opinion of 50 per cent (7) of the Administrators of *small* hospitals, 56 per cent (10) of *medium* hospitals and 54 per cent (7) of *large* hospitals, the 'tenure of office of members of the committee should not be more than three years'.

A large number of the Doctors including 39 per cent (26) from *small* hospitals, 44 per cent (65) from *medium* hospitals, and 30 per cent (38) from *large* hospitals also opined that 'the tenure of office of members of the committee should not be more than three years'.

The PTM staff comprising 37 per cent (35) from *small* hospitals, 38 per cent (65) from *medium* hospitals, and 33 per cent (62) from *large* hospitals also opined that the tenure of office of members of committee 'should not be more than three years'.

The analysis revealed that the majority of the respondents - 53 per cent (24) of the Administrators, 38 per cent (129) of the Doctors, and 36 per cent (162) of the PTM staff were of the opinion that the tenure of office of members of the committee 'should not be more than three years'.

The next large number of the respondents, i.e., 21 per cent (3) of the Administrators of *small* hospitals, 17 per cent (3) of *medium* hospitals, and 31 per cent (4) of *large* hospitals opined that the tenure of office of members of the committee 'should be according to position' only. A large section of the Doctors -29 per cent (19) of *small* hospitals, 25 per cent (37) of *medium* hospitals, and 39 per cent (49) of *large* hospitals- also opined that the tenure of office of members of the committee 'should be according to position' only. The same opinion was given by 29 per cent (27) of the PTM staff of *small* hospitals, 29 per cent (49) of *medium* hospitals, and 50 per cent (93) of *large* hospitals.

Another 22 per cent (10) of Administrators, 31 per cent (105) of Doctors and 38 per cent (169) of PTM staff held that the tenure of office of members of committee should be determined by 'representation according to position'. The survey results are given in Table 6.15. *(See on next page)*

By using the chi-square test, the association between the opinions on the 'tenure of office members of the committee' and different categories of staff in different types of hospitals were statistically examined [Table 6.15(a)]. *(See on page 180)*

The chi-square test at 5 per cent level of significance revealed that there was statistically significant association between the opinions about tenure of office of members of the committee and Doctors and PTM staff in different types of hospitals. But in the case of Administrators, the association was found statistically insignificant.

This leads to the conclusion that the majority of the employees prefer 'not more than three years' as their choice of tenure of office of members of committee.

This result would not only go a long way in proper implementation of participative management but also neutralize to a reasonable extent the negative impact of the mode of selection of committee members through 'nomination by management'. As the 'tenure of office is only for three years' everybody in a cadre is likely to get a chance to be an employee representative. This new blood in committees can be expected to infuse recent, novel and innovative ideas in hospital management which could be beneficial to all.

As a sequel to an analysis of these aspects of participative management, the next logical step is to study its implementation.

For or Against Implementing Participative Management

In view of the inherent benefits of participation, which ensures higher efficiency, better understanding, cooperation, coordination and enhanced satisfaction among members, it is only natural that employees would favour implementation of participative management in their institutions.

The research theory in social organizational psychology has also suggested that participation in group decision-making enhances satisfaction among members and removes tensions. Satisfaction was greater where participation was complete than where it was partial[10].

Table 6.15: Tenure of Office of Members of the Committee

Category	Type of hospital	Tenure of office				Total
		Not more than one year	Not more than three years	Until transfer, or retirement whichever is earlier	Represen-tation according to position	
Administrators	Small	3 21.4%	7 50.0%	1 7.1%	3 21.4%	14 100.0%
	Medium	3 16.7%	10 55.6%	2 11.1%	3 16.7%	18 100.0%
	Large	0 .0%	7 53.8%	2 15.4%	4 30.8%	13 100.0%
	Total	**6** **13.3%**	**24** **53.3%**	**5** **11.1%**	**10** **22.2%**	**45** **100.0%**
Doctors	Small	15 22.7%	26 39.4%	6 9.1%	19 28.8%	66 100.0%
	Medium	15 10.1%	65 43.6%	32 21.5%	37 24.8%	149 100.0%
	Large	4 3.2%	38 30.2%	35 27.8%	49 38.9%	126 100.0%
	Total	**34** **10.0%**	**129** **37.8%**	**73** **21.4%**	**105** **30.8%**	**341** **100.0%**
PTM staff	Small	11 11.7%	35 37.2%	21 22.3%	27 28.7%	94 100.0%
	Medium	20 11.8%	65 38.2%	36 21.2%	49 28.8%	170 100.0%
	Large	10 5.4%	62 33.3%	21 11.3%	93 50.0%	186 100.0%
	Total	**41** **9.1%**	**162** **36.0%**	**78** **17.3%**	**169** **37.6%**	**450** **100.0%**

Source: Field Survey

Hence, the opinions of employees in private hospitals in Kerala regarding implementing participative management in their institutions were collected and analysed. The choices given were:

(*i*) Yes

Table 6.15(a): Chi-Square Tests—Tenure of Office of Members of the Committee

Category		Value	df	Asymp. Sig. (2-sided)
Administrators	Pearson Chi-Square	3.711(a)	6	.716
	Likelihood Ratio	5.310	6	.505
	Linear-by-Linear Association	1.565	1	.211
	N of Valid Cases	45		
Doctors	Pearson Chi-Square	31.488(b)	6	.000
	Likelihood Ratio	31.826	6	.000
	Linear-by-Linear Association	17.139	1	.000
	N of Valid Cases	341		
PTM staff	Pearson Chi-Square	25.298(c)	6	.000
	Likelihood Ratio	25.722	6	.000
	Linear-by-Linear Association	11.306	1	.001
	N of Valid Cases	450		

Source: Computed

[a]9 cells (75.0%) have expected count less than 5. The minimum expected count is 1.44.

[b]0 cells (.0%) have expected count less than 5. The minimum expected count is 6.58.

[c]0 cells (.0%) have expected count less than 5. The minimum expected count is 8.56.

(*ii*) Yes, but not in health care

(*iii*) No.

The majority of the respondents were in favour of the concept of participative management but not ready to implement it in hospitals. Among the Administrators - 43 per cent (6) from *small* hospitals, 50 per cent (9) from *medium* hospitals, and 54 per cent (7) from *large* hospitals were in 'favour of implementing participative management but not in hospitals'. The Doctors also agreed to this idea- 50 per cent (33) of *small* hospitals, 46 per cent (69) of *medium* hospitals and 40 per cent (50) of *large* hospitals also were in 'favour of implementing participative management but not in hospitals'. The PTM staff - 40 per cent (38) from *small* hospitals, 42 per cent (72) from *medium* hospitals and 38 per cent (71) from *large* hospitals-were also in 'favour of implementing participative management but not in hospitals'.

Nearly one-third of the respondents were in favour of implementing participative management even in hospitals. Of the Administrators, 21 per cent (3) from *small* hospitals, 28 per cent (5) from *medium* hospitals, and 15 per cent (2) from *large* hospitals were in 'favour of implementing participative management'. Of the Doctors, 18 per cent (12) from *small* hospitals, 22 per cent (32) from *medium* hospitals, and 20 per cent (25) from *large* hospitals also were in 'favour of implementing participative management'. In the place of PTM staff—31 per cent (29) from *small* hospitals, 33 per cent (56) from *medium* hospitals, and 31 per cent (57) from *large* hospitals were also in 'favour of implementing participative management'.

Among the Administrators - 36 per cent (5) from *small* hospitals, 22 per cent (4) from *medium* hospitals, and 31 per cent (4) from *large* hospitals were 'not in favour of implementing participative management'. Among the Doctors, 32 per cent (21) of *small* hospitals, 32 per cent (48) of *medium* hospitals, and 41 per cent (51) of *large* hospitals were also 'not in favour of implementing participative management'. As regards to the PTM staff - 29 per cent (27) from *small* hospitals, 25 per cent (42) from *medium* hospitals and 31 per cent (58) from *large* hospitals were also 'not in favour of implementing participative management'.

The analysis revealed that 22 per cent (10) of Administrators, 20 per cent (69) of Doctors and 32 per cent (142) of the PTM staff were in 'favour of implementing participative management'. The majority of the respondents – 49 per cent (22) of Administrators, 45 per cent (152) of Doctors and 40 per cent (181) of PTM staff were in 'favour of implementing participative management but not in hospitals'. Another 29 percent (13) of the Administrators, 35 per cent (120) of Doctors and 28 per cent (127) of the PTM staff were 'not in favour of implementing participative management'. The survey results are given in Table 6.16.

By using the chi-square test, the association between opinions about 'implementation of participative management' and different categories of staff in different types of hospitals was statistically examined [Table 6.16(a)].

The chi-square test at 5 per cent level of significance revealed that there was no statistically significant association between the opinions on 'implementation of participative management' and the different categories of staff in different types of hospitals.

Though the majority (nearly 70 per cent) employees accepted the inherent benefits of the concept and were willing to implement it in any industrial organization, a significant number of employees expressed objection to it in the health care industry as a special situation. For employees, it is still an indigestible concept for the health care sector.

Table 6.16: Views of Employees for or Against Implementing

Participative Management

Category	Type of hospital	Implementing Participative Management			Total
		Yes	Yes, but not in health care industry	No	
Administrators	Small	3 21.4%	6 42.9%	5 35.7%	14 100.0%
	Medium	5 27.8%	9 50.0%	4 22.2%	18 100.0%
	Large	2 15.4%	7 53.8%	4 30.8%	13 100.0%
	Total	**10** **22.2%**	**22** **48.9%**	**13** **28.9%**	**45** **100.0%**
Doctors	Small	12 18.2%	33 50.0%	21 31.8%	66 100.0%
	Medium	32 21.5%	69 46.3%	48 32.2%	149 100.0%
	Large	25 19.8%	50 39.7%	51 40.5%	126 100.0%
	Total	**69** **20.2%**	**152** **44.6%**	**120** **35.2%**	**341** **100.0%**
PTM staff	Small	29 30.9%	38 40.4%	27 28.7%	94 100.0%
	Medium	56 32.9%	72 42.4%	42 24.7%	170 100.0%
	Large	57 30.6%	71 38.2%	58 31.2%	186 100.0%
	Total	**142** **31.6%**	**181** **40.2%**	**127** **28.2%**	**450** **100.0%**

Source: Field Survey

Reasons for Favouring Implementation of Participative Management

Of the different categories of respondents, 221 respondents (Administrators-10, Doctors-69 and PTM staff-142) favoured participative management in hospitals as per Table 6.16. The reasons for favouring this concept were analysed on the basis of responses obtained to one or more of the following suggestions: (*i*) to get better understanding and cooperation between management and employees; (*ii*) to improve coordination in the functioning of the hospital; (*iii*) to improve efficiency in patient care; (*iv*) to offer opportunity for prior consultation.

Table 6.16(a): Chi-Square Tests - Views of Employees for or Against Implementing Participative Management

Category		Value	df	Asymp. Sig. (2-sided)
Administrators	Pearson Chi-Square	1.220(a)	4	.875
	Likelihood Ratio	1.245	4	.871
	Linear-by-Linear Association	.000	1	.986
	N of Valid Cases	45		
Doctors	Pearson Chi-Square	3.062(b)	4	.547
	Likelihood Ratio	3.045	4	.550
	Linear-by-Linear Association	.666	1	.415
	N of Valid Cases	341		
PTM staff	Pearson Chi-Square	1.885(c)	4	.757
	Likelihood Ratio	1.898	4	.754
	Linear-by-Linear Association	.236	1	.627
	N of Valid Cases	450		

Source: Computed

a 5 cells (55.6%) have expected count less than 5. The minimum expected count is 2.89.

b 0 cells (.0%) have expected count less than 5. The minimum expected count is 13.35.

c 0 cells (.0%) have expected count less than 5. The minimum expected count is 26.53.

From the 221 respondents, 277 per cent (611) multiple responses were received and the analysis was made on the basis of these *multiple responses* (Table 6.17).

Administrators of *small* hospitals and *medium* hospitals favoured participative management equally for all the reasons suggested. In *large* hospitals, 50 per cent (2) responses were in favour of implementing participative management for the reason 'to get better understanding and cooperation with employees' and another 50 per cent (2) for the reason 'for better coordination in the functioning of the hospital'.

Doctors and PTM staff also gave nearly equal vote for all the reasons. 23 per cent (48) of the Doctors and 26 per cent (95) of the PTM staff favoured participative management for the reason 'to get better understanding and

Table 6.17: Reasons for Favouring Participative Management—Total Multiple Responses

Reasons	Code	Count	Per cent of responses	Per cent of cases
to get better understanding and cooperation between management and employees	1	153	25.0	69.2
to improve coordination in functioning of hospital	2	173	28.3	78.3
to improve efficiency in patient care	3	161	26.4	72.9
to offer opportunity for prior consultation	4	124	20.3	56.1
Total responses		**611**	**100.0**	**276.5**

Source: Field Survey
Note: 221 valid cases (respondents), 611 responses

cooperation between management and employees'. 27 per cent (55) of the Doctors and 29 per cent (108) of the PTM staff favoured participative management for the reason 'to improve coordination in the functioning of the hospital'. 28 per cent (58) of the Doctors and 26 per cent (95) of the PTM staff favoured participative management for the reason 'to improve efficiency in patient care'. Another group of respondents—22 per cent (46) of Doctors and 19 per cent (70) of the PTM staff favoured participative management for the reason 'to offer opportunity for prior consultation'. For survey results refer Table 6.17(a).

The responses from the various categories of staff who favoured participative management, regarding the reasons for doing so, were more or less evenly distributed among the given choices. Of these choices, to *improve coordination* in the functioning of the hospital and to *improve efficiency in patient care* got slightly higher ratings.

From this, we can conclude that there was no single reason for favouring participative management'. But the employees after understanding all the positive aspects of participative management were favouring its implementation.

Some respondents favoured implementation of participative management but not in hospitals.

Table 6.17(a): Reasons for Favouring Implementation of Participative Management

Category	Type of hospital	to get better understanding and cooperation between management and employees	to improve coordination in functioning of hospital	to improve efficiency in patient care	to offer opportunity for prior consultation	Total
Administrators	Small	3 25.0%	3 25.0%	3 25.0%	3 25.0%	12 33.3%
	Medium	5 25.0%	5 25.0%	5 25.0%	5 25.0%	20 55.6%
	Large	2 50.0%	2 50.0%	0 .0%	0 .0%	4 11.1%
	Total	**10 27.8%**	**10 27.8%**	**8 22.2%**	**8 22.2%**	**36 100.0%**
Doctors	Small	9 25.0%	11 30.6%	9 25.0%	7 19.4%	36 17.4%
	Medium	23 22.8%	25 24.8%	27 26.7%	26 25.7%	101 48.8%
	Large	16 22.9%	19 27.1%	22 31.4%	13 18.6%	70 33.8%
	Total	**48 23.2%**	**55 26.6%**	**58 28.0%**	**46 22.2%**	**207 100.0%**
PTM staff	Small	19 23.8%	25 31.3%	20 25.0%	16 20.0%	80 21.7%
	Medium	35 24.0%	42 28.8%	42 28.8%	27 18.5%	146 39.7%
	Large	41 28.9%	41 28.9%	33 23.2%	27 19.0%	142 38.6%
	Total	**95 25.8%**	**108 29.3%**	**95 25.8%**	**70 19.0%**	**368 100.0%**

Source: Field Survey

Note: Percentages and totals based on responses.

Reasons for Favouring Implementation of Participative Management but not in Hospitals

355 respondents (Administrators - 22, Doctors - 152 and PTM—181) were again in favour of implementing participative management but not in health care industry, as per Table 6.16. The responses from different categories of

employees, to the various reasons suggested below, were collected and analysed:

(*i*) Non-medical employees cannot be allowed to have a say in the running of the hospitals, since human lives are involved;

(*ii*) Para-medical staff cannot be allowed to partake in decision-making since their activities and outlook are restricted to too narrow a field;

(*iii*) Even doctors cannot be allowed since each of them is devoted to his special field and lacks an overall approach to total efficiency and profitability;

(*iv*) If a hospital is to run efficiently and successfully, it should be administered in a totalitarian way.

The survey revealed the following. Multiple responses were received for favouring implementation of participative management but not in hospitals. 150 per cent (534) multiple responses were received from 355 respondents (Table 6.18). The analysis was made on the basis of multiple responses.

The majority of the Administrators- 67 per cent (6) from *small* hospitals, 39 per cent (7) from *medium* hospitals and 78 per cent (7) from *large* hospitals- viewed that 'non-medical employees cannot be allowed to have a say in the running of the hospitals, since human lives are involved'. The Doctors also were of the same opinion: 39 per cent (20) from *small* hospitals, 53 per cent (50) from *medium* hospitals and 44 per cent (36) from *large* hospitals agreed to this point. The majority of the PTM staff - 61 per cent (30) from *small* hospitals, 48 per cent (54) from *medium* hospitals, and 43 per cent (47) from *large* hospitals - also opined that 'non-medical employees cannot be allowed to have a say in the running of the hospitals. The survey results are given in Table 6.18(a).

An analysis of the responses makes clear why so many of the respondents though favouring participative management were against its implementation in hospitals. 56 per cent (20) of the Administrators, 47 per cent (106) of the Doctors and 48 per cent (131) of the PTM staff, (total-257) did not favour it for the reason that 'non-medical employees cannot be allowed to have a say in the running of hospitals, as human lives are at stake'. Further 17 per cent (6) of the Administrators, 31 per cent (69) of the Doctors and 38 per cent (104) of the PTM staff (total-179) were against involving even the para-medical, technical staff to take part in decision-making, since their outlook is narrow. In short, a total of 81 per cent (257 + 179 = 436) of responses were against the non-medical and para-medical staff getting involved in decision-making in hospitals, since human lives are involved.

Table 6.18: Reasons favouring participative management but not in health care industry—Total Multiple Responses

Reasons	Code	Count	Per cent of responses	Per cent of cases
Non medical employees cannot be allowed to have a say in the running of the hospitals, since human lives are involved	1	257	48.1	72.4
Para-medical staff, cannot be allowed to partake in decision making since their activities and outlook are restricted to too narrow a field	2	179	33.5	50.4
Even doctors cannot be allowed since each of them is devoted to his special field and lacks an overall approach to total efficiency and profitability.	3	40	7.5	11.3
If a hospital is to run efficiently and successfully, it should be administered in a totalitarian way	4	58	10.9	16.3
Total responses		**534**	**100.00**	**150.4**

Source: Field Survey

Note: 355 valid cases (respondents), 534 responses

Another important finding is that objection to Doctors being involved in implementing participative management was very low, 8 per cent (40)-(Administrators-4, Doctors-21, PTM staff-15), even if they lacked an overall approach to total efficiency and profitability. This further leads us to conclude that *even at the expense of profitability the consideration for human lives reigns high.*

So the overall inference arrived at from this discussion is that the primary objection to implementing participative management in private hospitals can be that non-medical persons cannot decide on factors affecting patient care since human lives are involved.

Table 6.18(a): Reasons for Favouring Participative

Management but Not in Hospitals

Category	Type of hospital	Non-medical employees cannot be allowed to manage since human lives are involved	The activities of Paramedical staff are restricted to too narrow a field	Doctors cannot be allowed since they lack an overall approach to total efficiency and profitability	The hospital should be administered in a totalitarian way	Total
Administrators	Small	6 66.7%	1 11.1%	1 11.1%	1 11.1%	9 25.0%
	Medium	7 38.9%	3 16.7%	3 16.7%	5 27.8%	18 50.0%
	Large	7 77.8%	2 22.2%	0 .0%	0 .0%	9 25.0%
	Total	**20** **55.6%**	**6** **16.7%**	**4** **11.1%**	**6** **16.7%**	**36** **100.0%**
Doctors	Small	20 39.2%	21 41.2%	2 3.9%	8 15.7%	51 22.6%
	Medium	50 53.2%%	26 27.7%	8 8.5%	10 10.6%	94 41.6%
	Large	36 44.4%	22 27.2%	11 13.6%	12 14.8%	81 35.8%
	Total	**106** **46.9%**	**69** **30.5%**	**21** **9.3%**	**30** **13.3%**	**226** **100.0%**
PTM staff	Small	30 61.2%	13 26.5%	4 8.2%	2 4.1%	49 18.0%
	Medium	54 47.8%	42 37.2%	8 7.1%	9 8.0%	113 41.5%
	Large	47 42.7%	49 44.5%	3 2.7%	11 10.0%	110 40.4%
	Total	**131** **48.2%**	**104** **38.2%**	**15** **5.5%**	**22** **8.1%**	**272** **100.0%**

Source: Field Survey
Note: Percentages and totals based on responses

Reasons Not Favouring Implementation of Participative Management

260 respondents (Administrators—13, Doctors—120 and PTM staff—127) were not in favour of implementing participative management, as shown

in Table 6.16. The reason for this was analysed by giving the following options: (*i*) The decision making process will become highly time-consuming; (*ii*) No employee is professionally or temperamentally competent to assume managerial responsibility; (*iii*) The committee can degenerate into a body in which employees' grievances will dominate discussions; and (*iv*) Confidentiality of administrative policies and programmes will be lost.

From the 260 respondents, 292 per cent (760) multiple responses were received; the survey results were analysed on the basis of the multiple responses received (Table 6.19).

Table 6.19: Reasons for Not Favouring Participative Management –Total Multiple Responses

Reasons	Code	Count	Per cent of responses	Per cent of cases
The decision making process will become highly time consuming	1	189	24.9	72.7
No employee is professionally or temperamentally competent to assume managerial responsibility	2	212	27.9	81.5
The committee can degenerate into a body in which employees' grievances will dominate discussions	3	199	26.2	76.5
Confidentiality of administrative policies and programmes will be lost	4	160	21.1	61.5
Total responses		**760**	**100.0**	**292.3**

Source: Field Survey
Note: 260 valid cases (respondents), 760 responses

The survey results revealed the following. Administrators of *small*, *medium* and *large* hospitals gave nearly the same rating to 'all the reasons' for not favouring participative management in private hospitals, with the exception of 40 per cent (4) of the Administrators of *medium* hospitals whose reason was that 'no employee is professionally competent to assume managerial responsibility'. The responses of the Doctors of *small*, *medium* and *large* hospitals were in support of all these reasons more or less equally. The PTM staff of *small*, *medium* and *large* hospitals also supported this idea. The survey results are given in Table 6.19(a).

Table 6.19(a): Reasons for Not Favouring Participative Management

Category	Type of hospital	The decision making process will become highly time-consuming	No employee is professionally competent to assume managerial responsibility	Employees' grievances will dominate discussions	Confidentiality of administrative policies will be lost	Total
Administrators	Small	4 28.6%	4 28.6%	3 21.4%	3 21.4%	14 35.0%
	Medium	2 20.0%	4 40.0%	2 20.0%	2 20.0%	10 25.0%
	Large	4 25.0%	4 25.0%	4 25.0%	4 25.0%	16 40.0%
	Total	**10 25.0%**	**12 30.0%**	**9 22.5%**	**9 22.5%**	**40 100.0%**
Doctors	Small	14 21.9%	19 29.7%	16 25.0%	15 23.4%	64 16.6%
	Medium	38 26.6%	42 29.4%	33 23.1%	30 21.0%	143 37.1%
	Large	43 24.2%	49 27.5%	48 27.0%	38 21.3%	178 46.2%
	Total	**95 24.7%**	**110 28.6%**	**97 25.2%**	**83 21.6%**	**385 100%**
PTM staff	Small	19 27.1%	19 27.1%	19 27.1%	13 18.6%	70 20.9%
	Medium	25 24.5%	26 25.5%	31 30.4%	20 19.6%	102 30.4%
	Large	40 24.5%	45 27.6%	43 26.4%	35 21.5%	163 48.7%
	Total	**84 25.1%**	**90 26.9%**	**93 27.8%**	**68 20.3%**	**335 100%**

Source: Field Survey

Note: Percentages and totals based on responses

The analysis showed that the responses were more or less even in respect of the four choices. Of these, responses like 'no employee is professionally or temperamentally competent to assume managerial responsibility' and 'the committee can degenerate into a body in which employees' grievances will dominate discussions' were observed as the major objections to implementation of participative management.

Considering all these together, it is obvious that more than two-thirds of the employees favoured the implementation of participative management in an organization. Of those who favoured it, there were a significant number of employees who were highly sceptical about its implementation in hospital setup.

Further analyzing the reasons for the responses, we could safely come to the conclusion that the main objection aired by those who were against its implementation in hospital was not against the concept but against one important aspect, namely, 'non-medical employees cannot be allowed to take decisions' on the running of an organization whose prime objective is patient care in which human lives are involved.

Even though the number of respondents who favoured the implementation of participative management was small, *their* opinion regarding whether participative management should be made statutory or not was sought.

STATUTORY PARTICIPATION

One question frequently discussed is whether participation systems should be made obligatory by law or by agreements. Much depends on the national tradition: some countries resort to legislation to regulate industrial relations while others prefer to deal with these matters by negotiation at the national, regional, local or even undertaking level. In some cases, the law lays down a number of fundamental rights and corresponding rules, leaving the details to be worked out by collective bargaining. There are also instances of agreements preceding the adoption of laws or regulations. However, the choice between laws or agreements seems to be determined mostly by the form of participation selected.

Participative Management is to be understood in terms of organizational processes rather than structures created to satisfy legal requirements[11]. Participative forums cannot be made operational simply by a decision of the government or as a result of demand from the workers' representatives. Only a recipient of participation would allow this facility to his subordinates[12].

The opinion of employees regarding whether participative management should be made statutory or not was sought and analysed.

For or Against Making Participative Management Statutory

The question whether participative management should be made statutory or not was asked to 26 per cent (221) of the respondents (who were in favour of implementing participative management vide Table 6.16). The opinions collected from different categories of employees were analysed. The survey results revealed the following:

The majority of the Administrators—67 per cent (2) from *small* hospitals, 60 per cent (3) from *medium* hospitals and 50 per cent (1) from *large* hospitals opined that participative management should not be made statutory. Another 33 per cent (1) of Administrators of *small* hospitals, 40 per cent (2) of *medium* hospitals and 50 per cent (1) of *large* hospitals opined that participative management should be made statutory.

The majority of the Doctors—92 per cent (11) from *small* hospitals, 88 per cent (28) from *medium* hospitals and 84 per cent (21) from *large* hospitals, held that participative management should be made statutory. Like Doctors, the majority of the PTM staff—90 per cent (26) from *small* hospitals, 89 per cent (50) from *medium* hospitals, and 84 per cent (48) from *large* hospitals, viewed that participative management should be made statutory. Only a small percentage of Doctors and PTM staff were not in favour of making participative management statutory.

The analysis revealed that the majority—60 per cent (6) of the Administrators were *'not in favour'* of making participative management statutory. But the majority of the Doctors - 87 per cent (60) and PTM staff—87 per cent (124), were *'in favour'* of making participative management statutory. The survey results are given in Table 6.20. *(See on next page)*

By using the chi-square test, the association between opinions on making participative management statutory and the different categories of staff in different types of hospitals were statistically examined given in Table 6.20(a).

The chi-square test at 5 per cent level of significance revealed that there was no statistically significant association between the opinions on making participative management statutory and the different categories of staff in different types of hospitals.

This analysis revealed the fact that the majority of the Doctors and the PTM staff from *small*, *medium* and *large* hospitals were *in favour* of making participative management statutory, while the majority of the Administrators from different types of hospitals were *not in favour* of making it statutory.

This revealed that the majority of the Administrators who favoured implementation of participative management were against making it statutory either due to their inherent, inflexible and condescending mindset or due to lack of trust in employees or their capacity to take management decisions.

The Doctors and PTM staff favoured making it statutory, thereby revealing that with the present set up there was little or no scope for their effective participation in management and that they saw statutory participative management as the only feasible means for that.

Table 6.20: Opinions about Favouring or not Favouring Statutory Participation

Category	Type of hospital	Making participative management statutory		Total
		Yes	No	
Administrators	Small	1 33.3%	2 66.7%	3 100.0%
	Medium	2 40.0%	3 60.0%	5 100.0%
	Large	1 50.0%	1 50.0%	2 100.0%
	Total	**4** **40.0%**	**6** **60.0%**	**10** **100.0%**
Doctors	Small	11 91.7%	1 8.3%	12 100.0%
	Medium	28 87.5%	4 12.5%	32 100.0%
	Large	21 84.0%	4 16.0%	25 100.0%
	Total	**60** **87.0%**	**9** **13.0%**	**69** **100.0%**
PTM staff	Small	26 89.7%	3 10.3%	29 100.0%
	Medium	50 89.3%	6 10.7%	56 100.0%
	Large	48 84.2%	9 15.8%	57 100.0%
	Total	**124** **87.3%**	**18** **12.7%**	**142** **100.0%**

Source: Field Survey

The reasons in favour of making participative management statutory are analysed below:

Reasons Favouring Participative Management Statutory

The reasons suggested by employees who were in favour of making participative management statutory in the private hospitals in Kerala were collected. The following reasons were given as choices and the respondents were asked to record their choice. The reasons suggested were the following: (*i*) Only by making it statutory, the employers be persuaded to implement the scheme, (*ii*) By making it statutory, the employees will have an added consciousness of their responsibility towards the establishment where they are working; and (*iii*) Both the above.

Table 6.20(a): Chi-Square Tests—Opinion about Favouring or Not Favouring Statutory Participation

Category		Value	df	Asymp. Sig. (2-sided)
Administrators	Pearson Chi-Square	.139(a)	2	.933
	Likelihood Ratio	.138	2	.933
	Linear-by-Linear Association	.122	1	.726
	N of Valid Cases	10		
Doctors	Pearson Chi-Square	.436(b)	2	.804
	Likelihood Ratio	.454	2	.797
	Linear-by-Linear Association	.428	1	.513
	N of Valid Cases	69		
PTM staff	Pearson Chi-Square	.836(c)	2	.658
	Likelihood Ratio	.823	2	.663
	Linear-by-Linear Association	.669	1	.413
	N of Valid Cases	142		

Source: Computed

[a]6 cells (100.0%) have expected count less than 5. The minimum expected count is .80.

[b]3 cells (50.0%) have expected count less than 5. The minimum expected count is 1.57.

[c]1 cells (16.7%) have expected count less than 5. The minimum expected count is 3.68.

The opinion of 75 per cent (3) of the Administrators of *medium* and *large* hospitals were 'only by making it statutory, the employers can be persuaded to implement the scheme' and 'the employees will have an added consciousness of their responsibility towards the establishment where they are working'. 55 per cent (6) of the Doctors of *small* hospitals, 82 per cent (23) of the *medium* hospitals and 81 per cent (17) of the *large* hospitals also agreed to the views of the Administrators. Like that, 62 per cent (16) of the PTM staff of *small* hospitals, 68 per cent (34) of *medium* hospitals and 81 per cent (39) of *large* hospitals agreed to the views of Administrators and Doctors.

The analysis revealed that 75 per cent (3) of the Administrators, 77 per cent (46) of the Doctors and 72 per cent (89) of the PTM staff supported both the reasons: (*i*) statutory participation can persuade the employers to implement the scheme; and (*ii*) by making it statutory, the employees will have an added consciousness of their responsibility towards the establishment where they are working. The survey results are given in Table 6.21.

Table 6.21: Reasons for Favouring Statutory Participation

Category	Type of hospital	Reasons favouring statutory participation			Total
		Employers will be persuaded to implement the scheme	The employees will have an added consciousness of their responsibility	Both the above	
Administrators	Small	1 100.0%	0 .0%	0 .0%	1 100.0%
	Medium	0 .0%	0 .0%	2 100.0%	2 100.0%
	Large	0 .0%	0 .0%	1 100.0%	1 100.0%
	Total	**1** **25.0%**	**0** **.0%**	**3** **75.0%**	**4** **100.0%**
Doctors	Small	4 36.4%	1 9.1%	6 54.5%	11 100.0%
	Medium	1 3.6%	4 14.3%	23 82.1%	28 100.0%
	Large	0 .0%	4 19.0%	17 81.0%	21 100.0%
	Total	**5** **8.3%**	**9** **15.0%**	**46** **76.7%**	**60** **100.0%**
PTM staff	Small	5 19.2%	5 19.2%	16 61.5%	26 100.0%
	Medium	4 8.0%	12 24.0%	34 68.0%	50 100.0%
	Large	5 10.4%	4 8.3%	39 81.3%	48 100.0%
	Total	**14** **11.3%**	**21** **16.9%**	**89** **71.8%**	**124** **100.0%**

Source: Field Survey

The analysis leads to the conclusion that *compulsion in the form of statutory regulation only will bring the management and employees together,* thereby implementing participative management.

Reasons against making participative management statutory are also analysed now.

Reasons for Not Favouring Statutory Participation

The various reasons for opposing the making of participative management statutory were also gathered by suggesting various choices. The options suggested were: (*i*) Making participative management statutory will not change the employees' basic approach to the firm they work for; (*ii*) Compulsory participation will not yield the same results as voluntary participation; (*iii*) A statute cannot eradicate the existing distrust between the management and the employees; and (*iv*) The employers will find out ways and means to successfully circumvent the provisions of the statute.

The opinion of 100 per cent (2) of the Administrators of small hospitals and 33 per cent (1) of the *medium* hospitals was 'statute cannot eradicate the distrust between the management and the employees'. 100 per cent (1) of the Doctors of *small* hospitals, 50 per cent (2) of the *medium* hospitals and 25 per cent (1) of the *large* hospitals viewed that 'compulsory participation will not yield the same results as voluntary participation'. The majority of the PTM staff were also of the same opinion as that of the Doctors. 67 per cent (4) of the PTM staff of *medium* hospitals and 100 per cent (9) of the *large* hospitals also opined that 'compulsory participation will not yield the same results as voluntary participation'.

The analysis revealed that the majority—50 per cent (3) of the Administrators felt that making participative management statutory 'cannot eradicate the existing distrust between management and the employees'. A large number including 44 per cent (4) of Doctors and 72 per cent (13) of the PTM staff felt that 'compulsory participation will not yield the same results as voluntary participation'. The survey results are given in Table 6.22.

The obvious finding was that compulsory participation would not yield the same results as voluntary participation. Furthermore, a statute would not eradicate the existing distrust between the management and the employees. This leads to the conclusion that participative management need not be made statutory because the *successful implementation of this scheme depends more upon the willingness of both the parties,* i.e., a mental change from both the employees and managers than making it statutory.

Table 6.22: Reasons for Not Favouring Statutory Participation

Category	Type of hospital	Reasons for not favouring statutory participation					Total
		Making participative management statutory will not change employees basic approach	Compulsory participation will not yield same results as voluntary partici-pation	Statute cannot eradicate the distrust with management	The employers will find outways to escape from statute	All the above	
Administrators	Small	0 .0%	0 .0%	2 100.0%	0 .0%	0 .0%	2 100.0%
	Medium	0 .0%	1 33.3%	1 33.3%	1 33.3%	0 .0%	3 100.0%
	Large	0 .0%	0 .0%	0 .0%	0 .0%	1 100.0%	1 100.0%
	Total	**0 .0%**	**1 16.7%**	**3 50.0%**	**1 16.7%**	**1 16.7%**	**6 100.0%**
Doctors	Small	0 .0%	1 100.0%	0 .0%	0 .0%	0 .0%	1 100.0%
	Medium	1 25.0%	2 50.0%	1 25.0%	0 .0%	0 .0%	4 100.0%
	Large	0 .0%	1 25.0%	1 25.0%	0 .0%	2 50.0%	4 100.0%
	Total	**1 11.1%**	**4 44.4%**	**2 22.2%**	**0 .0%**	**2 22.2%**	**9 100.0%**
PTM staff	Small	0 .0%	0 .0%	3 100.0%	0 .0%	0 .0%	3 100.0%
	Medium	0 .0%	4 66.7%	1 16.7%	1 16.7%	0 .0%	6 100.0%
	Large	0 .0%	9 100.0%	0 .0%	0 .0%	0 .0%	9 100.0%
	Total	**0 .0%**	**13 72.2%**	**4 22.2%**	**1 5.6%**	**0 .0%**	**18 100.0%**

Source: Field Survey

The assessments made by the employees working in the private hospitals of Kerala regarding the implementation of this concept in their institutions could be analysed now:

PARTICIPATIVE MANAGEMENT IN KERALA

There has already been a move to a large extent from emphasis on the owner-manager to the professional manager, whether or not he is an owner. A move towards participative management has already begun in enlightened companies in India[13].

Availability of well-rewarded and motivated employees, along with adequately trained health care leaders, is the prime necessity for the success of the scheme. It is only through them the private health care institutions can meet the expanding health care needs of the people of Kerala. In general, the people of Kerala possess a high level of general awareness and a high potential for assuming any kind of responsibilities. In Kerala, it must be remembered that the new generation of children are more independent than their parents. While job opportunities may be less, union activities and instances of labour unrest are increasing.

Participative Management: Success or Failure in Kerala?

The opinions of different categories of employees regarding the success or failure of participative management in Kerala were collected. The survey was made with the parameters: (*i*) successful in Kerala; (*ii*) successful, but not in the health care industry; (*iii*) not successful in Kerala.

The majority of the Administrators—57 per cent (8) from *small* hospitals, 50 per cent (9) from *medium* hospitals and 62 per cent (8) from large hospitals, held that 'participative management will not be successful in Kerala'. Deviating from this view, 43 per cent (6) of the Administrators of *small* hospitals, 39 per cent (7) of *medium* hospitals and 39 per cent (5) of *large* hospitals opined that 'participative management will be successful in Kerala, but not in the health care industry'. Only 11 per cent (2) of the Administrators of *medium* hospitals viewed that participative management would be successful in Kerala.

Participative management 'will be successful in Kerala but not in the health care industry' was the opinion of 58 per cent (38) of the Doctors of *small* hospitals, 56 per cent (84) of *medium* hospitals and 46 per cent (58) of *large* hospitals. In addition to this, 8 per cent (5) of the Doctors of *small* hospitals, 19 per cent (28) of *medium* hospitals and 14 per cent (18) of *large* hospitals opined that participative management 'will be successful' in Kerala. But 35 per cent (23) of the Doctors of *small* hospitals, 25 per cent (37) of *medium* hospitals and 40 per cent (50) of *large* hospitals opined that 'participative management will not be successful' in Kerala.

37 per cent (35) of the PTM staff of *small* hospitals, 37 per cent (63) of *medium* hospitals and 41 per cent (77) of *large* hospitals opined that participative management 'will be successful in Kerala, but not in the health care industry'. To add more weight to this point, 15 per cent (14) of the PTM staff of *small* hospitals, 18 per cent (30) of *medium* hospitals and 24 per cent (44) of *large* hospitals opined that participative management 'will be successful' in Kerala. Another 48 per cent (45) of the PTM staff of *small* hospitals, 45 per cent (77) of *medium* hospitals and 35 per cent (65) of *large* hospitals held that participative management 'will not be successful' in Kerala.

The analysis revealed that only a small segment of staff in the health care industry consisting of 4 per cent (2) of the Administrators, 15 per cent (51) of the Doctors and 20 per cent (88) of the PTM staff held the view that the system will be successful in Kerala. Another 40 per cent (18) of the Administrators, 53 per cent (180) of the Doctors and 39 per cent (175) of the PTM staff were of the opinion that participative management would be successful in Kerala, but not in the health care industry. 56 per cent (25) of the Administrators, 32 per cent (110) of the Doctors and 42 per cent (187) of the PTM staff thought that participative management would not be successful in Kerala. The survey results are given in Table 6.23. *(See on next page)*

By using the chi-square test, the association between 'opinion on the success or not of this scheme in Kerala' and different categories of staff in different types of hospitals was statistically examined given in Table 6.23(a). *(See on page 201)*

The chi-square test at 5 per cent level of significance revealed that there was no statistically significant association between the opinions on 'success of this scheme in Kerala' and the Administrators and PTM staff in different types of hospitals. But with regard to Doctors, the association was found statistically significant.

The majority of the Administrators and the PTM staff felt that participative management 'will not be successful' in Kerala. But a significant number of employees gave the verdict that it would be successful in Kerala, but not in the health care industry. If these responses were counted along with those who felt it would be successful in hospitals also, the scale would tilt in favour of the opinion that it would be successful in Kerala.

Hence, it is mandatory that the reasons behind those responses, especially behind the response that it would not be successful in the health care industry, were examined in detail.

First, the reasons suggested by the employees why participative management could be a success in Kerala were analysed.

Table 6.23: Success or Failure of Participative Management in Kerala

Category	Type of hospital	Success of participative management			Total
		Yes	Yes, but not in the health care industry	No	
Administrators	Small	0 .0%	6 42.9%	8 57.1%	14 100.0%
	Medium	2 11.1%	7 38.9%	9 50.0%	18 100.0%
	Large	0 .0%	5 38.5%	8 61.5%	13 100.0%
	Total	**2** **4.4%**	**18** **40.0%**	**25** **55.6%**	**45** **100.0%**
Doctors	Small	5 7.6%	38 57.6%	23 34.8%	66 100.0%
	Medium	28 18.8%	84 56.4%	37 24.8%	149 100.0%
	Large	18 14.3%	58 46.0%	50 39.7%	126 100.0%
	Total	**51** **15.0%**	**180** **52.8%**	**110** **32.3%**	**341** **100.0%**
PTM staff	Small	14 14.9%	35 37.2%	45 47.9%	94 100.0%
	Medium	30 17.6%	63 37.1%	77 45.3%	170 100.0%
	Large	44 23.7%	77 41.4%	65 34.9%	186 100.0%
	Total	**88** **19.6%**	**175** **38.9%**	**187** **41.6%**	**450** **100.0%**

Source: Field Survey

Table 6.23(a): Chi-Square Tests—Success or Failure of Participative Management in Kerala

Category		Value	df	Asymp. Sig. (2-sided)
Administrators	Pearson Chi-Square	3.232(a)	4	.520
	Likelihood Ratio	3.897	4	.420
	Linear-by-Linear Association	.028	1	.867
	N of Valid Cases	45		
Doctors	Pearson Chi-Square	10.484(b)	4	.033
	Likelihood Ratio	11.013	4	.026
	Linear-by-Linear Association	.163	1	.687
	N of Valid Cases	341		
PTM staff	Pearson Chi-Square	6.904(c)	4	.141
	Likelihood Ratio	6.959	4	.138
	Linear-by-Linear Association	6.208	1	.013
	N of Valid Cases	450		

Source: Computed

[a]3 cells (33.3%) have expected count less than 5. The minimum expected count is .58.
[b]0 cells (.0%) have expected count less than 5. The minimum expected count is 9.87.
[c]0 cells (.0%) have expected count less than 5. The minimum expected count is 18.38.

Reasons for the success of Participative Management in Kerala

As per the above discussion (Table 6.23) it is seen that only 141 respondents (Administrators—2, Doctors—51 and PTM—88) viewed that participative management would be successful in Kerala. The various reasons for this view were gathered in the survey by giving the following alternatives: (*i*) Kerala has an educated, politicized and socially conscious labour force, which can be easily trained in managerial functions; (*ii*) They possess the capacity to equate rights and accountability with a high degree of general awareness and a high potential for assuming any kind of responsibilities; (*iii*) Kerala has been a pioneering state in trade union movement and the political and social atmosphere in Kerala is conducive to the implementation of participative management

The survey revealed the following: The Administrators had faith on the employees of Kerala. 50 per cent (1) each of the Administrators of the *medium* hospitals opined that 'Kerala has an educated, politicized and social conscious labour force which can be easily trained in managerial functions' and 'they possess the capacity to equate rights and accountability with a high degree of general awareness and a high potential for assuming any kind of responsibilities'.

The majority—60 per cent (3) of the Doctors of *small* hospitals, 54 per cent (15) of *medium* hospitals and 56 per cent (10) of *large* hospitals- also opined that 'Kerala has an educated, politicized and socially conscious labour force that can be easily trained in managerial functions'. The majority of the PTM staff - 64 per cent (9) of *small* hospitals, 50 per cent (15) of *medium* hospitals and 59 per cent (26) of *large* hospitals—also agreed to this point of view.

'Kerala has an educated, politicized and socially conscious labour force that can be trained in managerial functions and so participative management will be successful in Kerala - was the opinion of the majority —50 per cent (1) of the Administrators, 55 per cent (28) of the Doctors and 57 per cent (50) of the PTM staff. 50 per cent (1) of the Administrators, 33 per cent (17) of the Doctors and 16 per cent (14) of the PTM staff viewed that 'the employees possess the capacity to equate rights and accountability and a high potential for assuming any kind of responsibilities' and so participative management would be successful in Kerala. The survey results are depicted in Table 6.24. *(See on next page)*

From the analysis we can come to the conclusion that Kerala has an 'educated, politicized and socially conscious labour force, which can be easily trained in managerial functions'. This was quoted as the reason for the success of participative management in Kerala.

Some employees hoped that participative management would be successful in Kerala, but not in the health care industry. The reason for this had to be analysed now.

Participative Management Successful in Kerala, but Not in the Health Care Industry

As per Table 6.23, 373 respondents (Administrators-18, Doctors—180 and PTM staff–175) expressed the opinion that the concept of participative management would be successful in Kerala, but not in the hospitals. The reasons obtained were analysed:

(*i*) Employees will misuse this system and that will lead to loss of human lives;

(*ii*) Non-medical staff cannot be entrusted with the task of decision making in an institution that deals with health and human lives;

Table 6.24: Reasons for the Success of Participative Management in Kerala

Category	Type of hospital	Reasons for the success			Total
		Kerala has an educated, politicized and socially conscious labour force	Kerala employees possess the capacity to equate rights and accountability	Kerala has been a pioneering state in trade union movement	
Administrators	Small	0 .0%	0 .0%	0 .0%	0 .0%
	Medium	1 50.0%	1 50.0%	0 .0%	2 100.0%
	Large	0 .0%	0 .0%	0 .0%	0 .0%
	Total	**1** **50.0%**	**1** **50.0%**	**0** **.0%**	**2** **100.0%**
Doctors	Small	3 60.0%	2 40.0%	0 ,0%	5 100.0%
	Medium	15 53.6%	9 32.1%	4 14.3%	28 100.0%
	Large	10 55.6%	6 33.3%	2 11.1%	18 100.0%
	Total	**28** **54.9%**	**17** **33.3%**	**6** **11.8%**	**51** **100.0%**
PTM staff	Small	9 64.3%	0 .0%	5 35.7%	14 100.0%
	Medium	15 50.0%	6 20.0%	9 30.0%	30 100.0%
	Large	26 59.1%	8 18.2%	10 22.7%	44 100.0%
	Total	**50** **56.8%**	**14** **15.9%**	**24** **27.3%**	**88** **100.0%**

Source: Field Survey

(*iii*) Trade unions are almost non-existent in the private health care industry in Kerala.

The survey revealed the following. 83 per cent (5) of the Administrators of *small* hospitals, 86 per cent (6) of *medium* hospitals and 100 per cent (5) of *large* hospitals opined that 'non-medical staff cannot be entrusted with the task of decision making in an institution that deals with health and human lives'. The majority of the Doctors comprising 55 per cent (21) of *small* hospitals, 57 per cent (48) of *medium* hospitals, and 64 per cent (37) of *large* hospitals also agreed to the opinion of the Administrators. Like the Administrators and Doctors, the majority of the PTM staff—66 per cent (23) from *small* hospitals, 67 per cent (42) from *medium* hospitals, and 79 per cent (61) from *large* hospitals—also supported the idea of not giving the task of decision making to non-medical staff.

The analysis revealed that 89 per cent (16) of the Administrators, 59 per cent (106) of the Doctors and 72 per cent (126) of the PTM staff were of the view that 'non-medical staff cannot be entrusted with the task of decision making' in an institution that deals with health and human lives and so participative management will not be successful in the health care industry in Kerala'. The survey results are given in Table 6.25. *(See on next page)*

From this, we can conclude that the majority of the employees, irrespective of their category, from different types of hospitals thought *that participative management would be successful, but not in the health care industry in Kerala, mainly because non-medical staff could not be entrusted with the task of decision making in an institution that deals with human lives.*

From the above analysis it is evident that the main reason for holding the view that it will not be successful in the health care industry is that the non-medical ordinary employee cannot be allowed to take decisions in an institution that deals with health and human lives. So, the obvious conclusion is that the employees were not against the concept of participative management, but their objection was on the basis of the above mentioned points. So, as a whole, the positive responses received regarding this aspect can also be taken as the voice of those who felt that participative management would be successful in Kerala.

Participative Management will not be a Success in Kerala

It is often agreed that the Indian scene is different from the one in advanced countries, and therefore, the participative type of management is not likely to be successful here. For example, the culture in India is not permissive, being highly authoritarian. It is claimed that the caste system encourages the tendency to security and dependency. Besides, job opportunities in India are less, with the backlog of unemployment of a very high degree. Under these circumstances, it is claimed that the negative incentives such as disciplinary action and even lay-offs have more efficacy here[14]. So, it is difficult to say that the participative system of management will be successful in Kerala.

Table 6.25: Reasons for Favouring the Success of Participative Management in Kerala, but Not in Hospitals

Category	Type of hospital	Reasons for favouring success of participative management			Total
		Employees will misuse this system, leading to loss of human lives	Non-medical staff cannot be entrusted with the task of decision making in hospitals	Trade unions are almost non-existent in hospitals in Kerala	
Administrators	Small	1 16.7%	5 83.3%	0 .0%	6 100.0%
	Medium	1 14.3%	6 85.7%	0 .0%	7 100.0%
	Large	0 .0%	5 100.0%	0 .0%	5 100.0%
	Total	**2** **11.1%**	**16** **88.9%**	**0** **.0%**	**18** **100.0%**
Doctors	Small	12 31.6%	21 55.3%	5 13.2%	38 100.0%
	Medium	24 28.6%	48 57.1%	12 14.3%	84 100.0%
	Large	12 20.7%	37 63.8%	9 15.5%	58 100.0%
	Total	**48** **26.7%**	**106** **58.9%**	**26** **14.4%**	**180** **100.0%**
PTM staff	Small	8 22.9%	23 65.7%	4 11.4%	35 100.0%
	Medium	17 27.0%	42 66.7%	4 6.3%	63 100.0%
	Large	14 18.2%	61 79.2%	2 2.6%	77 100.0%
	Total	**39** **22.3%**	**126** **72.0%**	**10** **5.7%**	**175** **100.0%**

Source: Field Survey

Table 6.23 shows that 322 respondents (Administrators—25, Doctors—110 and PTM staff—187) thought that participative management would not be successful in Kerala. The analysis was made by the following reasons: (*i*) Almost none in the management in a private institution will subscribe to the scheme; (*ii*) Kerala is notorious for multiplicity of unions as well as for inter-union and intra-union rivalry; and (*iii*) Management and employees are still poles apart and cannot refrain from accusing each other of the responsibility for the omissions and commissions that occur; (*iv*) Managerial functions are alien to employees who have not so far attained the mental maturity to relate their personal growth to the growth of their organization.

The survey results revealed that in private institutions 'almost none in the management will subscribe to the scheme' was the opinion of the majority of the Administrators – 100 per cent (8) of *small* hospitals, 67 per cent (6) of *medium* hospitals, and 100 per cent (8) of *large* hospitals. The majority of the Doctors—78 per cent (18) of *small*, 70 per cent (26) of *medium,* and 88 per cent (44) of *large* hospitals also agreed to this reason. The majority of the PTM staff also supported this reason. 78 per cent (35) of the PTM staff of *small* hospitals, 53 per cent (41) of *medium* hospitals, and 62 per cent (40) of *large* hospitals also opined that 'almost none in the management will subscribe to the scheme'.

The analysis revealed that a good majority of the employees—88 per cent (22) of the Administrators, 80 per cent (88) of the Doctors, and 62 per cent (116) of the PTM staff were sure that 'almost none in the management in a private institution will subscribe to this scheme'. The survey results are given in Table 6.26. *(See on next page)*

The discussion leads to the conclusion that the main reason for the failure of the scheme was 'management's unwillingness to come forward to introduce this scheme'.

The overall results regarding the success of participative management in Kerala revealed some interesting points. A good number of employees who had favoured implementing participative management in private hospitals, in Table 6.16, expressed their opinion that it was not likely to be a success in Kerala. This would naturally make one to subscribe the fact that altercation among union members and the militant trade unionism rampant in Kerala were the reasons for this. But the survey results from all categories of employees suggested the unwillingness of a private management to adopt this concept as the main reason for its failure in Kerala.

Table 6.26: Reason Why Participative Management Will Not be a Success in Kerala

Category	Type of hospital	Reasons for failure				Total
		Almost none in the management in a private institution will subscribe to the scheme	Kerala is notorious for multiplicity of unions	Management and employees are still poles apart	Managerial functions are alien to employees	
Administrators	Small	8 100.0%	0 .0%	0 .0%	0 .0%	8 100.0%
	Medium	6 66.7%	0 .0%	0 .0%	3 33.3%	9 100.0%
	Large	8 100.0%	0 .0%	0 .0%	0 .0%	8 100.0%
	Total	**22** **88.0%**	**0** **.0%**	**0** **.0%**	**3** **12.0%**	**25** **100.0%**
Doctors	Small	18 78.3%	3 13.0%	2 8.7%	0 .0%	23 100.0%
	Medium	26 70.3%	1 2.7%	5 13.5%	5 13.5%	37 100.0%
	Large	44 88.0%	3 6.0%	3 6.0%	0 .0%	50 100.0%
	Total	**88** **80.0%**	**7** **6.4%**	**10** **9.1%**	**5** **4.5%**	**110** **100.0%**
PTM staff	Small	35 77.8%	4 8.9%	6 13.3%	0 .0%	45 100.0%
	Medium	41 53.2%	7 9.1%	6 7.8%	23 29.9%	77 100.0%
	Large	40 61.5%	8 12.3%	13 20.0%	4 6.2%	65 100.0%
	Total	**116** **62.0%**	**19** **10.2%**	**25** **13.4%**	**27** **14.4%**	**187** **100.0%**

Source: Field Survey

HURDLES TO SUCCESSFUL PARTICIPATIVE MANAGEMENT

The studies dealing with the feasibility of participative management seldom use a conceptual framework. The shortcomings or the failure of this mechanism are analysed on a case-by-case basis, and are blamed upon such factors as:

- — lack of proper leadership;
- — loss of confidence among workers;
- — lack of management initiative.

What is imperative is a deeper understanding of the environment which may or may not permit the actors to develop goals, attitudes and perception of roles necessary for the successful functioning of participative management[15].

For making participative management a successful proposition, different hurdles were forecast by the employees. The opinions of the employees regarding the following selected choices were collected and analysed: (*i*) The mere advisory nature of the existing participative bodies; (*ii*) Inter- and intra-departmental rivalries; (*iii*) Lack of education and managerial training among employee representatives and their lack of self-confidence, (iv) Restriction on employee representatives to voice their views; (*iv*) Managements' flair of superiority and the consequent distrust between managerial and employee representatives; and (*v*) All the above.

The survey results revealed that all the reasons suggested to them were hurdles to effective implementation of participative management in the private hospitals of Kerala, according to the opinion of the majority of the respondents. That is, 64 per cent (9) of the Administrators of *small* hospitals, 33 per cent (6) of *medium* hospitals, and 54 per cent (7) of *large* hospitals agreed with this idea. In the same way, 52 per cent (34) of the Doctors of *small* hospitals, 46 per cent (69) of *medium* hospitals and 52 per cent (66) of *large* hospitals also supported all the above reasons. Like that, a large number of the PTM staff – 44 per cent (41) from *small* hospitals, 35 per cent (59) from *medium* hospitals, and 48 per cent (89) from *large* hospitals also opined that all the above reasons were the hurdles to effective implementation of participative management. The survey results are given in Table 6.27.

A comparison among the different categories of employees revealed that a good number of the employees- 49 per cent (22) of the Administrators, 50 per cent (169) of the Doctors and 41 per cent (185) of the PTM staff were of the view that all the reasons given are pointed to the hurdles as realized by the employees of the private health care institutions in Kerala in the way of making participative management a successful one. A good number of the PTM staff had not surprisingly opined that lack of education and managerial training among employee representatives and their lack of self-confidence were the main hurdles to make participative management a successful one.

Table 6.27: The Hurdles to Participative Management

Category	Type of hospital	Hurdles						Total
		The mere advisory nature of the existing participative bodies	Inter union and intra union rivalries	Lack of education and training among employee representatives	Restriction on employee-representatives to voice their views	The managements flair of superiority and distrust with management	All the above	
Administrators	Small	0 .0%	2 14.3%	1 7.1%	1 7.1%	1 7.1%	9 64.3%	14 100.0%
	Medium	4 22.2%	0 .0%	2 11.1%	6 33.3%	0 .0%	6 33.3%	18 100.0%
	Large	2 15.4%	4 30.8%	0 .0%	0 .0%	0 .0%	7 53.8%	13 100.0%
	Total	**6** **13.3%**	**6** **13.3%**	**3** **6.7%**	**7** **15.6%**	**1** **2.2%**	**22** **48.9%**	**45** **100.0%**
Doctors	Small	0 .0%	8 12.1%	12 18.2%	5 7.6%	7 10.6%	34 51.5%	66 100.0%
	Medium	9 6.0%	2 1.3%	31 20.8%	35 23.5%	3 2.0%	69 46.3%	149 100.0%
	Large	8 6.3%	17 13.5%	14 11.1%	14 11.1%	7 5.6%	66 52.4%	126 100.0%
	Total	**17** **5.0%**	**27** **7.9%**	**57** **16.7%**	**54** **15.8%**	**17** **5.0%**	**169** **49.6%**	**341** **100.0%**
PTM staff	Small	3 3.2%	18 19.1%	20 21.3%	5 5.3%	7 7.4%	41 43.6%	94 100.0%
	Medium	4 2.4%	3 1.8%	55 32.4%	41 24.1%	8 4.7%	59 34.7%	170 100.0%
	Large	20 10.8%	21 11.3%	33 17.7%	13 7.0%	10 5.4%	89 47.8%	186 100.0%
	Total	**27** **6.0%**	**42** **9.3%**	**112** **24.9%**	**59** **13.1%**	**25** **5.6%**	**185** **41.1%**	**450** **100.0%**

Source: Field Survey

The analysis relating to the opinions of employees regarding the expected system of participative management revealed that the *controlling* and responsible authority should be the *investors* and that the hospital should be managed by *Doctors with professional training in management*. The majority of the employees favoured *consultative participation*. All categories of employees, irrespective of the size of the hospital, have a uniform concept regarding the participative management - *participation in all management functions but not in ownership*. The majority of the employees accepted the inherent benefits of the concept and was willing to implement it.

REFERENCES

1. David J. Hunter, Doctor as Managers Poachers Turned Gramakeepers in Rosemary Stewart (Ed), Management of Health Care, England: Dastmouth Publishing Company Ltd, 1998, pp. 355-357.
2. Fremont E. Kast, James E. Rosenzweig, Organization and Management—A Systems Approach, New York: McGraw-Hill Book Company, 1979, p. 538.
3. Manoj Kumar Sankar, Personnel Management, Delhi: Crest Publishing House, 2000, p. 353.
4. John Gratto Liebler, Charles R. McConnell, Management Principles for Health Professional, Maryland: An Aspen Publication, 1999, p. 88.
5. Clerc, J. M., Workers Participation in Management—Some Preliminary Considerations in Albeda Esasmus, W. (Ed), Participation in Management, Rotterdam: University Press, 1973, p. 10.
6. Kristi M. Branch, Participative Management and Employee and Stakeholder Inovlvement, Chapter 10, Google.com.
7. Clerc,J. M., *Op. cit.,* p. 10.
8. Ashmos, D. P., Daniel, R. R., Physician Participation in Hospital Strategic Decision Making: The Effect of Hospital Strategy and Decision, Health Services Research, Vol.26 (3), 1991, pp. 375-401.
9. John Gratto Liebler, Charles R McConnell, *op. cit.,* p. 318.
10. Michael Cooper, R., Wood T. Michael, Member Participation and Commitment in Group Decision-making on Influence Satisfaction and Decision Richness, *Journal of Applied Psychology*, Vol. 59, No.2, April 1974.
11. Alexander, K. C., Participative Management: The Indian Experience, Delhi: Sri Ram Centre for Industrial Relations and Human Resources, 1972, p. 108.
12. Thackur, C. P., Public Enterprise and Workers Participation in Management in Thackur, C. P., Sethi, K. C. (Eds), Industrial Democracy Some Issues and Experiences, Delhi: Sri Ram Centre for Industrial Relations and Human Resources, 1973, p. 26.
13. Rustom S. Davar, The Management Process—The Principles of Management, Madras: Progressive Corporation Private Ltd, 1978,p. 460.
14. *Ibid*, p. 459.
15. Syed, M. A., Hameed, Participative Management and Industrial Relation Setting in Thakur, C. P., Sethi, K. C. (Eds), Industrial Democracy: Some Issues and Experiences, Delhi: Sri Ram Centre for Industrial Relations and Human Resources, 1973, p. 35.

CHAPTER 7

Summary of Findings and Suggested Model

Health care industry being basically a human service organization, management with maximum human touch is a must in any hospital set up. In hospitals, maximum efficiency can only be achieved if all the staff in the hospital work together conscientiously and contribute to the management. For tapping the practical and intellectual resources of all the health personnel for the benefit of the organization, and as a way of making the work of the organization beneficial to everyone, they have to be properly motivated. Even though money is the best motivator, it is not the only motivator and those who have met their basic psychological needs need to be motivated by more serious factors like job satisfaction, achievement orientation, recognition, acceptability, etc. These can be provided only when the management creates a cordial atmosphere of mutual respect, where the individual is recognized and appreciated for the quality of work he or she is putting in. Our society is becoming increasingly democratic and people are learning to influence the policies and decisions of the management, directly or through their representatives. Viewed against the rapidly changing cultural context, employee participation in management is inevitable with inherent benefits.

The study was confined to the private health care institutions in the State of Kerala. The prime aim of the study was to find out the opinions of employees regarding the feasibility of participative management in the private health care industry in Kerala. The study focussed on the following specific objectives:

1. To study the human resource management practices followed in private health care institutions in the State of Kerala;

2. To examine the existing system of participation of employees in the management of private hospitals in the State of Kerala;
3. To ascertain the possibility of implementation of participative management in the private health care industry in Kerala;
4. To suggest a model of participative management system for private health care institutions in Kerala.

A sample of 30 hospitals has been selected on the basis of the number of hospitals existing in each size (small, medium and large) and in each zone (South, Central and North). Altogether 13 *small*-sized hospitals, 10 *medium*-sized hospitals and 7 *large*-sized hospitals were selected as sample units. The primary data were collected from the sample respondents using a structured interview schedule. The study covered a sample size of 836 respondents, consisting of 45 Administrators, 341 Doctors, and 450 PTM staff. Simple random sampling technique was applied for the selection of the respondents.

The data collected for the study were processed and analysed with the help of Computer Software-SPSS. The tools used for analysis of primary data were mathematical and statistical techniques such as Percentages, Mean, Two-way ANOVA technique, Chi-square analysis and Factor analysis.

The Introductory Chapter deals with the nature, importance, objectives, concepts and definitions used, methodology adopted, survey design, and the limitations of the study. The Second Chapter gives a brief review of earlier literature related to this research topic. The conceptual and theoretical framework of the study is dealt with in the next chapter.

In the analysis part, the major findings of the study with regard to the existing Human Resource Management practices and Participative Management practices are presented first, followed by the opinions of employees regarding the feasibility of Participative Management in the private hospitals of Kerala. In this chapter, the findings and the suggestions on participative management, including the proposal of a model of participative management system for private health care industry in Kerala is attempted followed by a note on the scope for further research.

SUMMARY OF FINDINGS

Now, an attempt is made here to summarise the *findings* of the study followed by the major *conclusions* drawn on the basis of the findings as regards participative management in the private health care institutions in the State of Kerala.

1. Human Resource Management Practices

Job-related Factors

The analysis revealed that the majority of the respondents in *small, medium* and *large* hospitals expressed a very *high* level of satisfaction with the 'method of staff selection'. This is because the highly skilled, qualified and experienced staffs were mostly inducted into their job with sufficient incentives by the management, and they in general had nothing to complain about. Most of the semi-skilled and unskilled workers, with the existing level of unemployment in the State, were only too happy to have landed in their present job and hence had no reason for complaint regarding their selection.

They however expressed the least satisfaction with 'training facilities', when compared to all other job-related parameters. The informal information gathered from most of the hospitals was that the management was keener on getting trained personnel from other hospitals than on training people in their own hospital. Real training is imparted only when a new procedure, protocol or equipment is pressed into service, about which all staff members appeared to have good opinion.

Regarding 'salary', the majority of the respondents in *small, medium* and *large* hospitals expressed a very *high* level of satisfaction. There is a big monetary divide, with the super-specialists getting monthly salary in lakhs, while an unskilled labourer has to be satisfied with a few hundreds. The highly-paid employee had nothing to complain, while the low-paid worker would rather be an employee with a low salary than be an ex-employee who complained about his salary.

Regarding the level of satisfaction with the 'work-place rules', 'working conditions' and 'welfare facilities', all the employees were found as satisfied and the same was the opinion regarding 'the status of the job'.

Opportunities for Personal Development

The study revealed that there were good opportunities for the employees to use and improve their knowledge and skills, and to take decisions about their own work. This is not surprising, considering the fact that each employee is qualified to perform independently in the field in which he is trained.

Regarding *'promotion opportunity'*, the rating was uniformly *poor* across all categories of employees in different types of hospitals. This can be explained by the organizational set up of a hospital, where highly skilled to unskilled labourers worked as a congregation with no scope for vertical promotion beyond a particular level.

Another interesting finding was the *poor* rating regarding the 'opportunities to influence managerial decisions at higher levels', which makes it clear that many hospitals are run in a totalitarian way with no effective participation of employees in managerial decisions.

Communication

The Administrators, Doctors and the PTM staff in general were satisfied about the effectiveness of the communication system. Also, the comparison across *small, medium* and *large* hospitals revealed no difference and the effectiveness of the communication system received more or less the same rating.

The fact that a hospital, unlike other industries, cannot survive without proper communication between all strata of employees, irrespective of its size, stands confirmed by our survey results which show more or less uniformly good rating for inter-personnel communication. This further leads us to conclude that there is at least informal participation among the peers, immediate superiors and subordinates.

The majority of the superiors and subordinates were satisfied with their respective communication skills, which leads to the conclusion that there was *proper two-way communication* between superiors and subordinates in the functioning of private hospitals.

Motivation

The important motivating factors among different categories of employees in hospitals of Kerala were then analysed. The foremost could be identified as the 'remuneration package', constituted by variables such as salary, job security and working condition. The second was found to be 'opportunity to participate in the decision making process', constituted by variables such as opportunity in managerial decision making and opportunity in making decision with regard to own job. The third factor of motivation was found to be non-interference in own job by others.

All these brings to the fore the stark reality that the finer aspects of motivation like 'opportunity to participate in management decision', 'opportunity to participate in decisions connected with the job' and 'non-interference in one's work', can become determinants only when the basic factors like salary, and job security are met. This situation unfortunately leaves a lot to be desired in private hospitals where poor salary (very difficult to ascertain), long and tedious working schedules and job insecurity are the rule rather than the exception.

Human Relations

The analysis revealed that there is good relationship between the employee, his immediate superior, the management and his subordinates - which is not surprising, considering the fact that in a work environment where cooperation and coordination is a must, an employee with poor interpersonal or superior-subordinate relationship can adversely affect the functioning of the hospital itself, and in all probability, in private hospitals, may lose his job.

The levels of support and cooperation received from superiors, colleagues, and subordinates were also deemed good by the respondents. This is because no hospital without the support and cooperation of its employees can survive in this fiercely competitive field, and the management and the employees are equally aware that it is a matter of survival.

Irrespective of the category of staff or type of hospital or category of personnel from various levels, the extent of resistance exercised when a new project is implemented was very low. The fear of losing job or other repercussions, coupled with the fact that human lives are involved rather than the existence of proper participation in the management was the most plausible explanation for this survey finding.

Conflicts, Disputes, Discipline and Grievances

Conflicts occurred only very rarely in hospitals. The presence of good two-way communication in hospitals could prevent conflicts to a large extent.

The results reveal that there was high level of satisfaction regarding settlement of disputes. The two levels at which disputes were resolved were at the 'concerned Department level' and at the 'top level management'. The good rating for resolution of disputes at Department level suggests a reasonable amount of Intra-departmental participation. The faith expressed by employees in the top level management for dispute resolution indicates the high level of control the management had over lower level employees thereby showing poor delegation of power and very low level of employee participation in higher level management process. Also, the poor rating given to the involvement of committees in dispute settlements denotes very poor level of employee participation in management. Delving deeper into the data, one finds that employees of medium-sized hospital showed a slightly better satisfaction with committees, probably because of the presence and satisfactory working of many committees in such hospitals.

The analysis revealed that the *level of discipline was quite good* and employees at all levels understood the importance of it in health care.

The employees were satisfied with all the parameters regarding redressal of grievances. This leads to the conclusion that in the private hospitals, complaints and grievances were expressed and dealt with immediately so that they did not persist as a disturbing factor affecting the functioning of the hospital.

Strikes and Unions

All the employees reported that strike in hospitals was unjustified. The employees of hospitals did not see strikes as a justifiable means of achieving their goals as lives of patients would be at stake.

The data shows total absence of strikes in private hospitals which goes hand in glove with the opinion that strikes are not justified in hospitals. Even though many hospital authorities feel that the recognition of the union is a direct invitation to strike, in the two hospitals in our sample where union is functioning there was no instance of strike.

The survey results show very low prevalence of unions in private hospitals. One of the strongest means by which an employee can influence management decision or participate in management function is through a truly representative, responsible union, the lack of which is a strong indicator of poor or no employee participation in management in private hospitals. Another point that needs mention is the difficulty in forming an effective single union or association as the hospital personnel belong to different cadres, classes and professions.

The available data indicate that though union is present in a very few hospitals it's functioning is unsatisfactory leading us to believe that just the presence of unions does not lead to participation in management.

2. Existing System of Participation

Forms of Participation

The 'informative participation', the least effective among all forms of participation, was dominant in *small* and *medium* size hospitals, while 'consultative participation' was dominant in the *large* size hospitals. The most noteworthy point is the total absence of 'joint decision making' or 'collective bargaining', which is a true indicator of effective participative management, in any of the *small, medium* or *large* hospitals.

Participation at Lower Level

The majority of the Administrators, Doctors and the PTM staff reported that the employees' *opportunity to participate in decisions connected with their job was 'high'*. Even though the Administrators, Doctors and PTM staff gave a high rating regarding the opportunity to take decisions connected with their job, the rating given by the PTM staff was low when compared to the other two categories of staff, irrespective of the size of the hospital. From this we can conclude that the Administrators and Doctors had freedom to plan their work, irrespective of size, and the PTM staff did not enjoy the same freedom.

Participation at Higher Level

The survey result revealed that managerial decisions were taken by the investors. The Administrators had limited opportunity while the Doctors and the PTM staff had low or very low opportunity to influence managerial decisions. The fact that even the Doctor, who is central in making decisions regarding patient care activities, starting from diagnosis, investigations and treatment, did not have much say in the management is quite surprising and does not augur well for these organizations. On the whole, the results indicate that there existed little opportunity for employees to influence managerial decisions, thereby making it amply clear that there was no effective ascending participation.

Considering ascending and descending participation together, it is obvious that the *Administrators had moderate participation at the higher level and high level of influence over the lower level. The Doctors reported poor ascending participation with high level of descending participation,* which could be explained by their unique professional authority. *The PTM staff had low level of ascending and relatively low level of descending participation.* Taken together, all these factors indicate *poor employee participation in management activities in private hospitals.*

Informal Participation

Informal consultation was there among all employees, but its degree was low with the PTM staff. When comparing *small*, *medium* and *large* hospitals, informal consultation was found present in all the three types of hospitals; however, it was more in *medium* hospitals than in *small* and *large* hospitals.

From the results the obvious conclusion is that informal consultation, the least effective form of participative management, *was prevalent* in hospitals. In the hospital settings, as time is an important factor, it is very difficult and cumbersome to arrange formal meetings and take decisions regarding issues which require immediate solution. So, depending on situations, whenever necessary, the persons actually in the field will be consulted informally and decisions taken. Such being the situation in any hospital, it is quite natural that so many of the employees acknowledge the fact that there is informal consultation.

Regarding the extent of influence of informal consultation, the majority of the Administrators gave a *good* rating about their influence in managerial decisions through informal discussions, while both the Doctors and the PTM staff gave *average* to *low* rating regarding their influence in management decisions. The relatively low rating given by the Doctors and the PTM staff indicates that the Administrators by virtue of their position or proximity to the owners are imposing decisions on other staff rather than making joint decisions. Hence, it may be inferred that though *there is good amount of informal consultations in hospitals,* it cannot be counted as a true manifestation of participative management.

Team Work in Hospitals

The survey result revealed that 'the extent of superiors' ability to promote team work' as well as 'the extent of team work' existing in the private hospitals in Kerala was *good.*

Hospitals, unlike other industries, where the whole unit can be considered as a team, are run by multiple task-centred teams. Each patient care activity is carried out by a team comprising a limited category of workers only, and the satisfaction level expressed by an employee can only be taken as that of this task-oriented small team. This sort of teams, even though limited to a few categories of employees, lead to cross-category involvement of employees in a task. This is inevitable in each and every patient care activity, and as such, there is no task or platform other than celebrations or formal events which can bring all the staff in a hospital together as a team. Participation cutting across categories as a concept in the true sense is far different from this task-oriented team approach. Hence, we can safely conclude that the satisfaction expressed by employers in team work is *not an indicator of the presence of participative management.*

Employee's Participation through Committees

There is total absence of committees in any form in *small* hospitals; only a small percentage of *medium* and *large* hospitals have it to a limited extent.

In hospitals, joint committees can be considered as the single most effective mechanism by which participative management can at least be attempted. From the total absence of committees in any form in *small* hospitals and very small percentage of hospitals in the *medium* and *large* sectors having committees, it is apparent that there is *no effective participative management.*

In all hospitals where there are committees, the *members are nominated by the management* and there is *not even a single elected representative.* Hence, the members of such committees cannot be considered as true employee representatives and their views and decisions will be in line with those of the management rather than those of the employees. So, the obvious conclusion is that even in hospitals where committees are present, the mode of selection of members *negates the true concept of participative management.*

In the hospitals where there are committees, the existing *tenure of office of members of committees is unlimited 'until transfer or retirement whichever is earlier'*. This *unlimited tenure,* coupled with the *undemocratic selection* of the members, would *lead only to near total absence of true employee representation* in committee meetings.

The analysis apparently leads to the conclusion that the committees wherever they are present seemed to be effective on all parameters and particularly in 'its involvement in patient care', according to the Administrators, Doctors and PTM staff of *medium* hospitals and Administrators of *large* hospitals.

It seemed highly unlikely that this positive response was actually due to effective employee participation in management through committees. The nomination of committee members by management and unlimited tenure of office of members of the committee, in effect, annul the true concept of participative management. Hence, it is concluded that *the high rating of effectiveness of committees can be due rather to overt or covert coercion by the management* than to employee participation in management.

The observations made in the field survey revealed that the management called the 'Heads of Departments' or "In-charges of Departments' for committee meetings and the committee meetings in many institutions were just rituals with no meaningful discussion or decision. A management-nominated committee is usually biased and the true problems of lower level employees are not taken up earnestly. Furthermore, the HOD being a member of the committee which is close to the controlling authority, the subordinate staff is naturally forced to toe the line with the HOD.

Control and Participation

The survey results revealed that irrespective of the size of the hospitals, the private hospitals in Kerala were *controlled by the investors only*.

Doctors who have high status in the hospital and are the actual decision makers regarding patient care had good control over the PTM staff. Doctors, though not promoting participative management, directly or indirectly control or coordinate the activities of others to ensure better patient care.

All these factors together indicate *poor employee participation existing in management activities in the private hospitals of Kerala.*

Feasibility of Participative Management in Private Health Care Industry in Kerala

Opinion about Managing Personnel

The analysis revealed that the majority of the employees from all categories wanted hospitals to be controlled by 'the investor' only because they felt that the controlling authority should be a single source.

Doctors and the PTM staff were unanimous in their opinion that 'non-medical professional administrator' would not be efficient in managing a hospital. A 'Doctor without professional training in management' also was considered to be *average* in his capacity to run a hospital efficiently. *Good* rating was given for: (*i*) 'Doctor with professional training in management'; (*ii*) jointly by non-medical professional administrator and doctors; and (*iii*) a committee consisting of representatives from all cadres. Of the three choices with *good* rating, '*Doctor with professional training in management'* was the most preferred and a 'committee consisting of representatives of all cadres' came only third. Hence it is concluded that, as per the opinion of Doctors and the PTM staff, *the highest level of efficiency in managing a hospital would be achieved when it was managed by Doctors with professional training in management*. Here, the belief that medical knowledge and management skill ought to be combined was found strong.

The satisfaction of the Doctors and the PTM staff was 'good' if working under any of the following parties in the order of their preference:

(*a*) Doctor with professional training in management; or
(*b*) Non-medical professional Administrator and Doctors; or
(*c*) A committee consisting of representatives from all cadres.

Non-medical managers simply will not understand the needs and priorities in health care delivery. If they are in control, then clinical care will be effectively dictated by people who do not have the ability to comprehend it. In other words, the reason why doctors should get involved in management is that, if doctors do not take collective actions to rationalize their own behaviour, then others will seize on this evidence and use it for their own, probably unacceptable, ends.

The *Doctors felt that the control of the PTM staff should be with them* and not with a Non-medical Administrator. The PTM staff of different types of hospitals opined that their professional relationship with the treating physician was 'good'. This presence of good professional relationship between the PTM staff and Doctors enables us to conclude that *the PTM staff did feel comfortable to work under Doctor-managers*.

The observation revealed that the Doctors and the PTM staff from *all the different types of hospitals* opined that coordination was a better option than control, to a 'good' extent. The obvious conclusion is that both Doctors and the PTM staff viewed coordination among staff as the most viable proposition for efficient patient care activities.

Concept of Participative Management

All *categories of employees, irrespective of the size of the hospital, have a uniform concept regarding participative management, (ie) 'participation in all management functions but not in ownership'.* It is interesting to note that all categories of employees have in-depth understanding regarding participative management as revealed by the low rating given to informal consultation and limited extent participation in management Also, the employees are practical in their outlook as they don't conceptualize participation in ownership.

Forms of Participation

The analysis revealed that, as a whole, the majority of the respondent Administrators, Doctors and the PTM staff suggested *consultative participation as the best form of participation.* Another point noticed in the findings from *small* hospitals was that the Administrators and Doctors (who were part of the ownership) reported that informative participation, the least effective form of participation, was enough, while the PTM staff expected consultative participation, thereby making it apparent that many *small-sized* hospitals were being run in a totalitarian way.

The majority of the employees opined 'consultative participation' as the best form of participation. Even though the employees do not want joint decision making and collective bargaining, they want to be consulted in all management activities. This could be due to the fact that each employee trained in a particular field could only give authentic suggestion regarding that field or do not want any management decision to affect him adversely.

Often, we are forced to conclude that as the age-old mindset of management and employees leading to distrust between them, any extent of participation beyond consultative participation is beyond the realms of their imagination.

Degrees of Participation Expected

There was no unanimity in the opinions of the Administrators, the Doctors and the PTM staff regarding the level of hierarchy at which the concept of participative management should operate. *The PTM* staff was the only group that gave the highest rating for starting from the bottom rather than starting simultaneously at all levels. This apparently was a reflection of the wish of the *PTM staff* for participation, thereby leading to *freedom in work at least at their level.* The Doctors' responses were divided between administrative level, departmental level and 'starting from below', from which no special conclusions could be drawn. The *Administrators'* opinions were more or less evenly distributed between administrative level and 'starting at the bottom', which denoted a reasonable understanding and willingness to accept the concept.

Opinion Regarding Sharing of Equal Powers

Most of the respondents did not favour the idea of giving equal powers to employee and manager representatives. The analysis revealed that the majority of all categories of the employees in all types of hospitals were of the idea that the power should be in the hands of the management only. Employees felt that they should be given freedom to express their opinion, and that all reasonable suggestions from them should be considered before taking important managerial decisions.

The *reasons for favouring equal powers to managers' and employees' representatives* were analyzed, and the majority of the employees viewed that 'without equal powers the very intention behind the scheme will be defeated'.

The *reasons for not favouring equal powers to managers' and employees' representatives* were analyzed. The analysis revealed that all *the reasons* suggested, like: (*i*) The employee representatives might become manager-representatives, trade unions becoming managerial organizations; (*ii*) The joint forum might degenerate into a collective bargaining counter or an arena for ego clash; (*iii*) Employee representatives might develop hunger for power and cease to represent employees; and (*iv*) Employee representatives might be lacking in managerial competence and executive capacity, were the reasons contributing to the opinion against granting equal powers to manager and employee representatives.

Extent of Participation

The survey reveals that only a limited number of employees were competent to take managerial responsibility. They hoped that in hospitals, an institution dealing with human lives, where experience is very important, control should not be disbursed to incapable and inexperienced persons.

From the results, it may be concluded that there is not much scope for increasing the extent of participation of employees in management to high levels. But the important point is that, as per the survey data, the employees who are competent to participate in management can effectively represent the employees found incompetent. Lack of competence to participate is the belief behind centralized control and unwillingness to share power.

Committees and Participation

The opinion of the majority of all categories of employees regarding the *mode of selection of members of the committee* was in favour of retaining the existing system, i.e., through 'nomination by management'; the second best option expressed was 'through consensus'. Regarding Administrators and Doctors, this result was understandable, as by both nomination and consensus the employee representative most likely would be a person who toes the management's line. Furthermore, this would reflect the innate distrust of the management towards lower level employees. What was quite unexpected was the response of the PTM staff who also favoured nomination by management. This could be due to many factors like:

(*i*) Absence of committees in a majority of hospitals, leading to lack of proper knowledge about their functioning;

(*ii*) The PTM staff is subordinated to such an extent that they are afraid to demand an election;

(*iii*) HODs or in-charges are nominated by the management in committees, and as the PTM staff has to work under the HODs and in-charges at Departmental level, they don't want to antagonize them by speaking against their nomination.

Another mode of selection which got good rating was by *consensus*. This can be easily explained by the work culture of hospital where cooperation rather than confrontation is the rule.

The majority of the employees were of the opinion that the tenure of office of the members of the committee 'should not be more than three years'. This would not only go a long way in proper implementation of participative management but also neutralize to a reasonable extent the negative impact of the mode of selection of committee members through nomination by management. When the tenure of office is only for three years, everybody in a cadre is likely to get a chance to be an employee representative. This new blood in committees can be expected to infuse recent, novel and innovative ideas in hospital management which could be beneficial to all.

For or against Implementing Participative Management

Though the majority of the employees accepted the inherent benefits of the concept and was willing to implement it in any industrial organization, a significant number of employees expressed objection to it in the health care industry as a special situation. For employees, it is still an indigestible concept for the health care sector.

The *responses from the various categories of staff who favoured participative management, regarding their reasons* for doing so, were more or less evenly distributed among the choices: (*i*) to get better understanding and cooperation between management and employees; (*ii*) to improve coordination in the functioning of the hospital; (*iii*) to improve efficiency in patient care; and (*iv*) to offer opportunity for prior consultation. Of these choices, to *improve coordination* in the functioning of the hospital and to *improve efficiency* in patient care got slightly higher ratings. From this, we can conclude that there was no single reason for favouring participative management, but the employees, being aware of all its positive aspects, favoured its implementation.

Reasons for favouring implementing participative management but not in hospitals were analyzed. The majority of the respondents gave the reason that 'non-medical employees cannot be allowed to have a say in the running of hospitals', as human lives are at stake.

Reasons for not favouring implementing participative management were also analyzed and it revealed that 'no employee is professionally or temperamentally competent to assume managerial responsibility' and 'the committee would degenerate into a body in which employees' grievances will dominate discussions'. These are the grounds for the major objections to the implementation of participative management.

In the light of these responses, it was found that more than two-thirds of the employees favoured the implementation of participative management in an organization. Of those who favoured it, a significant number were highly sceptical about its implementation in the hospital setup. Further analyzing the reasons for the responses, we could safely come to the conclusion that the main objection aired by those who were against its implementation in hospital was *not against the concept but against one important aspect, namely,* the possibility of *'non-medical employees taking decisions' on the* running of an organization whose prime objective is patient care, in which human lives are involved.

Statutory Participation

The majority of the Doctors and the PTM staff from *small, medium* and *large* hospitals were in *favour* of making participative management statutory while the majority of the *Administrators* from different types of hospitals were *not in favour* of making it statutory. This revealed that the majority of the Administrators who favoured implementation of participative management were against making it statutory, either due to their inherent, inflexible and condescending mindset or due to lack of trust in employees or their capacity to take management decisions. The Doctors and the PTM staff favoured making it statutory, thereby revealing that, with the present set up, there was little or no scope for their effective participation in management and that they saw statutory participative management as the only feasible means for that.

Reasons favouring statutory participation revealed that *compulsion in the form of statutory regulation only will bring the management and employees together,* thereby implementing participative management.

Reasons not favouring statutory participation were also analyzed. The obvious finding was that *compulsory participation would not yield the same results as voluntary participation.* Furthermore, a statute would not eradicate the existing distrust between the management and the employees. This leads to the conclusion that participative management need not be made statutory because the successful implementation of this scheme depends more upon the willingness of both the parties, i.e., a mental change from both the employees and managers, than making it statutory.

Participative Management in Kerala

The majority of the Administrators and the PTM staff felt that participative management 'will not be successful' in Kerala. But a significant number of employees gave the verdict that it would be successful in Kerala, but not in the health care industry. If these responses were counted along with those supporting that it would be successful in hospitals also, the scale would tilt in favour of the opinion that *it would be successful in Kerala.*

The opinions of the employees regarding the *reasons for the success of participative management in Kerala* were analyzed. The majority of the respondents opined that 'Kerala has an educated politicized and socially conscious labour force that can be trained in managerial functions' and so participative management would be successful in Kerala.

The majority of the employees, irrespective of their category, from different types of hospitals thought that *participative management would be successful, but not in the health care industry in Kerala, because non-medical staff could not be entrusted with the task of decision making in an institution that deals with human lives.* So, the obvious conclusion is that the employees were not against the concept of participative management. So, as a whole, the positive responses received regarding this aspect can also be taken as the voice of those who felt that participative management would be successful in Kerala.

The opinions of the employees regarding the *reasons for the failure of participative management in Kerala* were analysed. The discussion leads to the conclusion that the main reason contemplated for the failure of the scheme was 'management's unwillingness to come forward to introduce this scheme'.

So, the obvious conclusion is that the employees were not against the concept as they expressed that participative management would be a success in Kerala. So, as a whole, the positive responses received regarding this aspect can also be taken as the voice of those who felt that participative management would be successful in Kerala.

Hurdles to Participative Management

A comparison across the different categories of employees in different types of hospitals revealed that: (*i*) the mere advisory nature of the existing participative bodies; (*ii*) inter-and intra-departmental rivalries; (*iii*) lack of education and managerial training among employee representatives and their lack of self-confidence; (*iv*) restriction on employee representatives' opportunity to voice their views; and (*v*) managements' flair of superiority and the consequent distrust between managerial and employee-representatives, were actually the hurdles to making participative management a success. A good number of the PTM staff had opined that lack of education and managerial training among employee representatives as well as their lack of self-confidence was the main hurdle to making participative management a success.

Test of the Hypotheses

The analysis of the data collected substantiates the different hypotheses set for the study. The first hypotheses was tested by using Two-way Anova test and second by Factor Analysis. The remaining hypotheses were tested by using Chi-square Test.

$\mathbf{H_1}$: The extent of satisfaction regarding *communication system* for different parameters *relating to communication* were collected and the differences in the mean level *among different categories, types of hospitals and their interaction* were *statistically* examined. The test revealed that the *mean difference by category, type of hospital* and their *interaction effect* on all the different parameters studied were *statistically insignificant.*

When comparing the views of Administrators, Doctors and the PTM staff, all parties had a *good rating about the effectiveness of the communication system.* Also, the comparison across small, medium and large hospitals revealed *no difference* and the effectiveness of the communication system received no significant difference in the rating.

$\mathbf{H_2}$: Data regarding the factors which motivate the employees of the private hospitals in Kerala were collected and analyzed. The analysis revealed that for all categories of employees in all types of hospitals, the *remuneration package is the major motivating factor.* This brings to the fore the stark reality that the finer aspects of motivation like 'non-interference in one's work', 'opportunity to participate in management decision', and 'opportunity to participate in decisions connected with the job' can become determinants only when the basic factors like salary and job security are met.

$\mathbf{H_3}$: The association between 'form of participation' and 'different types of hospitals' was statistically examined and the analysis revealed that there is *statistically significant association* between 'form of participation' and 'different types of hospitals'.

The analysis leads to the conclusion that *informative participation, the least effective among all forms of participation, was widely prevalent in hospitals* irrespective of their size. However, its presence was more prevalent in the *small* and *medium* scale sector. Even though the prevalence of 'consultative participation', which is slightly better than informative participation, was more in *large*-sized hospitals, the difference was not statistically significant. The most noteworthy point is the *total absence of joint decision making or collective bargaining, which is a true indicator of effective participative management, in any of the small, medium or large hospitals.*

H_4 : The association between 'the parties controlling the hospital' and 'different types of hospitals' were statistically tested and the analysis revealed that there was *no statistically significant association* between the parties controlling the hospital and the different types of hospitals. This leads to the conclusion that irrespective of the size of the hospitals, the private hospitals in Kerala were controlled by the investors only.

H_5 : The association between 'tenure of office of the members of the committee' and 'different types of hospitals' was statistically examined and it revealed that there was *no statistically significant association* between tenure of office of the members of the committees in different types of hospitals. It was found that the existing tenure of office of members of committees was unlimited i.e., 'until transfer or retirement whichever is earlier' in different types of hospitals.

H_6 : The association between opinions about 'the concept of participation' in different categories of staff in different types of hospitals was statistically examined and the analysis revealed statistically significant association between the opinions on 'the concept of participation' and the Doctors and the PTM staff in different types of hospitals. For administrators, the association was found statistically insignificant.

It was concluded that all categories of employees, irrespective of the size of the hospital, have a uniform concept regarding participative management, i.e., 'participation in all management functions but not in ownership'.

H_7 : The association between opinions about 'implementation of participative management' and different categories of staff in different types of hospitals was statistically examined and the test revealed that there was no statistically significant association between the opinions on 'implementation of participative management' and the different categories of staff in different types of hospitals.

H_8 : The association between 'opinion on the success or not of this scheme in Kerala' and different categories of staff in different types of hospitals was statistically examined and it revealed that there was no statistically significant association between the opinions on 'success of this scheme in Kerala' and the Administrators and PTM staff in different types of hospitals. But with regard to Doctors, the association was found statistically significant.

SUGGESTIONS

In the light of the aforesaid findings about the various aspects relating to participative management practices, the researcher would like to suggest a model for effective implementation of participative management in the private hospitals of Kerala.

Before suggesting such a model, many factors need to be considered. First and foremost is that the hospital is a private enterprise and it goes without saying that profit is one of the prime motives. But being an institution concerned with human health and lives, a significant number of humanitarian and social considerations come into play. Striking a balance between the investor and employee interests, resulting in optimum patient care, should be its main objective. The survey results are balanced and obviously give due importance to all the aspects considered.

The broader framework for implementation of participative management has been obtained by analyzing the survey data. Keeping this in mind, the researcher would like to suggest the following model.

Three-tier Participative Management Model

A three-tier participative model is suggested with Work Committee at the grass root level followed by Inter-Departmental Committee at the intermediate level and Joint Management Committee at the top level. The model, the structural role positions and Committee workings are explained below.

Ownership and Control

The legally binding authority or the *owner is the investor and hence the controlling authority*. This has been proved in the survey also, where the employees neither expect nor wants any part in ownership. This leaves the investor free to make policy decision, and handle financial matter or any other matter, as he deems fit, for the profitable functioning of the institution. Moreover, in an institution engaged in patient care activities, it is advisable that authority emanates from a single source, thus minimizing or eliminating conflicts of ideas and that every employee from top to bottom has a clear cut idea regarding his position, role, duties and responsibilities, as stated in the Organization Structure. In summary, participation in ownership is not practical in the present scenario and as per the survey not desired by the employees too.

Management Personnel

The next issue is who should be running the hospital as a day-to-day routine as per the policy guidelines of ownership, with the cooperation of employees whose demands and aspirations are met, while keeping in mind the nuances of patient care, as human lives are at stake. The analysis of the primary data has clearly spelt out that it is a *doctor, with professional management qualification, who should manage a hospital.* One informal observation during the survey is that in most of the hospitals a doctor with professional management qualification doesn't seem to find a place in the hierarchy.

Over and above, a good number of employees who support the concept of participative management are apprehensive about implementing it in hospitals, for the sole reason that a ***non-medical person cannot make decisions regarding the running of a hospital as human lives are involved.*** Hence, as per the employees' opinion, only a medical person can be allowed to take decisions regarding the management of a hospital and non-medical and even paramedical employees are not expected to take management decisions. Further, with the growing complexity of modern-day hospital set up, professional management qualification must be mandatory for the proper administration of the hospital. So a doctor with qualification in professional management should hold the key post for the proper running of the hospital and implementing participative management without compromising the patient welfare.

Clinical Director

It is in this context that the researcher would like to suggest a new cadre of management personnel called *'Clinical Director'*. The Clinical Director should:

(*i*) be a doctor;

(*ii*) have professional management degree;

(*iii*) be sufficiently senior to command the respect of all cadres of employees;

(*iv*) have firsthand experience in hospital administration;

(*v*) have rapport with the owner and not be the owner or part of ownership;

(*vi*) have rapport with all categories of employees;

(*vii*) be receptive to newer concepts and innovation; and

(*viii*) have freedom and authority to take decisions regarding the function of both clinical and non-clinical departments.

The number of Clinical Directors in a hospital can vary according to the size of the hospital, from one in a small hospital to a Board of Clinical Directors in large corporate hospitals. The mode of selection of the Clinical Directors, considering the work culture of a hospital, can be through consensus (even though a secret ballot may be ideal) among the investors and all the employees. This would not be difficult, as the majority of the Doctors and the PTM staffs were of the opinion that Clinical Directors would be the most efficient in management and that they were willing to work under a Doctor with management qualification. The tenure of office of Clinical Directors can also be three years, as suggested for committees in the survey.

Regarding the *duties of the Clinical Director,* ideally, he should be the ultimate authority in matters concerning the day-to-day running of the hospital. But with the explosion of specialties, investigation and other facilities and the multi-faceted nature of recent-day patient care requiring the services of so many personnel who are specialized in their own fields, the Clinical Directors cannot effectively manage a hospital all alone. Moreover, as matrix design rather than one-line authority is prevalent in hospitals, it is imperative that there should be a set of Administrators or Assistant Administrators or HODs who assist the Clinical Directors. Hence, the work of Clinical Directors becomes more of coordination rather than control, as envisaged by employees in our study. Under each of the Administrators/Assistant Administrators will be nonclinical employees, either based on category or task, while the clinical departments will function under HODs under whom will be the doctors and many other categories of employees concerned with a particular field, i.e., patient care by that department.

Implementation of Participative Management

The next step is to study the actual *implementation of participative management* in this complex hierarchical setup, keeping in mind the various conclusions arrived at like:

(*i*) freedom to decide about their work;

(*ii*) consultative participation in all managerial decisions but not joint decision making or collective bargaining;

(*iii*) no need for equal powers;

(*iv*) nominated/consensus committee members;

(*v*) no statutory status for members; and

(*vi*) PTM not allowed to take decisions in hospital management.

A confrontationist type of militant trade unionism is absent in hospitals, and strikes have been identified as unjustifiable by almost all the employees.

In such a set up, the employees want to participate in all management decisions through consultation. Hence, the only option through which such participation can be implemented is **committees**. But the greatest difficulty is in formulating a viable committee in a hospital, where there is a very wide gap between the different categories of employees, intellectually, academically, socially and financially.

Over and above, there are so many functional units in a hospital which can only be considered together, even though employees from the highest to the lowest cadre as a team provide patient care activity. For example, the various clinical departments like Medicine, Gynaecology, Paediatrics, Radiology, Pathology, and so on, vary in their function but have a common aim, patient care. Hence, the researcher would like to suggest a *Work Committee* for each functional unit at the grass roots level.

Even though compartmentalization as functional units and departments is easy on paper, in actual practice, every patient care activity requires the services of more than one functional unit and at times many. For example, a patient being treated under the Surgery unit depends on the Radiology Unit for X-rays, the Microbiology Department for bacterial studies, the Catering Department for his food requirements, and so on. Each of these departments may have its own requirements, mode of functioning and limitations in resources. Hence, for smooth patient care activity, a high level of co-ordination among the departments is mandatory. Proper participation of employees or employee representatives for each of these departments is of utmost importance in coordinating the patient care activities of these departments. The researcher would therefore suggest a second tier Committee, *Inter-Departmental Committee,* above the Work Committee, in which the employees can participate in taking decisions regarding the running of hospitals.

The next level at which participation can be mooted is a level above the Inter-Departmental Committees, i.e., at the highest level of hospital administration. Before deciding on participation at this level certain important factors are to be considered. Foremost is the fact that, a hospital being a private institution, the investor's interest is to be considered and profitability guaranteed. However, being an institution that deals with human lives, profitability can't be the motive at the expense of patient care either qualitatively or quantitatively. In this context, a satisfied employee can meet the interests of both the investor and the patient as improved patient care benefits the patient and in turn increases profitability. So, involvements of employees or employee representatives at this level can only further the employee commitment towards the organization. Hence, the researcher would like to recommend a *Joint Management Committee* which is the top administrative body of a hospital. It would contain employee representatives, but as envisaged in our study, should not be in a position to influence decisions which can adversely affect patient care in any way.

One unique point, especially regarding patient care activities, is that as the health care need of each patient is unique, unexpected, situational problems or management bottlenecks may arise which require immediate decisions and which can't wait for any committee. So, a single point authority to solve such emergency situation is a must in any hospital set up. Hence, all hospitals should have a *Clinical Director* with sufficient authority to take such need-based decisions without which a hospital cannot function effectively. Decisions so taken by the Clinical Director can be ratified in the Joint Management Committee in its next sitting.

Next, the researcher would like to explore each of these committees with reference to its:

— structure and constitution;
— terms of reference;
— process at each level; and
— parameters to evaluate the participation of elected and nominated members with special reference to the employee participation angle.

1. Work Committees

The Work Committees can be classified as *medical or non-medical*. The core function of any hospital is patient care and grass roots level problem-solving starts through primary examination and clinical testing of patients. Hence, Medical Work Committees are the key source in the participative models. The number of Medical Work Committees depends on the functional medical units in the hospital.

However, due support from office administration and maintenance units is inevitable for comprehensive patient care, for which non-medical Work Committees function.

(i) Work Committees—Medical

Even though the Work Committee is considered as the grass roots level *Committee in Clinical Departments,* there are many unique features in a hospital when compared to a low level committee in any other industry. In an industry, the grass roots level committee would be formed by the lowest category of employees with or without junior managers. But, in a hospital, the patient care activities revolve around the treating physician who takes most of the decisions regarding patient care, which can be broadly seen under two heads—(*a*) professional decisions; and (*b*) non-professional patient support activities. All decisions regarding the former – diagnosis, treatment, surgery and so on are absolute and do not in any way come under the purview of any committee or level of participation. Moreover, the treating physician is legally responsible and answerable for his decisions, and he cannot hide behind any committee.

In addition, all the activities carried out by the PTM staff regarding any patient are as per the explicit instructions of the treating physician. Hence, the Work Committee of a clinical department should essentially be one that *coordinates activities* rather than *controls* them, as the survey results showed. At this level, a non-medical administrator has no relevance and the committee can be headed only by the head of the unit who is medico-legally responsible along with two junior staff- one Doctor and one PTM staff whose role is consultative, in line with our survey results.

The Work Committee can consider matters like diagnostic approach, clinical tests, nursing care, house keeping, hygiene, patient preparation, theatre preparation, instrument sterilization, resource mobilization, and so on.

From the above discussion, it becomes apparent that though considered by the grass roots level committee, it involves the treating specialist to the attender. Work Committees- Medical, may comprise the following members:

Convener—Head of the clinical department and two junior staff—one Doctor and one PTM staff.

The treating physician by consensus is the head of the Work Committee, and the other members can be selected by consensus, seniority or election, as suggested in the survey. The tenure of office can be fixed as three years, as obtained from our survey results.

(ii) Work Committee—Non-medical can be of two categories: Work Committee Front office and Work Committee Integrated Services.

Work Committee—Front Office, unlike clinical departments, can be more like what is seen in industries with professional administrators. The Committee members would be:

(*a*) Convener—Chief Medical Superintendent;

(*b*) Chairman—Administrator (non-medical); and

(*c*) Two nominated/elected staff of front office (not Doctors).

The terms of reference of the Work Committee are receptions, waiting time management, customer enquiries, dealing with patient complaints and grievances, conveying hospital services, public relations, etc. Here also the member's tenure can be fixed as 3 years.

Work Committee—Integrated Services, may comprise the following members:

(*i*) Convener—Clinical Director,

(*ii*) Chairman—In-house Officer; and

(*iii*) Two nominated/elected staff from Integrated Service Department.

The terms of reference of the Work Committee are co-ordination between functional units, use of common resources, assessment of unit level impact on patient care, documentation of patient history, data base management, hospital information system, maintenance of common facilities, infrastructure support, etc. Here also, the member's tenure can be fixed as 3 years.

As one of the major findings in our study is that a non-medical person cannot make decisions in hospital management, the above two Work Committees' decision should be ratified by the Clinical Director who is medically qualified. The decisions of the Work Committees are 'Implementable Decisions' (ID) and 'Implementable subject to ratification (I/R) Decisions'.

Inter-departmental Committee

This forms the second tier in the model, as already suggested. It is constituted with the following members:

(*i*) Convener—Clinical Director;

(*ii*) Chairman—Chief Medical Administrator/Non-Medical Administrator;

(*iii*) Chairman of the concerned Work Committee, and

(*iv*) One consensus/nominated/elected member from each Work Committee.

The scope of this committee is wide. It has to take up all issues brought to its notice by the Work Committee. It should be the coordinator/arbitrator between the various Work Committees, which have to work in coordinated manner. It should be the authority referring issues to the Joint Management Committee. Also, it is the hub for upward, downward and lateral communication of decisions, reports, and feedback and performance appraisals. The tenure of office of this committee can also be fixed at 3 years. The elected members from Work Committees can participate in this Committee.

Joint Management Committee

This is the topmost decision making committee in a hospital with employee participation. The membership pattern suggested is as follows:

(*i*) Chairman—Managing Director/Chief Executive Officer of the hospital;

(*ii*) Two nominated Directors - of which one should be a Clinical Director;

(*iii*) Conveners of Work Committees and Interdepartmental Committees;

(*iv*) One Responsible Representative (RR) - Responsible Representative is an external member from the society. She/he should be an educated, independent and well-informed person who reflects the true feelings and aspirations of patients, and

(*v*) Eight elected members - Four each from Doctors and the PTM staff (depending upon the size of the hospital)

This is the highest decision-making body and the presence of employee representatives allows the employees directly to participate in the decision-making. Here also, the tenure of the nominated, consensus or elected candidate can be fixed as three years.

Irrespective of whether the committee be of the low level or high level, for employee participation to be effective, all the members should be given due importance and there should be free flow of ideas in either direction.

There would be exclusive decisions reserved for the Joint Management Committee and, in addition, they would decide on issues referred to them by the Work Committees and Inter-departmental Committees. The final decision based on Work Committees and Inter-departmental Committees will be taken by the Joint Management Committee with a right to withhold decisions of lower Committees, considering consequences and implications.

A diagram showing the suggested Model for the implementation of Participative Management is given in figure 7.1. *(See on next page)*

For committees to be effective, the following basic *processes* should be followed in their meetings:

(*i*) Sourcing information from all levels of employees regarding the day-to-day functioning plus their creative suggestions;

(*ii*) Studying the information so gathered and understanding its implications in patient care and employee efficiency;

(*iii*) Thorough cordial discussion with all the committee members about the problem or process;

(*iv*) Getting expert opinion when needed;

(*v*) Reaching a decision by consensus and implementing it with the co-operation of the whole unit.

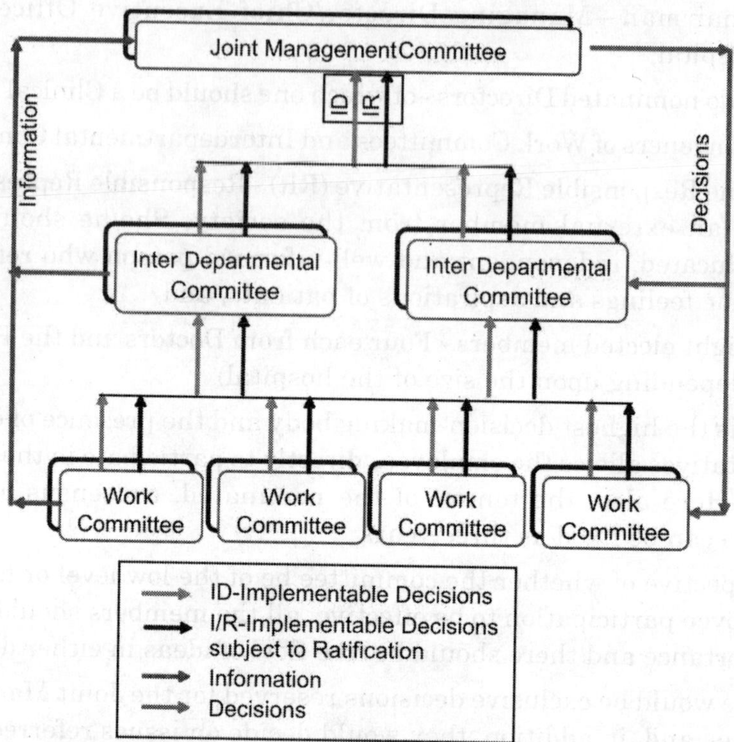

Fig 7.1. Model for the implementation of Participative Management

Note: The number of Work Committees and Inter Departmental committees may vary depending on the number of departments and variety of services provided by each hospital.

There should be a mechanism for the **review** of the results of a decision implemented and to study its impact and ultimate success or failure in terms of the following parameters regarding its members:

(*i*) involvement in decision-making process;

(*ii*) efforts to seek information;

(*iii*) efforts and ability to elicit ideas and suggestions from other members;

(*iv*) Effort and ability to accurately assess pros and cons;

(*v*) contribution to the final decisions;

(*vi*) ability to communicate ideas and decisions convincingly.

Only such *evaluation* and corrective measures will help in fine-tuning the employee participation in management, which can ultimately result in a win-win situation for both the management and employees in private hospitals.

The study has revealed that all categories of employees in private hospitals have a reasonably clear concept regarding employee participation in management. Also, the desire of the employees to partake in such venture stands revealed. The understanding of the ground realities in a private hospital as well as the maturity of the employees by placing the institutional interest ahead of their personal interest is made amply clear as they opted for consultative participation through consensus or nominated representatives rather than for a collective bargaining through elected representatives. With all this in mind, the researcher has suggested the above model for employee participation in management, which is believed to be both effective and practical.

Participation is not something that can be forced upon someone. In Kerala, or for that matter anywhere in the world, it can't be brought about by unions or statutory laws. Participation in its true sense can only be brought about by appropriate mindset of both the employer and employee. It is high time that such mindset was nurtured at all levels of an institution like a hospital where it can produce amazing results.

The researcher sincerely hopes that this humble beginning through the suggested model would in future usher in a change in mindset of all concerned, resulting in extra-efficient hospitals which reap rich dividends for the society at large.

SCOPE FOR FURTHER RESEARCH

During the review of literature and survey for data collection, it was observed that there is vast potential for research on various aspects of hospital management. The general belief is that the failure of health care institutions is essentially born out of inefficient management. Therefore, there is the need to investigate further the finer aspects and various dimensions of Human Resource Management in general and especially the concept of Participative Management. The researcher would like to suggest the following areas for further research:

(*i*) This study is confined to the participation of employees in the management of private allopathy hospitals in the State of Kerala. Further research may concentrate on the participation of employees in the management of Government hospitals, because the management style of government hospitals is different from that of private hospitals;

(*ii*) A comparison of the participation of employees of private and government hospitals in their management can be undertaken;

(*iii*) A comparative study on the management practices in private hospitals and other industries can be expected to yield fruitful results;

(*iv*) Comparative studies can also be conducted which should include private hospitals from other States so that a wide frame of reference may be developed;

(*v*) Case study analysis on Participative Models implemented in the health care segment of other nations and the implication of such models can be studied.

It is hoped that the present study would provide a base for further research in the above mentioned areas of health care institutions.

Bibliography

Books

Abdo S.Yazbeek and David H. Peters (Eds), *Health Policy Research in South Asia: Building Capacity for Reforms,* Washington: The World Bank, 2003.

Ajit K. Dala and Subha Ray (Eds), *Social Dimensions of Health,* Jaipur, Rawat Publications, 2005.

Albeda Erasmus, W. (Ed), *Participation in Management,* Rather dam, University Press, 1973.

Alexander S. Preker and Guy Carrin, *Health Financing for Poor People, Resource Mobilisation and Risk Sharing,* Washington: The World Bank, 2004.

Alexander, K.C., *Participative Management: the Indian Experience*, Delhi: Sri Ram Centre for Industrial Relations and Human Resources, 1972.

Alice Anne Andrews, *Manual of Medical Office Management*, Pennsylvania: WB Saunders Company, 1996.

Amrik Singh Sudan and Kumar N., *Management Process and Organisational Behaviour,* New Delhi: Anmol Publications Pvt. Ltd, 2003.

Anand, K.K., *Hospital Management: New Perspectives*, New Delhi: Vikas Publishing House, 1996.

Andrew Green and Ann Matthias, *Non Governmental Organisations and Health in Developing Countries,* New York: S T Martins Press Inc., 1997.

Andrew Green, *An Introduction to Health Planning in Developing Countries,* Tokyo: Oxford University Press, 1994.

Andrew Pearse and Matthias Stiefel, *Popular Participation Programme*, Switzerland: United Nations Research Institute for Social Development, 1980.

April Harding and Alexander S. Preker, *Private Participation in Health Services*, Washington: The World Bank, 2003.

Biswanath Ray, *Welfare, Choice and Development,* New Delhi: Kanishka Publications, 2001.

Brian Abel and Smith, *An Introduction to Health Policy, Planning and Financing,* New York: Longman Group Ltd., 1994.

Brian Abel, Smith Josep Figueras, *et al., Choices in Health Policy,* Singapore: Office for Official Publications of the European Committees, 1995.

Calum Paton, *Health Policy and Management*, London: Chapman & Hall, 1996.

Chantler, C., *Management Reform in a London Hospital—Managing for Health Result,* London: King's Fund, 1990.

Charney, C.Y., *The Instant Manager*, Great Britain: Kogan Page Ltd., 2001.

Christopher G Worley, *Implementing Participation Strategies in Hospitals: Correlates of Effective Problem Solving Teams*, California: School of Business and Management, 2006.

Clive Harris, *Private Participation in Infrastructure, Trends in Developing Countries in 1990-2001,* Washington: The World Bank, 2003.

Coile, R.C., *The New Medicine: Reshaping Medical Practice and Health Care Management,* Rockville: Aspen Publishers, 1990.

Colin Chase, John Garnett, *et al., Handbook of Management Skills,* Bombay: Jaico Publishing House, 1993.

Culyer, A.J., et al., *Competition in Health Care,* London: The Macmillan Press Ltd., 1990.

Davar, S.R., *Personnel Management and Industrial Relations,* New Delhi: Vikas Publishing House, 1976.

David Calkins, *et al.* (Eds), *Health care Policy*, USA: Blackwell Science, 1995.

David Calkins, Rushika J Fernandopulle, Bradley S.Marino, *Health Care Policy*, USA: Blackwell Science, 1995.

David H. Peters, et al., *Better Health Systems for India's Poor: Findings, Analysis and Options,* Washington: The World Bank, 2002.

David M Hansell and Brian Salter (Eds), *The Management of Health Care,* London: WB Saunders Company Ltd, 1995.

David M Hansell and Brian Salter (Eds), *The Management of Health Care*, London: W B Saunders Company Ltd, 1995.

David, K., *Human Behaviour at Work*, New York: McGraw-Hill, 1977.

Disken, S., Dixon, M., *et al., Models of Clinical Management*, London: Institute of Health Services Management, 1990.

Douglas McGregor, *Human Side of Enterprise*, New York: McGraw-Hill, 1960.

Duggal, R. and Amin, S., *Costs of Health Care, Household Survey in an Indian District*, Mumbai: Foundation for Research in Community Health, 1989.

Dunlop, R.J. and Hockley, J.M., *Hospital based Palliative Care Teams,* Oxford: Oxford University Press, 1998.

Durbin and Springall, *Organisation and Administration of Health Care: Theory, Practice, Environment,* The C.V. Mosby Company, 1969.

Einar Thorsrud and Fred E. Emery, *Form and Content of Industrial Democracy*, London: Tavistock Publications, 1969.

Eli Ginzberg, *Tomorrows Hospital: A Look to the Twenty-first Century,* London: Yale University Press, 1996.

Ellencweig, A.Y., *Analysing Health Systems,* Oxford: Oxford University Press, 1990.

Fremont E. Kast and James E. Rosenzweig, *Organisation and Management: A Systems Approach*, New York: McGraw- Hill Book Company, 1970.

Goel, S.L, *Health Care Organisation and Structure*, Delhi: Deep & Deep Publications Pvt. Ltd., 2004.

Goel, S.L., Modern Management Techniques, New Delhi: Deep & Deep Publications Pvt. Ltd., 2000.

Goel, S.L., *Health Care Management and Administration*, Delhi: Deep & Deep Publications Pvt. Ltd., 2004.

Goyal, R.C., *Human Resource Management in Hospitals,* New Delhi: Prentice-Hall of India, 1999.

Goyal, R.C., *Health Care Management and Administration*, Delhi: Deep and Deep Publications Pvt. Ltd., 2004.

Goyal, R.C, *Handbook of Hospital Personnel Management,* Delhi: Prentice Hall of India Pvt. Ltd., 1993.

Graham Moon and Rosemary Gillespie, *Society and Health,* London: Routledge, 1995.

Grey, B., *The Profit Motive and Patient Care,* Cambridge: Harvard University Press, 1991.

Griffiths, R., *The NHS Management Enquiry,* London: Department of Health and Social Security, 1983.

Gro Harlem Brundtland, *A World Without WHO..... Fifty Years of WHO in South East Asia,* New Delhi: World Health Organisation, 1999.

Gupta, J.P. and Sood, A.K., *Contemporary Public Health Policy Planning Management,* Delhi: Apothecaries Foundation, 2005.

Hansell, M. and Brian Salter, *The Management of Health Care: The Clinicians Management Hand Book*, London: WB Saunders Company Ltd, 1995.

Harrison, S., *Managing the National Health Service,* London: Campman and Hall, 1989.

Harrison, S., Hunter, D.J., et al., *Health before Health Care,* London: Institute for Public Policy Research, 1991.

Heinz Weihrich and Harold Koontz, *Management: A Global Perspective*, Singapore: Mc Graw-Hill Book Co, 1994.

Herzlinger, R., *Creating New Health Care Ventures,* Gaithersburg, Aspen Publishers, 1992.

Jack Durcan, W., Peter M. Ginter and Linda E. Swayne, *Hand Book of Health Care Management,* Oxford: Blackwell Publishers, 1998.

James A Willian, *Hospital Management,* Hong Kong: McMillan Education Ltd, 1990.

Jean Barrett, *Ward Management and Teaching,* Delhi: Konark Publishers Pvt. Ltd., 1989.

Jennifer, Rietbergen, *Participation and Social Assessment Tools and Techniques,* USA: Mc Cracken Deepa Narayan, 1998.

Jo Owen, *Management Stripped Bare,* Delhi: Koyan Page India Pvt. Ltd., 2003.

John and Shirley Payne, *Management How To Do It,* England: Gower Publishing Ltd., 1999.

John Gratto Liebler, Charles R. McConnell, *Management Principles for Health Professionals*, Mary Land: An Aspen Publication, 1999.

John J Glynn, David A Perkins and Simon Stewart (Eds), *A Management of Health Care: Achieving Value for Money,* Tokyo: W B Saunders Company Ltd., 1996.

John J. Hanlan, *Principles of Public Health Administration,* Saint Louis: The C.V. Mosby Company, 1969.

John Leslie Livingston, *Accounting for Social Goals*, New York: Hooper and Raw, 1974.

John Sutherst and Veronica Glasscott, *The Doctor Manager*, Tokyo: Churchill Livingstone, 1994.

Joseph L. Massie, *Essentials of Management*, Delhi: Prentice Hall of India Pvt. Ltd., 1985.

Judith Allsop and Linda Malcahy, *Regulating Medical Work Formal and Informal Controls,* Buckingham: Open University Press, 1996.

Keith Davis, Human *Relations at Work*, New York: McGraw-Hill Publishing Company, 1957.

Korrie de Koning and Marion Martin, *Participatory Research in Health Issues and Experiences,* United Kingdom: Redwood Books, 1996.

Kothari, C.R., *Quantitative Techniques,* Delhi: Vikas Publishing House Pvt. Ltd., 1991.

Kristi M. Branch, *Participative Management and Employee and Stakeholder Involvement,* Google.com.

Kumar, N. and Amrik Singh Sudan, *Management Process and Organisational Behaviour,* New Delhi: Anmol Publications, Pvt. Ltd.,2003.

Kumar, R., *Labour Participation in Management,* Delhi: Ajantha Publications, 1992.

Lallan Prasad and Bannerjee, A. M., *Management of Human Resources,* Delhi: Sterling Publishers Pvt. Ltd., 1985.

Lee, K. and Mills, A., *Policy Making and Planning in the Health Sector,* London: Croom Helm, 1982.

Lloyds G. Reynods, *Micro Economic Analysis and Policy*, New Delhi, Universal Book Stall, 1990.

Manoj Kumar Sankar, *Personnel Management*, Delhi: Crest Publishing House, 2000.

Martin Henser and Lauron Rose (Eds), Implementing Health Sector Reform in Central Asia, Washington: The World Bank, December 1998.

Martins, M. and David W. Dunlop, *An International Assessment of Health Care Financing- Lessons for Developing Countries-EDI,* Washington: The World Bank, November 1995.

Maurice Burrows, Roger Dyson and Peter Jackson, *Management for Hospital Doctors,* Great Britain: Bath Press Ltd., 1994.

Medical Services Development Committee, *Nursing Strategy; Towards the Year 2000,* Hong Kong: Hospital Authority of Hong Kong, 1995.

Melinda S. Meade and Robert J. Erickson, *Medical Geography,* New York: The Guilford Press, 2005.

Michael Armstrong, *A Handbook of Management Techniques,* London: Kogan Page Ltd, 1986.

Michael Harris, *Human Resource Management,* USA: The Dryden Press, 2000.

Michael M. Cernea, *Testing Bottom-up Planning*, The Building Blocks of Planning, Washington D.C: The World Bank, 1992.

Michael M. Cernera, *The Building Blocks of Participation,* Washington: The World Bank, 1992.

Michael Poole, *Workers' Participation in Industry,* London: Routledge & Kegan Paul Ltd, 1975.

Michael U. Klein-Bita Hadjimichael, *The Private Sector in Development Entrepreneurship, Regulation and Competitive Disciplines,* Washington: The World Bank, 2003.

Michael Ward, *Fifty Essential Management Techniques,* England: Gower Publishing Ltd., 1995.

Mohammed Akbar Ali Khan, *Hospital Management*, Delhi: A.P.H. Publishing Corporation, 1999.

Moi Ali, Stephen Brookson, *et al., Managing for Excellence,* Great Britain: 2001.

Nancy North and Yvonne Brakshaw (Eds), *Perspectives in Health Care,* Hong Kong: Macmillan, 1997.

Neville Bain, *Successful Management,* London: The Macmillan Press Ltd, 1995.

Oommen Philip, *Management of Hospitals: Text and Cases*, Trivandrum, Institute of Management in Government, 1990.

Parameswaran, E.G., *Perspective in HRD*, Hyderabad: Neelkamal Publication, 2003.

Peter D. Lucash, *Medical Practice Change Management: Strategies and Techniques for the Changing Business of Health Care*, Singapore: IRWIN Professional Publishing, 1997.

Peter Orton and John Fry, *UK Health Care: The Facts*, London: Kluwer Academic Publishers, 1995.

Pylee, M.V., *Worker Participation in Management: Myth and Reality,* Delhi: N.V Publications, 1975.

Radrabasavarj, M.N., *Dynamic Personnel Administration: Management of Human Resources*, Bombay: Himalaya Publishing Company, 1979.

Rajasenan D., Gerard de Groot, *Kerala Economy: Trajectories Challenges and Implications*, Cochin: Directorate of Publications and Public Relations, 2005.

Rao, V.S.P. and Narayana, P.S., *Management Concepts and Thoughts*, Delhi: Konark Publications Pvt. Ltd, 1987.

Rejasekharan Nair, K. *Evolution of Modern Medicine in Kerala,* Trivandrum: St. Mary's Press, 2001.

Rensis Likert, *New Patterns of Management*, New York: McGraw-Hill, 1961.

Richard Normann, *Service Management Strategy and Leadership in Service Business,* New York: John Wiley and Sons Ltd, 2000.

Rob Baggott, *Health and Health Care in Britain*, London: Macmillan Press Ltd, 1998.

Robert Blake and Jane S.Monton, *The Management Grid*, Texas: Gulf Publishing Co., 1964.

Rockwell Schulz, Alton C. Johnson, *Management of Hospitals and Health Services: Strategic Issues and Performance,* USA: Bread Books, 2005.

Rosemary Stewart (Ed), *Management of Health Care*, England, Dastmouth Publishing Company Ltd, 1998.

Rosemary Stewart (Ed), *Management of Health Care,* England: Dastmouth Publishing Company Ltd, 1998.

Russell F Whaley and Talal J Hashim, *A Text Book of World Health*, USA: The Parthenon Publishing Group, 1995.

Russell L Colling, *Hospital and Health Care Security,* Oxford: Butter worth Heinemann, 2001.

Rustom S. Davar, *The Management Process: The Principles of Management,* Madras: Progressive Corporation Private Ltd, 1978.

Saini, A. K., *Management Information System in Hospitals: A Computer-Based Approach for Quality in Hospital Services and Administration,* New Delhi: Deep & Deep Publications, 1999.

Sankara Rao, M., *Hospital Organization and Administration,* Delhi: Deep & Deep Publications, 1992.

Sara Bennett, Barbara McPake, Anne Mills, *Private Health Providers in Developing Countries*, USA: Zed Books, 1997.

Savita Sharma K'Cherry, *Hospital Management*, Delhi: Commonwealth Publishers, 1996.

Sheila Twinn, Barbara Roberts and Surah Andrews, *Community Health Care: Nursing Principles and Practice,* Oxford: Butterworth-Heinemann, 1996.

Shenoy, G.V., Sharma, S.C. and Srivastava, V.K., *Operations Research for Management*, Delhi: Willey Eastern Ltd., 1991.

Sheth, N.R., *The Joint Management Council: Problems and Prospects*, Delhi: Sri Ram Centre for Industrial Relations and Human Resources, 1972.

Shirley A White (Ed), *The Art of Facilitating Participation*. Delhi: Sage Publications, 1999.

Srinivasan, A.V. (Ed), *Managing a Modern Hospital*, Delhi: Response books, Sage Publications, 2000.

Steve Cropper and Paul Forte, *Enhancing Health Services Management,* USA: Open University Press, 1997.

Subratesh Ghosh, *Styles of Human Resource Management in India and Japan: A Comparative Study,* Calcutta: Indian Institute of Management, 1988.

Sudhir Dawra, *Hospital Administration and Management,* Delhi: Mohit Publications, Vol. II, 2002.

Syed Amin Tabish, *Hospital and Health Services Administration—Principles & Practice,* Oxford: Oxford University Press, 2001.

Thackur, C.P., Sethi K.C. (Eds), Industrial Democracy: Some Issues and Experiences, Delhi: Sri Ram Centre for Industrial Relations and Human Resources, 1973.

Tony White, *Text Book of Management for Doctors,* Tokyo: Churchill Livingstone, 1996.

Tuteja, S.K. (Ed), *Management Mosaic,* Delhi: Excel Books, 2005.

Venkat Reddy, *Hospital Materials Management*, New Delhi: Response Books, 2002.

Viswanathan, V. and Rohde, J.E., *Diarrhea in Rural India: A Nation-wide Study of Mothers and Practitioners,* New Delhi: Vision Books, 1990.

Whitmore, D.A., *Management for Administrators,* London: Heinemann Ltd, 1985.

William O Cleverley and Andrew E Cameron, *Essentials of Health Care Finance,* Canada: Jones and Bartlett Publishers, 2003.

Winston and Albright, *Practical Management Science,* Singapore, Thomson Asia Pvt. Ltd, 2002.

Wohl, S. *The Medical Industrial Complex,* New York: Harmony, 1984.

Yesudian, C.A.K., *Health Services Utilization in Urban India: A Study,* New Delhi: Mittal Publications, 1988.

Zivan Tanic, *Worker's Participation in Management: Ideal and Reality in India,* New Delhi: Shri Ram Centre for Industrial Relations, 1969.

Journals, Reports, Dissertations, Working Papers, Etc

Anand, K.K., 'Professionalising Management in Hospitals', *Paper presented at National Hospital Convention,* New Delhi: IHA, December 1985.

Anil Kumar, V., A Study of Human Resource Management in the Travancore Industries Ltd, M. Phil Dissertation, Kerala University, 1995.

Basu Gopa, 'A Study of Job Motivations of a Sample of Indian Executives', Unpublished Ph.D.Thesis, Banaras Hindu University, 1973.

Bhagyalakshmi Sankar, 'Human Resources Management in the Apollo Hospital Administration', Unpublished Ph.D.Thesis, Department of Public Administration, University of Madras, September 2000.

Brian Abel, Smith Josep Figueras, *et al., Choices in Health Policy- An Agenda for the European Union,* Luxembourg, Office for Official Publications of the European Communities, 1995.

Census of India 2001, Provisional Population, 'Report on Private Medical Institutions in Kerala-2004', *Department of Economics and Statistics,* Government of Kerala, Thiruvananthapuram, 2006.

Dayanandan, R., 'Human Resource Management in Co-operative Banks'. Unpublished Ph.D.Thesis, Kerala University, 1977.

Florence Eid, 'Hospital Governance and Incentive Design', *Policy Research Working Paper,* The World Bank, Operations Evaluation Department, 2001.

George, A., 'Household Health Expenditure in Madhya Pradesh, Mumbai', *Foundation for Research in Community Health,* 1993.

Government of Kerala, 'Health Care Infrastructure', *Economic Review 2005,* Thiruvananthapuram, State Planning Board, February 2006.

Government of Kerala, *Economic Review 2003,* Trivandrum, State Planning Board, Feb. 2006.

Government of Kerala, *Office Records,* Trivandrum, Directorate of Health Services, 2004.

Government of Kerala, *Report on Private Medical Institutions in Kerala-1985,* Thiruvananthapuram, Department of Economics and Statistics, 1985.

Government of Kerala, *Report on the Census of Private Medical Institutions in Kerala-1995,* Thiruvananthapuram, Department of Economics and Statistics, 1995.

Government of Kerala, *Report on the Private Medical Institutions in Kerala-2004,* Kerala, Thiruvananthapuram, Department of Economics and Statistics, 2006.

Government of Kerala, *Tenth Five Year Plan 2002-2007,* Fourth Years Programme 2005-2006, State Planning Board, Thiruvananthapuram, February 2006.

Guleria, M.S., 'A Study of Hospital Information System with Particular Reference to Patient Information System and Inpatient Medical Records', *MHA Dissertation,* New Delhi, AIIMS, 1986.

Hella, A.K. and Thoshniwal, A.K., 'Material Management Practices and Procedures in a Hospital', *Project Report*, Mumbai, Bombay Management Assn., 1986.

Hemavathy, C.S., 'Evaluation of the Motivational Techniques for Managerial Development in Selected Public and Private Enterprises', Unpublished Ph.D. Thesis, Kerala University, 1990.

International Labour Office, *Workers Participation in Decisions within Undertakings,* Geneva, 1985.

Jacob Thomas, 'Human Resource Management and Organisational Commitment-A Study of Managers in Co-operatives', Unpublished Ph.D. Thesis, Kerala University, March 2001.

Thomkuzhy Joseph Thomas, *Personnel Management in Apex Co-operatives in Kerala: An Empirical Study on Employee's Perspective,* Unpublished Ph.D. Thesis, University of Kerala, 1993.

Jyothi, S.S., 'Human Resources Management in Co-operative Sector', Published Ph.D.Thesis, New Delhi, Inter-India Publications, 1985.

Khanna, B.B., 'Relationship between Organizational Climate and Organizational Effectiveness: A Case Study', Unpublished *Ph.D Thesis*, Banaras Hindu University, 1986.

Khurana and Renu. B., 'Computers in Indian Hospitals—A Market Study' *IIM Project Report*, Bangalore, 1984.

Llewelyn, R. Davies and Macaulay, H.M.C., 'World Health Organisation', *Hospital Planning and Administration,* Geneva, 1996.

Lohe, L.P., 'Drug Inventory Control in Nursing Homes', *Project Report*, Mumbai, Management Association, 1987.

Magnus Lindelow. Pieter Serneels., and Teigist Lemma, 'The Performance of Health Workers in Ethiopia – Results from Qualitative Research', *Policy Research Working Paper,* The World Bank Development Research Group, Public Services Team, April 2005.

Mala Ashok, 'Doctor's Day', *The Hindu*, 28 June, 2003.

Mandip Basi, 'Biomedicine as a Health Option in Contemporary Rural Punjab', *Discussion paper No.103, Centre for Developing Area studies (CDAS).* Canada, Mc Gill University, May 2003.

Martin Henser, *The Rationalization and Management of Hospitals* in Zuzana Feachen, Martin Henser, Lauron Rose (Eds), Implementing Health Sector Reform in Central Asia, Washington, The World Bank, December 1998.

Mendhi and Nayana, 'A Study of Job Satisfaction of Managers in Public and Private Sector Organisations', Unpublished Ph.D. Thesis, Bombay, Tata Institute of Social Sciences, 1985.

Mitra, S. and Pestonjee, D.M., Job Satisfaction, Job Involvement and Participation amongst Different Categories of Bank Employees', Unpublished Working Paper, Ahmedabad, IIMA., 1990.

Mohanan Nair, V.R., 'A Study on the Working of the Hospital Industry in Kerala', Unpublished Ph.D.Thesis, Department of Commerce, University of Kerala, 2005.

Mohanty, P.K., *Andhra Pradesh: Improving Governance through Performance Management* in Surendra Kumar (Ed), A Journal of Administrative Reforms-Management in Government, Vol.XXXIV, No.1&2, April-Sept. 2003.

Nanda Kumar Damodara Prasad, 'Human Resource Management in the Textile Units in Kerala', Unpublished Ph.D. Thesis, University of Kerala, May 2002.

Padmavathy Amma, K., 'Work Attitude of the Employees of the Industrial Sector of Kerala- A Comparative Study of Public Sector and Private Sector', Unpublished M.Phil. Dissertation, University of Kerala, 1992.

Percy, B.J., *The Role of the Physician Manager,* Hospital Management forum, 1984.

Pillai K. Soman, 'HRM in Kerala Minerals and Metals Ltd., Chavara'. Unpublished M.Phil. Dissertation, University of Kerala, 1993.

Premavathi, K., 'Health Care Administration in Tamil Nadu; A Study in Public Policy', Unpublished Ph.D Thesis, Anna Centre for Public Affairs, University of Madras, November 1998.

Pushpa, S., 'Workers' Participation in Management', Unpublished Ph.D Thesis, University of Kerala, 1993.

Rao, M.N., *Development of Computerized MIS for Small Hospitals*, Bangalore, Unpublished *Ph.D.Thesis*, IIM, 1986.

Sagaya Doss, S., 'An Economic Analysis of Health Care Services', Unpublished *Ph.D. Thesis*, Department of Economics and Research, University of Madras, June 2003.

Sagaya Doss, S., 'An Economic Analysis of Health Care Services', Unpublished *Ph.D. Thesis*, Department of Economics and Research, University of Madras, June 2003.

Saumya Panda, 'Evaluation of India's Health Policy', Indian Academy of Social Service, January 2002.

Sinha, R.K., 'A Study to Assess Staffing Requirements of Doctors in Surgical Units of a Large Hospital', *MHA Dissertation*, AIIMS, New Delhi, 1987.

Staff Reporter, 'A doctor is a workman, says High Court', *The Hindu,* Wednesday, Feb.28, 2007.

Sundaresan, P.K., 'Cost Accounting and Cost Control- Hospitals', Unpublished Ph.D. Thesis, Cochin University of Science and Technology, 1993.

Thattil Gabriel Simon, 'The Personnel Management of Public Enterprises—A Case Study of Cochin Shipyard Ltd.' Unpublished M.Phil. Dissertation, University of Kerala, 1991.

Thomas Joseph, 'Personnel Management in Apex Co-operatives in Kerala: An Empirical Study on Employees' Perspectives', Unpublished Ph.D Thesis, University of Kerala, 1993.

Venkataraman, *HRM: Present Trends and Anticipated Developments,* The Hindu, Opportunities, June 28, 1995.

Voluntary Health Association of India; (VHAI) India's Health Status, New Delhi, 1998.

Wilson, K., 'Job Satisfaction and Commitment of Employees' in Selected Public and Private Sector Undertakings in Kerala', Unpublished Ph.D Thesis, University of Kerala, 1995.

Workers Participation in decisions within undertakings, International Labour Office, Geneva, 1981, p.81.

Yovanan Vargheese, Employment Security measures in unorganized sector of Kerala – An Evaluative Study, Unpublished Ph.D Thesis, University of Kerala, December 2004.

Published Articles

Abhay Shukla, 'Jan Swasthya Abhiyan', *Yojana,* Vol. 49, July 2005.

Adnan A Hyder, Tasleem Akhter and Abdul Quayyum, 'Capacity Development for Heath Research in Pakistan: The Effects of Doctoral Training', *Health Policy and Planning,* Vol. 18, No.3, September 2003.

Alastair Ager and Katy Pepper, 'Patterns of Health Service Utilisation and Perceptions of Needs and Services in Rural Orissa', *Health Policy and Planning,* Vol. 20, No. 3, May 2005.

Alexander, K.C., *For a survey of Workers' Participation in Management in France,* Federal Republic of Germany and the United States of America, Bulletin, International Institute of Labour studies, No.6, June 1969.

Alison Katz, 'The SACHS Report: Investing in Health for Economic Development-or Increasing the Size of the Crumbs from the Rich Man's Table?' *International Journal of Health Services,* Vol. 35, No.1, 2005.

Anand, T.R.. and Nath, D.H., 'Hospital Services and Management Methods', *Hospital Administration,* Vol. 14, No. 3, September 1977.

Anantha Padmanabhan, U.K, 'Relevance of Cost Control and Cost Reduction Techniques in Hospital Material Management', *Hospital Administration,* Vol. 23, No.6, 1986.

Ashmos, D.P. and Daniel, R.R., 'Physician Participation in hospital strategic decision making: The effect of hospital strategy and decision content', *Health Services Research,* Vol.26, No. 3, 1991.

Austin, M., 'Evaluating the Training of Mental Health Administrators', *Administration in Mental Health,* Vol.3, 1975.

Baghotia, K.S. and Sethi, N.K., 'A Study of Hospital Waste Management in a Territory Care Hospital', *Health and Population Perspectives and Issues,* Vo. 21, No.1, Jan–March 1998.

Barger, G., *et al.,* 'Improving Patient Care through Problem Solving Groups', *Health Progress,* Vol. 68, No.7, September 1987.

Basu Ghosh, 'MIS for Health Care Human Resource Management: A Case', *Journal of Health Management,* Vol. 2, No. 1, January-June 2000.

Bhadkamkar, S.M., 'Management Information System and Ranking of the Hospitals', *Hospital Administration,* Vol. 21, No. 2, September/December 1983.

Bhaskaran, M., 'IMA and Medical Profession', *Kerala Medical Journal,* Vol. 41, No.2, April 2000.

Bhat, R., 'The Private/Public Mix in Health Care in India', *Health Policy and Planning,* Vol.8, No. 1-4, 1993.

Bhola, R.S. and Anand, T.R., 'Some Aspects of Hospital Management Requiring Personal Attention of a Hospital Administrator', *Hospital Administration,* Vol. 15, No. 2, June 1978.

Birna Trap and Charles H. Todel, Heather Moore and Richard Laing, 'The Impact of Supervision on State Management and Adherence to Treatment Guidelines: a Randomized Controlled Trial', *Health Policy and Planning,* Vol. 16, No.3, September 2001.

Boissoneau, R. and Mc Pherson, J., 'Practicing Participative Management in the Clinical Laboratory: Foster a Productive and Satisfying Staff', *Clinical Laboratory Management Review,* Vol.5, No.3, May-June 1991.

Brenda Scott, Ladd, Verena Marshall, 'Participation in Decision Making: A Matter of Context', *Leadership and Organisation Development Journal,* Vol. 25, No. 8, 2004.

Brigid, L. Bechtold, 'Towards a Participative Organizational Culture: Evolution or Revolution', *Empowerment in Organisations,* Vol. 35, No.1, 1997.

Brijesh C Purohit, 'Private Initiatives and Policy Options: Recent Health System Experience in India', *Health Policy and Planning,* Vol. 16, No. 1, 2001.

Buwa Drugudi, 'A day in the Life of a District Medical Officer', *Health Policy and Planning,* Vol. 19, No.1, January 2004.

Carol Vlassoff and Sharon Fonn, 'Health Workers for Change as a Health Systems Management and Development Tool'. *Health Policy and Planning,* Vol. 16 (Suppl. 1), September 2001.

Chandan, J.S., 'A Queuing Model for Hospitals with Reference to Routine X-rays', *Journal of Hospital Administration,* Vol. 21, No. 2, June 1984.

Chandan, J.S., 'Hospital Administration and Some Issues', *Hospital Administration,* Vol. 17, No. 4, December 1980.

Chang-Yup Kim, 'The Korean Economic Crisis and Coping Strategies in the Health Sector: Pro-welfarism or Neoliberalism?' *International Journal of Health Services,* Vol. 35, No. 3, 2005.

Charles Andrews, 'Concentration of U.S. Hospitals, 1991-1999 and its Implications for a National Health Problem', *International Journal of Health Services,* Vol. 35, No.1, 2005.

Chauhan Daisy, 'Challenges for HRD in the Changing Environment', *Personnel Today,* Vol. XV, No.4, January-March 1995.

Chet N. Chaulagai, Christon M. Mayo, et al., 'Design and Implementation of a Health Management Information System in Malawi: Issues, Innovations and Results', *Health Policy and Planning,* Vol. 20, No.6, November 2005.

Chris Holden, 'Privatization and Trade in Health services: A Review of the Evidence', *International Journal of Health Services,* Vol.35, No.4, 2005.

Cox, T., Griffiths, A. and Cox, S., 'Work-Related Stress in Nursing: Controlling the Risk to Health', *International Labour Organisation (ILO) Manual,* 1996.

David H. Peters, Sujatha Rao, K., Robert Fryatt, 'Lumping and Splitting: The Health Policy Agenda in India', *Health Policy and Planning,* Vol. 18, No. 3, September 2003.

David Heel, John Sparrow, Robert Ashford, 'Work Place Interactions that Facilitate or Impede Reflective Practice', *Journal of Health Management,* Vol. 8, No.1, Jan–June 2006.

Desai, V. B., 'Principles of Management as Applicable to Hospitals', *Hospital Administration,* Vol. 21, No. 1&2, March and June 1984.

Ekta Sharma, 'Role Stress among Doctors', *Journal of Health Management,* Vol. 7, No.1, Jan-June 2005.

Elisa, J. Sobo and Blair, L. Sadler, 'Improving Organizational Communication and Cohesion in a Health Care Setting through Employee-Leadership Exchange', *Human Organisation,* Vol. 61, No. 3, 2002.

Eric J. Thomas, *et al.,* 'Hospital Ownership and Preventable Adverse Events', *International Journal of Health Services,* Vol.30, No. 4, 2000.

Gadwale, H. H., 'Worker's Participation in Management in India', *Southern Economist,* Vol. 43, No. 10, September 2004.

Geetika Tankha, 'A comparative study of Role stress in Government and Private Hospital Nurses', *Journal of Health Management,* Vol. 8, No.1, January–June 2006.

Ghei, P.N., 'Hospital Organisational Development', *Hospital Administration,* Vol. 15, No. 2, June 1978.

Ghei, P.N., 'Hospital Material Management', *Hospital Administration,* Vol. 12, No. 1 & 2, March-June 1975.

Ghei, P.N., 'Principles of Hospital Management', *Hospital Administration,* Vol.14, No. 2, June 1977.

Gladwin, J., Dixon, R A., Wilson T D. 'Rejection of an Innovation: Health Information Management Training Materials in East Africa', *Health Policy Planning,* Vol. 17, No. 4, December 2002.

Gouri S.Gupta, 'Complaint Management in Hospital', *Hospital Administration,* Vol. 19, No.1 & 2 March & June 1982.

Goyal, S.P. 'Management By Objectives', *Hospital Administration,* Vol. 16, No. 3 & 4, September/ December 1979.

Green, A., Ali, B., Naeem,A. and Vassall,A. 'Using Costing as a District Planning and Management tool in Balochistan, Pakistan', *Health Policy and Planning,* Vol. 16, No.2, June 2001.

Gupta, J.P. and Juyal, R.K., 'An Exploratory Study on Cost Analysis of an Urban Maternal and child Health and Family Welfare Centre', *Hospital Administration,* Vol.15, No.3, 1978.

Harold Trader, 'Management Accounting in a Hospital', *Hospital Administation,* Vol. 23, No.3, 1986.

Hebrang A., Henigsberg, N., et al., 'Privatization in the Health Care System of Croatia: Effects on General Practice Accessibility', *Health Policy and Planning,* Vol.18, No.4, Dec. 2003.

Hellander, 'Data on U.S. Health Sector', *International Journal of Health Services,* Vol. 35, No.2, 2005.

Herman J Gilligan, 'Evaluating self-managed Learning part-3: developing leaders in a US Health System', *Health Manpower Management,* Vol. 21, No. 6, 1995.

Hugh Waters, Laurel Hatt and David Peters, 'Working with the Private Sector for Child Health', *Health Policy and Planning,* Vol.18, No.2, June 2003.

Iyer, R.S., 'Modern Management Systems in Hospitals', *Hospital Administration,* Vol. 20, No. 2, September and December 1983.

Jacob, K.K. and Giri,V.V., 'Grievance Redressal Procedure and Labour Management Relations in State Level Public Enterprises', *Labour and Development,* International Labour Institute, Vol.11, No.1, June 2001.

Jagdish C. Bhatia and John Cleland, 'Health Care Seeking and Expenditure of Young Indian Mothers in the Public and Private Sectors', *Health Policy and Planning.* Vol.16, No. 1, March 2001.

James, J. Polezynski and Larry.E.Shirland, 'Determining Readiness of Hospital Administrators to Accept Management by Objectives', *Hospital Administration,* Vol.20, No.2, September, December 1983.

Janat Shah and Murty, L.S., 'Compassionate, High Quality Health Care at Low Cost: The Aravind Model', *IIMB Management Review,* Vol. 16, No.3, September 2004.

JDH Porter, *et al.,* 'Introducing Operations Research into Management and Policy Practices of a Non-governmental Organisation (NGO): A Partnership Between an Indian Leprosy NGO and an International Academic Institution', *Health Policy and Planning,* Vol. 19, No.2, March 2004.

John L Fiedler and Javier Suazo, 'Ministry of Health User Fees, Equity and Decentralisation: Lessons from Honduras', *Health Policy and Planning,* Vol.17, No.4, December 2002.

John W. Hennessey, 'The Administrator and Policy Processes', *Hospital Administration,* Fall 1965.

Joseph Mani, *'Quality Health Care'*, Kerala State Branch *IMA News Letter*, No.91, December 2005.

Kailash, B.L. and Srivastava, 'Work Place Diversity Helps Bring Success', *Indian Management*, Vol. 40, No. 2, February 2001.

Kapilashrami, M.C., Sood, A.K. and Sharma, B.B.L., 'Involvement of Private Sector in Health: Suggested Policy Guidelines and Mechanisms', *Health and Population Perspectives and Issues*, Vol. 23, No.2, April-June 2000.

Kimsujin, 'The Impact of Team Diversity on Team Outcomes: Meta-analytic Findings of Team Demography', *.Dissertation Abstracts: International,* Vol. 65, No. 11, May 2005.

Kinsey, Mc., 'Health Care – Expansion for Profit', *Economic and Political Weekly*, Vol.37, No.34, 2002.

Klinger, P., 'Protocols for Pharmacists Intervention in a 160 Bed Hospital', *Health Policy Economic and Management,* Vol. 27, Issue.1, 1991.

Lakshman Rao, H. K., 'Application of OR to Management Practice: An Introduction', *Management Review*, Vol. 12, No.4, 2000.

Lee, Hyun–Jung, 'Willingness and Capacity: The Determinants of Pro-social Organizational Behaviour among Nurses in the UK', *International Journal of Human Resource Management*, Vol. 12, No.6, 2001.

Lunblad and Jennifer Paige, 'Team Work and Safety Climate in Small Rural Hospitals', *International Dissertation Abstracts,* Vol. 65, No.10, April 2005.

Lydia Kapiriri, *et al.*, 'Public Participation in Health Planning and Priority Setting at the District Level in Uganda', *Health Policy and Planning,* Vol. 18, No. 2, June 2003.

Lynn. M. Morgan, '*Community Participation in Health- Perpetual Allure, Persistent* Challenge', *Health Policy and planning,* Vol.16, No. 3, Sept. 2001.

Maathai K Mathiyazhagan, 'People's Choice of Health Care Provider: Policy Options for Rural Karnataka in India', *Journal of Health Management,* Vol. 5, No.1, January–June 2003.

Mahendra Dutta, Chawla, D. R. and Sharma, R. S. 'Pattern of the Bed Utilization in Large Hospitals of India', *Hospital Administration*, Vol. 20, No.1 & 2, March & June 1983.

Margitta, B. and Beil- Hildebrand, 'Instilling and Distilling a Reputation for Institutional Excellance—A Critical Reflection on Organizing Practice', *Journal of Health Organisation and Management,* Vol.19, No.6, 2005.

Michael Cooper, R., Wood T. Michael, 'Member Participation and Commitment in Group Decision-making on Influence Satisfaction and Decision Richness', *Journal of Applied Psychology*, Vol. 59, No.2, April 1974.

Mitra, P. and Anand, T. R., 'Ward Planning and Management', *Hospital Administration,* Vol. 20, No. 1 & 2, March & June 1983.

Mogli, G.D., 'Organisational Needs of Hospital Reception', *Hospital Administration,* Vol. 17, No. 4, December 1980.

Morse, N.C. and Riemer, E., 'The Experimental Change of a Major Organisational Variable', *Journal of Abnormal and Social Psychology*, Vol.52, 1956.

Mowday, 'Unit Performance, Situational Factors and Employee Attitudes in Spatially Separated Work Units'. *Organisational Behaviour and Human Performance,* Vol. 12, No.2, 1974.

Mox and Chan, 'Work and Family Roles of Female Nurses: Sources of Stresses and Coping Strategies', *The Hong Kong Nursing Journal*, Vol.73, 1996.

Nahra, J., 'Top Ten Compliance Program Challenges for the Health Care Industry', *The ICFAI Journal of Health Care Law,* Vol.III, No. 3, August 2005.

Nair, V.M., *et al.,* 'Changing Roles of Grassroot Level Health Workers in Kerala, India', *Health Policy and Planning,* Vol. 16, No. 2, June 2001.

Narayan, L. S. Menon and Spector, P. E. 'Stress in the Work Place: A Comparison of Gender and Occupations', *Journal of Organisational Behaviour,* Vol.20, No.1, 1999.

Nayar, K. R, Anant Kumar, 'Kerala and Bihar: A Comparison', *Yojana,* Vol.49, July 2005.

Nguyen Thi Hong Ha, *et al.,* 'Household Utilization and Expenditure on Private and Public Health Services in Vietnam', *Health Policy and Planning,* Vol. 17, No.1, March 2002.

Nico, W. Van Yperen, *et al.,* 'Towards a Better Understanding of the Link Between Participation in Decision-making and Organizational Citizenship Behaviour: A Multilevel Analysis', *Journal of Occupational and Organizational Psychology,* Vol. 72, No.3, 1999.

Nilambar Jha, K.C., *et al.,* 'Five Star Doctors for the 21st Century: A BPKIMS Endeavour for Nepal', *Journal of Health Management,* Vol. 7, No.2, July - December 2005.

Norbert Dreesch., *et al.,* 'An Approach to Estimating Human Resource Requirements to Achieve the Millennium Development Goals', *Health Policy and Planning,* Vol. 20, No.5, September 2005.

Onyango-Ouma, Frederick W Thiong'o, *et al.,* 'The Health Workers for Change Impact Study in Kenya', *Health Policy and Planning,* Vol. 16, Supplement 1, September 2001.

Onyango-Ouma, Rose Laisser, *et al.,* 'An Evaluation of Health Workers for Change in Seven Settings: A Useful Management and Health System Development Tool', *Health policy and Planning,* Vol.16, Supplement 1, September 2001.

Padmini, E V K. and Syam Chand, R. 'Workers Participation in Management, A Field Study', *Indian Management,* Vol. 39, No. 5, May 2000.

Parikh, P., Taukari, A. and Bhattacharya T, 'Occupational Stress and Coping among Nurses'. *Journal of Health Management,* Vol. 6, 2004.

Pestonjee, D.M., Kajal H.Sharma and Sonal Patel, 'Image and Effectiveness of Hospitals: An HR Analysis', *Journal of Health Management,* Vol. 7, No.1, Jan–June 2005.

Pol De Vas, 'No One Left Abandoned Cuba's National Health System Since the 1959 Revolution', *International Journal of Health Service, Vol. 35, No.1,* 2005.

Ramesh Bhat and Sunil Kumar Maheswari, 'Human Resource Issues. Implications for Health Sector Reforms', *Journal of Health Management,* Vol. 7, No.1, January-June 2005.

Ravinder, H.V., 'How to Make Better Decisions', *Management Review,* Vol. 8, No. 2, April-June 1996.

Ray, D.B., 'A Study of the Filter Clinic of a Large Size Hospital', *Hospital Administration,* Vol. 20, No.1 & 2, September& December 1983.

Redwariur Rahman, M., 'Health Services System in Bangladesh: An Overview', *IASSI Quarterly,* Vol. 18, No. 3, January-March 2000.

Reeta Dhingra, 'NGOs and Health Insurance Schemes in India', *Health and Population Perspectives and Issues,* Vol. 24, No. 4, October, December 2001.

Rudolf Klein, 'Control Participation and the British National Health Service', *Health and Society,* Vol. 57, No. 1, 1979.

Sampath, 'Programme on Personnel Management', *Tamil Nadu Journal of Co-operation,* February 1979.

Schrubb, D.A., 'The Implementation of Self-managed Teams in Health Care', *Health Information Management,* Vol. 13, No.1, August 1992.

Schwartz, R.H. 'Nurse Decision Making Influence: A Discrepancy between the Nursing and Hospital Literatures', *Health Policy, Economics and Management,* Vol.27, Issue 1, 1991.

Sena Eken David A., Rabilino and George Schieber, 'Living Better', *Finance and Development,* Vol. 40, No.1, 2003.

Sethi, A.S., 'Application of Administrative Theory to Hospital Operations', *Hospital Administration,* Vol. 16, No. 1 & 2, March/ June 1979.

Sharma, S.C. and Usha Agrawala, 'Human Relations in Hospital Administration: Need, Importance and Scope', *Hospital Administration,* March-June 1975.

Sharon Fonn and Makhosazana Xaba, 'Health Workers for Change: Developing the Initiative', *Health Policy and Planning,* Vol. 16, Supplement 1, September 2001.

Sheela Datta, 'Application of Computers in Hospitals', *Hospital Administration,* Vol. 25, No.11, 1988.

Shubhra Singh, 'National Rural Health Mission', *Yojana,* Vol. 49, No. 1&2, July 2005.

Singh Shailendra, 'Relationship between Manager's Authority Power and Perception of their Subordinates Behaviour', *Indian Journal of Industrial Relations,* Vol.35, No.3, January 2000.

Sinha, R. P., 'Financial Management in Hospitals', *Hospital Administration,* Vol. 19, No. 3&4, September/December 1982.

Smith, R., Grabvam, A. and Chantler, C., 'Doctors Becoming Managers', *British Medical Journal,* 1989.

Sweta D'Cunha and Sanjeev Rai, B., 'A Study on the Management Information System Used in the Outpatient Department', *Journal of the Academy of Hospital Administration (JAHA),* Vol. 16, No.2, July–December 2004.

Terry H Wagan and Kent V. Rondeau, 'Labour-Management Forums and Work Place Performance: Evidence from Union Officials in Health Care Organisations', *Journal of Management in Medicine,* Vol. 16, No. 6, 2002.

Thomas Bossert, *et al.,* 'Decentralization in Zambia: Resource Allocation and District Performance', *Health Policy and Planning,* Vol.18, No.4, December 2003.

Tiwani, C. K., 'Hospital Budgeting', *Hospital Administration,* Vol.27, No.3, 1990.

Tony De Groote, Pierre De Paepe and Jean-Pierre Unger, 'Colombia: In Vivo Test of Health Sector Privatisation in the Developing World', *International Journal of Health Economics,* Vol. 35, No. 1, 2005.

Tran Tuan, *et al.,* 'Comparative Quality of Private and Public Health Services in Rural Vietnam', *Health Policy and Planning,* Vol. 20, No.5, September 2005.

Vander Plaetse, B., *et al.,* 'Costs and Revenue of Health Care in a Rural Zimbabwean District', *Health Policy and Planning,* Vol.20, No.4, July 2005.

Varatharajan, *et al.,* 'Assessing the Performance of Primary Health Centres under Decentralized Government in Kerala, India', *Health Policy and Planning,* Vol. 19, No.1, January 2004.

Vivek Handa, A. K., Sood and Rajini Bagga. 'Human Resource Development in a Government Health Organization: Views of Doctors', *Health and Population Perspectives and Issues,* Vol. 27, No.2, April—June 2004.

William Jack, 'Contracting for Health Services: An Evaluation of Recent Reforms in Nicaragua', *Health Policy and Planning,* Vol. 18, No. 2, June 2003.

Dailies

The Business Line, Chennai

The Economic Times, Mumbai

The Financial Express, Chennai

The Hindu, Thiruvananthapuram

The New Indian Express, Thiruvananthapuram

Index